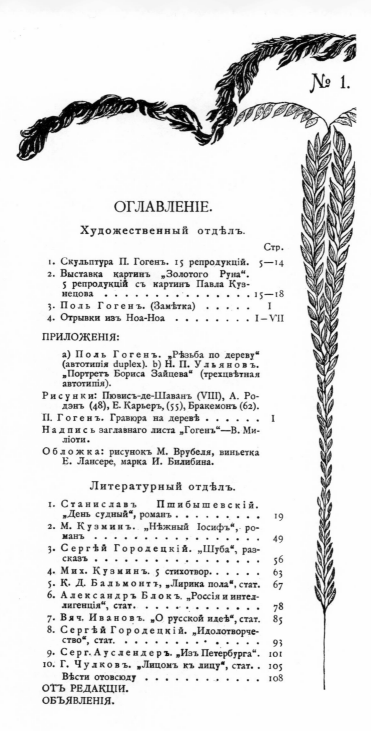

ОГЛАВЛЕНІЕ.

Художественный отдѣлъ.

Литературный отдѣлъ.

William Richardson

Zolotoe Runo
and
Russian Modernism: 1905-1910

Ardis, Ann Arbor

316322

William Richardson, *Zolotoe Runo and Russian Modernism, 1905-1910*
Copyright © 1986 by Ardis Publishers
All rights reserved under International and Pan-American Copyright Conventions.
Printed in the United States of America

Ardis Publishers
2901 Heatherway
Ann Arbor, Michigan 48104

Library of Congress Cataloging in Publication Data

Richardson, William.
Zolotoe runo and Russian modernism, 1905-1910.

Bibliography: p.
1. Russian literature—20th century—History and
criticism.   2. Modernism (Literature)—Soviet
Union.   3. Symbolism (Literary movement)—Soviet
Union.   4. Zolotoe Runo.   I. Title.
PG3020.5.M6R53   1986   891.7'09'1   86-1100
ISBN 0-88233-795-5 (alk. paper)

CONTENTS

ACKNOWLEDGMENTS

This study originated as a doctoral dissertation for the History Department at the University of California, Berkeley, and it is to those with whom I worked there that I owe the greatest gratitude. Nicholas Riasanovsky was particularly helpful in his intellectual support, criticism, counsel, and guidance. Indeed, without him, the book could have not been written. Martin Malia, Robert Hughes, and Simon Karlinsky gave me much useful advice in understanding the intricacies of Russian intellectual life and the Russian language. While the book's drawbacks are of my own making, the positive features derive from the great help these four men gave me in understanding Russian culture.

Research for this study was carried on in a number of places, but especially valuable was the library of the University of California, Berkeley. Its extraordinary collection and helpful staff made my work much easier than it would otherwise have been.

I would also like to thank Edward Chmielewski of the University of Tennessee for stimulating my early interest in Russian history, and especially Albert Kaspin, now retired from the University of California, Santa Barbara, who first led me to an appreciation of Russian literature, and who has continued to provide me with sound advice and stimulating conversation.

Finally, I wish to thank my wife Carol for her unfailing support, and my sons, Caleb and Micah, who gave up more than a little of their time with me so that I might complete this book.

A NOTE ON TRANSLITERATION

In general, the Library of Congress system of transliteration has been used in the text of this work, but with the following simplifications:

a. -' to indicate the Russian soft sign is not used, although in some cases, the soft sign is indicated by i; e.g., Prokofiev.

b. -y is used at the end of surnames instead of -ii; e.g., Riabushinsky, Kursinsky; -yi is retained in the case of such names as Belyi.

c. proper names that have an accepted form in English differing from their direct transliteration will appear in the established form, with the transliterated form in parenthesis the first time the name appears; e.g., Benois (Benua), Roerich (Rerikh).

d. in keeping with pre-revolutionary practice, the titles of periodicals (but not of books) published before 1917 will have each major word capitalized; e.g., *Mir Iskusstva, Zolotoe Runo.*

Part One

The "Silver Age" of Russian Culture

I

INTRODUCTION: PETERSBURG ESTHETES, MOSCOW MERCHANT MAECENASES, AND THE RUSSIAN *FIN DE SIECLE*

I

The life of at any rate the cultured classes was rich and full during these twenty years. It was also a little feverish, perhaps. Even during the war, on the very outbreak of the revolution, the reading of a new poem by Alexander Blok or Anna Akhmatova was for many an important personal event, a joy or an anguish, an intimate communion with reality. When Scriabin was at the piano, his music evoked an emotion that was very much more than mere esthetic pleasure. To hear Shaliapin or Sobinov, to see a Meyerhold production or one at the Art Theater, to be transported once more by that strange voice of the great Kommissarjevskaia, young students of both sexes would queue at the box-offices in their hundreds all night. New writers and artists seemed to be born every day; universities and picture-galleries, every institution devoted to the arts or sciences or letters, were being transformed or modernized under one's very eyes; the country's past was being studied with more love than ever, and with more objectivity. Icons, the most beautiful painting that Russia ever produced, were being discovered once more after being forgotten for centuries. Privately, too, there were fine collections being made of pictures and drawings, books, engravings and all works of art; exhibitions, both of ancient and modern art, could always be sure of attracting crowds. Ancient churches throughout the country, ancient towns and dwelling houses were now for the first time being gazed on with wonder not only by artists but by ordinary travelers.

Wladimir Weidlé, *Russia: Absent and Present*, pp. 103-104.

Weidlé's reminiscence of what is sometimes cautiously called the "cultural renaissance"[1] of early twentieth-century Russia, but more generally known as the Russian "Silver Age," points out a fundamental aspect of the period: it exhibited a range of creativity and a diffusion of talent unequalled in previous Russian history. While the "Golden Age" of Russian poetry was dominated by such giants as Pushkin, no individual possessed similar authority within the modernist culture of turn-of-the-century Russia.[2] In fact, that the exact opposite was true qualitatively defines the nature of this Silver Age. As Camilla Gray remarked a number of years ago, the cultural "truth" of these years was in their very chaotic confusion, in which so much happened, so rapidly, and in so many places.[3]

To recognize this is to approach an understanding of the Russian Silver
Age, an age when a vital, multifaceted rebirth was taking place.

At the end of the nineteenth century, Russia was undergoing a period
of constantly accelerating economic, political, and social change that was
at times bewildering, but which created an atmosphere of eagerness and
expectation among Russian intellectuals. After a long period of semi-
isolation and cultural stagnation, contacts with the West were intensified
and extended after the death of Alexander III in 1894. In relatively few
years, Russians were among the most cosmopolitan of Europeans: while
Ibsen and Strindberg were hardly known in France, for example, they were
passionately admired in Russia.[4]

The Russians actively rejoined a Europe itself experiencing a great
physical and spiritual transformation, and both the dangers and benefits of
what Jean Cassou called an age "condemned to genius"[5] found expression
in the new Russian culture that was developing. Russians adopted and
modified what they were newly discovering in the West: while the Russian
"esthetic movement"of the 1880's admired Wilde and Baudelaire, it did not
adopt unquestioningly the theory of "art for art's sake." On the contrary,
this tentative Russian "estheticism" was basically the expression of an
interest in finding some justification for art beyond the confines of
Chernyshevsky's or Stasov's social utilitarianism.[6]

The Russian version of European "decadence" found its initial
expression in the early works of Dmitry Merezhkovsky (1865-1941),
Konstantin Balmont (1867-1941), and Valery Briusov (1873-1924), poets
clearly inspired by the symbolism of Mallarmé, Verlaine, and Baudelaire.
They were soon joined by other young Russians, and a modernist literary
camp, if not movement, was established. Though not very popular, their
works did continue the "esthetics' " attacks on social utilitarianism in art
and literature, and while what success they did have was due more to their
attempts at "shocking the philistines" than to anything else, their poetry
was an unmistakable indication of a new current in a previously moribund
Russian cultural life. A more concrete step in the development of a truly
independent Russian modernism was taken with the founding of *Mir
Iskusstva (The World of Art)* in St. Petersburg in 1898.

Ever since Petersburg's establishment at the beginning of the
eighteenth century, the city had been the focus for Western influences
entering Russia. Russian modernist poetry of the 1890's owed much to
foreign models, and when the first significant Russian modernist journal
began publication, it must have surprised no one that it appeared in the
most European city of the Russian Empire. The background of *Mir
Iskusstva* has been discussed in a number of places,[7] and need not be
recounted here in any great detail. The magazine was begun at the initiative

of Alexandre Benois (1870-1960) and Sergei Diaghilev (1872-1929), two men whose influence on early twentieth-century Russian culture was to prove unequalled,[8] and its contributors included Konstantin Somov (1869-1939), Lev Bakst (Leonid Rosenberg, 1866-1924), Valentin Serov (1865-1911), Evgeny Lanseray (Lansere, 1875-1946), and Mstislav Dobuzhinsky (1875-1957). The program and philosophy of the new journal (and the "society and exhibiting organization" of which it was a part) were to be based on anti-academism and a hatred, in Benois' words, of the "typical *peredvizhnichestvo,* meaning by this everything which reflected a literary, political, or social tendency. Our slogan was 'art, pure and unfettered.' "[9] Diaghilev's long programmatic essay in the magazine's first issue stressed this position: "The great power of art resides precisely in the fact that it is an end in itself, that it is self-availing, and above all— free."[10] To the Russian public, it appeared that with *Mir Iskusstva,* the Western "art for art's sake" esthetic had made a firm entrance into Russian culture.

As had been the intention of the editors and contributors, *Mir Iskusstva*'s first two years of publication were dedicated almost entirely to art, and particular attention was given to the development of the European art nouveau, with reproductions of the works of Beardsley, Burne-Jones, Mackintosh, Van der Velde, Puvis de Chavannes, and Olbrich predominating. Only in 1904, in the magazine's last few issues, were such post-Impressionists as Gauguin or Van Gogh given any attention. Foreign as well as Russian contributions were accepted, and at times esthetic views differing decidedly from those of many of the *miriskusniki* were published, as was the case when Diaghilev insisted on including in one issue a Russian translation of an essay by John Ruskin on the Pre-Raphaelites. Every aspect of the "world of art" was considered, including both traditional and more modern applied arts. A chronicle appearing with each issue dealt with contemporary cultural developments in Russia and abroad, and proved to be an important resource in continuing the artistic education of *Mir Iskusstva*'s Russian readers. One of the journal's fundamental aims was to acquaint a relatively ignorant Russian public with the most recent developments in European and Russian art.

Mir Iskusstva included a section devoted to "literary and esthetic criticism," the responsibility for which was given to Dmitry Filosofov (1872-1942), an old friend of Benois' and a cousin of Diaghilev's. The decision to include literary criticism was a fortuitous one for the development of Russian symbolism, since *Mir Iskusstva*'s literary section was the first place critical work by Russian symbolist poets was readily accepted for publication. These poets were still much too small in numbers to support a journal of their own, and joining with *Mir Iskusstva* was an effective means for them to strengthen their position and to publicize their esthetic views. On the other hand, little of the symbolists' original prose appeared in the new magazine, since Filosofov adhered to his original intention of giving almost no space to fiction. The literary section soon gained a decidedly religious and philosophical orientation because of Filosofov's mystical connections with Merezhkovsky and his wife Zinaida Gippius, and it became a source of continual argument within the magazine's entire editorial board. Finally, small musical and theatrical sections were also included in *Mir Iskusstva*, but both proved of little significance.[11]

It was not *Mir Iskusstva*'s content that most impressed its readers, however, but the magazine's innovative and unique external production. The "cult of form" so typical of the *Mir Iskusstva* artists' works was nowhere better represented than in the magazine's luxurious physical appearance. Each issue averaged 350 pages, two-thirds occupied by full-page illustrations, in addition to those included in the body of the text. Its cover and the headpieces and illustrations for articles were all designed by the *miriskusniki*. The editors demanded the highest-quality European polygraphy and autotype (executed in Germany and Finland). Each issue was considered an artistic whole and every one was a contrast to a periodical press dominated by the stodgy, esthetically conservative and artistically unimaginative Russian "thick journals." *Mir Iskusstva* set standards against which all subsequent Russian publications would be judged.

Such constant innovation in the magazine and in the exhibitions of contemporary art it sponsored inevitably led to an outcry from the more conservative sectors of Russian society. The activities of the group of artists associated with the magazine were met with ridicule from most of the press and with shocked concern from the majority of the entrenched literary and art critics. Ilya Repin, an early supporter, soon broke with *Mir Iskusstva*, deploring what he called the magazine's "dilettantism and decadence." Benois wrote that their position

> remained incomprehensible to the Russian public as well as to the contemporary Russian press, and so our undertaking encountered definite hostility. The accusations which had already been directed at the young Russian poets were now turned against us painters. We were immediately labeled "the Decadents"...[12]

Mir Iskusstva earned the title "decadent" by promoting a close association between Russian and European art, and in most Russian eyes, the modern art of the time was permeated with "decadence."

Such hostility caused continual difficulties for the magazine throughout its period of publication. Financial problems (which were to prove endemic to Russian modernist periodicals) had afflicted *Mir Iskusstva* from the beginning: because of its very limited circulation (rarely exceeding a thousand subscribers), the magazine needed a patron who could afford the necessary financial loss represented by each issue. Princess Maria Tenisheva (1867-1928) provided initial support, but eventually withdrew it because of the general reception of the magazine as "decadent," and because of humiliating personal attacks on her in the press.[13] Later support was given by the wealthy industrialist Savva Mamontov and even by Nicholas II, but both of them discontinued their aid because of financial pressures. Increasing economic difficulties were accompanied by a loss of interest on the part of the magazine's editors: Filosofov left *Mir Iskusstva* to work on the Merezhkovskys' new magazine *Novyi Put (The New Path),* Diaghilev underwent a period of depression and was constantly away from the capital, and Benois wrote that he felt "that everything that had to be said and shown had been said and shown."[14] All three were tired of working on the magazine, and agreed to end its publication in December 1904.

Mir Iskusstva's achievement was immense, and these few pages can in no way pretend to do it justice. One of the best summaries of *Mir Iskusstva*'s place in Russian culture has been given in a recent Soviet book by Alla Gusarova, however:

> For us *Mir Iskusstva* is not only drawings, paintings, books, the embodiment of mental grace, the mind, the high culture of its creators, the reverential love of nature and art. It is a noble enthusiasm for the study of Russian antiquity, a discovery of entire sections of Russian art, almost unknown before; it is Rokotov's, Levitsky's, Borovikovsky's, and Kiprensky's having secured a deserved place in the best museums of the country. It is examples of artistic criticism, intelligent, sensitive and tolerant of the searchings of their young contemporaries, even those alien in spirit.
>
> The encyclopedic spread of interests and knowledge of the *miriskusniki* and their preparedness to share them, the striving to make them general is especially valuable. The sphere of influence of *Mir Iskusstva* was uncommonly wide, it could be seen in painting and in graphic design, in music, in literature, in decorative and applied arts, even in fashion.
>
> The sweep of creations of *Mir Iskusstva* was vast: from miniatures to monumental frescoes, including easel pictures, books, theater. The artists were concerned with decorative art, worked on interior decoration, created toys and furniture.[15]

Despite the overly reverential tone of Gusarova's evaluation, it is a measure of *Mir Iskusstva*'s accomplishment that all of what she writes is true.

With *Mir Iskusstva*'s discontinuation during the early months of the 1905 revolution, a subtle but noticeable reorientation was taking place in modernist Russian cultural life. In spirit, as one observer remarked, *Mir Iskusstva* was

a legitimate fruit of Western European life, saturated with its essence; it ripened on a
Russian trunk as a natural result of our cultural-artistic Europeanization, as "the last
word" in this domain of the St. Petersburg period.[16]

As John Bowlt has pointed out, despite its "decadent" reputation, *Mir
Iskusstva* possessed a quality as decidedly aristocratic and reserved as that
of the city in which it was formed and flourished. The high level of
intellectual and cultural sophistication found in St. Petersburg could be
equalled neither by Moscow nor by any of the provincial cities. In contrast
to the *miriskusniki,* many of the new cultural figures arising in this
"renascent" Russia betrayed a woeful ignorance of both their own and
foreign cultural history, and little sense of measure could be found in their
work. But these new people from Moscow and the provinces possessed a
kind of energy the Petersburg founders of *Mir Iskusstva* no longer seemed
to have by 1905, a vital energy that distinguishes a true *avant-garde* from
simple innovators and reformers, and a further indication of the rapid pace
of change in all aspects of Russian life at the beginning of our century.[17]
The poet Mikhail Kuzmin noted this change:

> And the loud, Moscow dialect, the peculiar words, and their manner of tapping their
> heels while walking, the Tatar cheekbones and eyes, the moustaches twisted upward,
> the *épater*-ing neckties, the colored waistcoats and jackets, the well-known grating and
> irreconcilability in opinions and judgements—it was all so unlike those representatives
> of *Mir Iskusstva* whom I had known in Petrograd, that I involuntarily felt that new
> people had come forward.[18]

These new people included, and were supported and financed by, a
new group of Maecenases, not members of the aristocracy as had been the
case previously in Russian history, but men from a newly-rich, merchant-
industrial class that was seeking tangible proof of its financial success and
of its cultural sophistication.

The old peasant saying "everything rolls into the city" was at no time
truer than it was of Moscow at the beginning of the twentieth century. It
was more than ever the economic center of the country, and much of its
prominence derived from the expanding Old Believer community whose
families controlled much of the city's commerce and industry. They
founded, invested in, and controlled banks, newspapers, retail businesses,
printing and publishing houses throughout Russia, but maintained a
common center in Moscow for political, social, religious, and economic
reasons. As a result, the city underwent a construction boom previously
unequalled in its history, these new entrepreneurs commissioning build-
ings for business enterprises and private homes that would be representative of the new economic and social power and position they felt they now
held in their country. In the next few years, Moscow was to be adorned

with Gothic, Kremlinesque, and art nouveau villas, austere and functional business offices, and native arts and crafts train stations. The men who encouraged such eclecticism, like the newly-rich English bourgeoisie of Victorian times, hoped to find those roots in society which money alone could not give them, but which, they felt, a home built in a historicist style might.

The desire of these merchant-industrialists to be accepted into society was accompanied by a common sense of social responsibility, a felt need to repay society for the success it had permitted them. They were active in municipal government, attempted to improve working conditions in their factories, built hospitals and schools in the countryside, and following the example of Pavel Tretiakov (1832-98), opened their houses and collections of artistic and historical treasures to the public.

This fervor for "collecting" spread among these merchant families, and because of their economic prominence, not only was there a change in the Russian art market, but the nobility's former dominance as lawgivers of artistic taste was destroyed, and their places taken by men such as Tretiakov. Further, while the nobility tended to buy the academic works of Semiradsky or Aivazovsky, the new "Maecenases" generally appreciated and invested in the rather more modern paintings of Levitan or Vrubel.

Russian artists, and writers as well, became heavily dependent on these Maecenases for direct material aid, and also for the general propagation of their esthetic theories. The merchant-industrialists not only provided financial support for literary and artistic journals (as Mamontov had done for *Mir Iskusstva*), but they also edited them personally (as Riabushinsky did for *Zolotoe Runo)*. They established artists' colonies (Mamontov's Abramtsevo) and opened salons that provided opportunities for buying, selling, and auctioning works of art. While they bought works of art for investment, they also did so to help impoverished artists and to satisfy their own personal esthetic sensitivities. In general, as Valentine Marcadé has remarked, in this multi-faceted cutural activity, their role was not unlike that of the seventeenth-century Dutch merchants, who embellished Amsterdam in much the same way as these Russian families of Maecenases did Moscow.[19]

One such family was the Mamontovs, who controlled a network of Moscow industrial and commercial concerns. Savva Mamontov (1841-1918) managed his own industrial affairs, was a sculptor, stage manager, singer, and dramatist. He founded the country's first private opera company, and attracted the most progressive painters, singers, architects, archeologists, art historians, writers, and actors to his Abramtsevo art colony near Moscow.[20] The Morozovs were even more typical of the merchant-industrial class as a whole, and have been described by Valentine

Bill as the "archetype of the Russian bourgeoisie."[21] They were a large, closely knit group sharing an Old Believer tradition, and had made their fortune in textiles and cotton. Ivan (1871-1921) and Mikhail (1870-1904) were famous for their collections of French art, and Savva (1861-1905) helped found and finance the Moscow Art Theater, gave money to Maxim Gorky (bailing him out of jail on one occasion) and to the Social Democrats, and eventually committed suicide on the French Riviera after his mother, head of the family firm, removed him from its management when he devised a plan to share the company's profits with its workers. Considerably less touched by scandal was the Shchukin family, all of whom were inveterate collectors: photographs of the house of Peter (1852-1912), for example, make it appear to be more an overcrowded museum than a home. Sergei (1869-1936) made a systematic collection of paintings by artists rejected in the West, and the walls of his home were covered with works by Cézanne, Gauguin, Matisse, and Picasso. His home was open on Sundays to anyone interested, and Sergei acted as guide and propagandist for the new artists and their works. He introduced the post-Impressionists to Russia (it should be remembered that *Mir Iskusstva* had given them only grudging attention) and provided an international foundation upon which later Russian artists could build.[22] While the aristocracy was not entirely eclipsed by these new people, as Princess Tenisheva's activities indicated (particularly her Talashkino arts and crafts colony), as cultural patrons they were clearly overshadowed by these ambitious, imaginative, and wealthy Muscovites.

One major family that has received little attention in this regard are the Riabushinskys. Because of their importance in the social, economic, and cultural life of the Silver Age, as well as the fact that one of the brothers was the founder and editor of *Zolotoe Runo,* they deserve a rather more lengthy discussion than has been given the other Moscow merchant-industrialist families. Originating in Kaluga, in 1824 the Riabushinsky family moved to Moscow, where its head, Pavel Mikhailovich (d. 1889), laid the foundations for the growth of his descendents' fortune in banking, cotton, and paper industries. He, his wife, and their children maintained the strong familial discipline typical of Old Believer families, and with the father's death all the sons deferred to their oldest brother in business and social life. All Pavel Mikhailovich's sons probably attended the Moscow Practical Academy of Commercial Sciences, and as they grew older became enormously influential and powerful in Muscovite financial life. In 1902, for example, the family firm was expanded with the founding of the Riabushinsky Bank, whose phenomenal success could be seen in the geometric growth of its reserves: in 1902, they were 5 million rubles; in 1903, 33.7 million rubles; 1905, 313.4 million rubles; and by 1908, they had reached 742.3 million rubles.[23]

The oldest son, and head of the family after his father's death, was Pavel Pavlovich (1871-1924). His interests centered on industry and banking, and he founded and financed a large number of new industries and factories in the Moscow region, in 1916 building Russia's first automobile factory. He was an astute businessman, well thought of by his contemporaries, and a member of the Moscow Stock Exchange Committee. He became interested in social questions after 1905, and was one organizer of the "progressivist party" of the industrial and commercial bourgeoisie, he himself being recognized as the head of the progressive Moscow merchants. He owned and edited a weekly newspaper, *Utro Rossii* (1907, 1909-18), which he envisioned and used as an organ of the Moscow merchants holding beliefs similar to his own,[24] and sponsored the publication of a weekly political and literary newspaper, *Rannee Utro* (1907-18). He considered the newspapers means to express his belief that merchants should not simply attempt to join the nobility once they had attained great wealth, but should return to society some of the riches it had given them. Pavel was an outspoken opponent of the 1917 Bolshevik Revolution and was so active as an émigré leader of anti-Soviet activities in the early 1920's that he was made a popular Soviet bogeyman.[25]

The second brother, Vladimir (1873-1955), was director of the family's Moscow bank and head of several textile factories. He too was active in social work, was a member of the Moscow Duma, and in 1917 held a position in the provisional government. Vladimir was best known, however, as a popularizer of icons, and in emigration was the creator of an international society dedicated to their study, preservation, and popularization.

The third brother, Stepan (1874-1943), was also a collector and promoter of icons, and was regarded as one of the world's greatest experts on them. He was the family's commercial head and distinguished as well by his ownership of Moscow's only truly art nouveau structure, his home on the Malaia Nikitskaia (now the Gorky Museum).

Mikhail (1880-1960) was co-director of the family's Moscow bank and was renowned as a collector of modern art. He purchased works by Benois, Degas, Pissarro, and Renoir, but particularly those of Mikhail Vrubel, furnishing his house with as many of the artist's panels and sculptures as he could obtain, although as a contemporary remarked, Vrubel's works must have looked rather peculiar in the "absurdly showy,"[26] neo-Gothic house on the Spiridonovka that Mikhail had bought from Savva Morozov.

Dmitry, the youngest brother (1882-1962), was a scholar, professor, and corresponding member of the French Academy of Sciences. Interested mainly in aerodynamics, he is remembered for having built the world's first aerodynamical laboratory on the family estate at Kuchino.

But certainly the most interesting of the Riabushinsky brothers was Nikolai Pavlovich (1876-1951). Most of his contemporaries, perhaps mistakenly, saw Nikolai as typical of the Muscovite merchant Maecenases of his time, although they were rarely quite as vindictive as was Andrei Belyi:

> Tall, blond, with the beard of a Yankee, with a face distorted by a tic and similar to a rosy but already spent suckling pig, the long-legged Nikolai Riabushinsky shoved his way in everywhere, very proud that he had acquired a bad poem by Merezhkovsky and that Balmont patronized him; he imitated Balmont in everything; and the rosy bud of a rose always hung from the buttonhole of his striped, bright yellow coat; about him lashed rumors, of whether or not he would be among that small society of suicides found among the sons of capitalists; and organized orgies on the graves of those who had killed themselves by lot; he had been in Australia, and exchanged shots with savages who had almost killed him; at first he tried to publish poems; then suddenly exhibited dozens of his loud canvases at the show of [*Golubaia roza*]; the canvases were not terribly bad: they were fireworks of raspberry-orange and wine-yellow flames; this neurasthenic, a drunkard who could also efface himself, flatter lispingly, and cede his place to "talent"; he also had enough slyness to simulate the intuition of a poet-artist and thereby to justify a merchant's stupid willfulness; it was with this that he captivated Balmont; in questions of ideology he showed an impassable stupidity, which he was able to put away in his pocket when necessary, accustoming himself to the flow of opinion, and squatting first by Briusov, then by Chulkov and Blok, he would whisper "I think the same way."[27]

Nikolai Pavlovich was described as a "major industrialist," a "money bag," a "talentless upstart," and a "Muscovite Petronius."[28] One (often repeated) story about him dealt with the thousands of rubles from his inheritance he allegedly spent on an incognito mission to India, having hired the maître d'hôtel of Moscow's Iar Restaurant to be his master of ceremonies and emissary to the Indian rajahs.

Despite popular opinion that he was merely an eccentric, Riabushinsky considered himself a perfect esthete. He liked to paint, and produced still-lifes and portraits that often included allegorical images. He wrote poetry, printed some of it in *Zolotoe Runo,* and in 1907 published a small volume of poems under his pseudonym, N. Shinsky. As John Bowlt has remarked, however, "to a large extent his creative activity was valueless and acted merely as a pretext for enjoying the license which an artist's life afforded."[29]

His exercising of this "license" is what is usually noted in reminiscences of him. His extravagant lifestyle was based on a devotion to the ideal of producing the "grand gesture":

...tall, fair-haired, the very picture of health, a really fine fellow who looked as though he'd just walked out of a Kustodiev picture, Nikolai Pavlovich Riabushinsky— sometime poet, sometime dilettante artist, sometime musician—tried to be as visible as possible. A stalwart, self-assured figure dressed in a dinner-jacket or a suit from a fashionable tailor, the rosy face of N.I. Riabushinsky, bordered with a light brown beard, could be seen at all the theatrical premieres, at every "varnishing-day"— everywhere the artistic aristocracy of Moscow gathered.[30]

His penchant for epicureanism, a wish to impress rather than to discern, to be appreciated rather than to appreciate, led him into disagreements and feuds with numerous Moscow intellectuals,[31] and his personal lack of tact would be responsible for many of his magazine's difficulties.

A concrete expression of Riabushinsky's personality could be found in his notorious Petrovsky Park villa, which he called the "Black Swan." In the words of a visitor,

It was a symbol of the inner composition of this young and playful Maecenas, rash with money, and stopping at no caprice nor any venture. Poisoned arrows, taken from savage countries, vases and sinister dragons from Mallorca, Russian graphics, canvases of...young artists of leftist trends, decadent rich furniture and a luxurious "sleeping-room," welling with exotic scents, where the owner-sybarite, like any Roman during the time of the decline, would recline with constantly smiling mistresses...and wives.[32]

Petrovsky Park was a new, fashionable residential area north-west of Moscow's center, intended as a pleasant setting for "country" villas. Constructed between 1907 and 1909, the "Black Swan" was given a surprisingly modest and rigorously neo-classical design by the architect V. D. Adamovich.[33] In 1912, Riabushinsky hired Leonid and Viktor Vesnin (famous in the 1920's as Constructivist architects) to redesign the building's interior with the intent of making it a better showcase for his art collection, but their plans were never completed, and in 1914, the building and its collection of art and furnishings were entirely destroyed by fire.

At the house's entrance was a large bronze ox above a "tomb" in which Riabushinsky's ashes were to be placed when he died. In the surrounding extensive gardens, he had cages built for lions and tigers (with which Riabushinsky said he had a kind of "affinity") but was forced to give up the idea of a personal zoo after receiving an order from the Moscow police forbidding it. It is reported that at Christmas he burned in-numerable electric lights in the fir trees and under the snow in the garden, and one winter night even gave a "garden party" at which he made gifts of art objects and jewels to his guests.

Moscow society talked of Riabushinsky's drunken gatherings in the Metropol Hotel's restaurant, of the extravagant parties he gave in his villa for the Muscovite literary and artistic *avant-garde,* of the way he so

thoughtlessly spent money in search of immediate gratification. On Prince
Sergei Shcherbatov's one visit to the "Black Swan," the single remark he
remembered Riabushinsky making was "I love beauty and I love many
women."[34] His emotional spontaneity inevitably involved Riabushinsky in
scandal, at times as an apparently innocent bystander, as Mikhail
Bakhrushin remembered:

> In c. 1910 a very sensational event took place. The well-known playboy Prasolov shot
> his wife in the Strelnia Restaurant—with whom as a matter of fact he was no longer
> living—after finding her in the company of a group of young merry-makers, which
> included Nikolai Pavlovich Riabushinsky. The latter lifted up the wounded and dying
> young beauty, carried her out to his car and took her to hospital, but she died on the
> way. Nikolai Riabushinsky appeared in court as a witness. He said that the young lady
> and her sister had visited him several times in his villa, the Black Swan. The judge asked
> him just what his relations had been with the deceased and Nikolai Pavlovich replied
> that they had been friendly, no more, and that she used to visit him simply because she
> found it interesting to be in his house. In response to the question, what is it that's so
> interesting in your house, Nikolai Pavlovich answered: "Everything's interesting in my
> house. My pictures, my porcelain, and after all is said and done, I myself. My habits are
> interesting..." Incidentally, Prasolov was acquitted, his action being regarded as a *crime
> passionel.*[35]

Like most stories of this nature, this one tells a great deal more about
Riabushinsky than about Prasolov and his estranged wife, and provides a
valuable insight into Riabushinsky's character and his high self-esteem.

Nikolai Pavlovich was active in more than amorous and extravagant
adventures, of course. He supported a number of serious artistic projects,
and was a charter member of the "Society of Free Esthetics" when it was
founded in Moscow in 1907. One of his most interesting proposals was for
a "Palace of Arts," a building that would be a permanent exhibition hall
and a museum of modern Russian art, and which would include facilities
for auctioning. But with little support from other sponsors because of their
common dislike of the founder, he was unable to realize the plan after his
financial collapse in 1909-10.[36]

Riabushinsky's greatest importance was in his role as publicist for,
and patron of, new artists and writers. He was an enthusiastic collector of
paintings and sculptures: he first bought works by Brueghel, Cranach,
Poussin, and Van Ruysdael, but soon transferred his attention to modern
French and Russian works. With great foresight, he concentrated on
artists still ignored in France, and was the first among his brothers, or in
fact among any of the Russian art patrons, to sponsor the generation of
Russian artists arising after 1905, and to support the new *avant-garde*
trends appearing in Moscow. He gave early public exposure to such artists
as Arapov, Fonvizin, Goncharova, Kuznetsov, Larionov, Sapunov,

Sarian, and Sudeikin, and some of their best works hung in the "Black Swan." Riabushinsky stood almost alone among Russian art patrons in supporting these artists, particularly by publishing their works in *Zolotoe Runo,* and by organizing and financing a series of exhibitions between 1907 and 1910, the Russian sections of which were devoted almost entirely to their paintings.

Because of a lavishness on the scale of the *Mir Iskusstva* exhibitions, those sponsored by Riabushinsky never returned more than a small fraction of the money he expended on them. Actually, his entire financial career was rather a dismal one. He played only a minor role in his family's business enterprises, took no real part in his family's almost constant economic expansion, and was a source not only of social, but also financial embarassment to his brothers.[37] He preferred to make his money as an investor, and despite the lack of respect such a position was accorded by his fellow merchant-industrialists, he did feel a certain sense of responsibility toward his business background: he was, for example, a loyal member and supporter of his brother Pavel's Moscow Merchants' Society, although what such support involved remains unclear.

Not unexpectedly, unwise expenditures and the relatively small income available to an "investor" ensured continual financial difficulties for Riabushinsky. His first serious problems arose in 1909 (by which time he had spent most of his original inheritance), and continued until 1913. 1910 saw not only the end of publication of his magazine *Zolotoe Runo,* but also his declaration of bankruptcy. In 1911, he was forced to auction off part of his art collection (although the works sold were the ones of which he had grown rather less fond) and to sell a portion of his share of the family estate at Kuchino.

By 1914, he had transferred most of his business and personal interests to Western Europe and in that year opened an antique shop in Paris, later moving it to the Riviera. His dealings with the new Soviet government were minimal, and he was never as virulent in his hatred of the new regime as were his brothers, perhaps because he had lost a great deal less to the new government than had either Pavel or Vladimir, for example.

Nikolai Riabushinsky himself was not typical of the new Moscow merchant-industrialist Maecenases who had come to such prominence in Russian cultural life by the end of the nineteenth century, rather he was almost a parody of them. Yet his tastes, his personality, his cultural and even his economic activities proved him a product of his age in a way the Petersburg "esthetes and decadents" surrounding *Mir Iskusstva* could no longer be in post-1905 Russia.

II

> The years following the suppression of the revolution were a period of anti-political individualism, which found its expression in the growth of estheticism and sexual freedom on one hand, and of the productive forces of capitalism on the other.
>
> D.S. Mirsky, *Contemporary Russian Literature*, p. 152

> These were the times of a characteristically fin de siècle cult of vice (mostly theoretical with an admixture of mysticism which sometimes turned into mystification).
>
> Alexandre Benois, *Memoirs*, volume 2, p. 123.

The political and social developments leading to the Russo-Japanese War and the revolution of 1905 have been recounted in several places, are well-known, and need not be repeated here.[38] A summary of the events themselves is not as useful as a description of the impact the upheavals had on the cultural figures with whom this work is concerned. The real significance of the two years of war and revolution could not be seen objectively at the time, but there was a reflection of it in the varying attitudes and positions taken by Russian modernist artists and writers, none of whom seriously influenced the course of events. This brief section does not intend to be an in-depth examination of "1905 and literature" or "1905 and art," but merely a summary of some aspects of the revolution's influence on cultural figures.[39] The broader impact of the revolution on Russian cultural life will be one of the principal motifs of the post-1905 years discussed in this study.

The initial Russian modernist reaction to the 1904 war with the Japanese was neither enthusiastically patriotic, nor was it defeatist; in fact, since a Russan victory was assumed, there seemed to be little concern or interest in the war's outcome at all. Benois has left an interesting and thoroughly honest picture of his own, and his closest acquaintances' feelings at the time:

> The attitude of almost everybody to it was extraordinarily frivolous, as if it were a minor adventure from which Russia would certainly be the victor. Just fancy, those insolent Japs, those yellow-faced monkeys, suddenly attacking the immense Russian state with its population of more than a hundred and eighty million! Many of us even pitied them, that if the war moved over to their islands it would mean the end of their wonderful art. A number of us had collections of prints by such Japanese masters as Hokusai, Hiroshige, Kunyoshi and Utomaro. Just a year before the outbreak of war Grabar had brought a traveling Japanese antiquarian to see me, from whom we had all bought, for fairly reasonable prices, the most beautiful pages and prints. Later there were rumors that the man had been a spy, but during his stay in Petersburg this possibility had never occurred to anybody.
> ...I must confess that we, the artists, were simply not interested in the war. We would glance through the war news and leave it at that.[40]

Benois' lack of concern about a war he felt had little relation to his own life was shared by most of his friends. The war itself demanded no serious position-taking on the part of people who were by this time Russian cultural leaders, but the revolution growing out of it did.

A number of prominent figures left Russia almost immediately after the beginning of revolutionary activity. Benois moved to Versailles as unrest grew, and remained there for two years. He made his decision ostensibly in the interests of his son's health, but also because of his own dislike of the disorder and irrationality inherent in the spontaneous and undirected uprisings he saw about him. In early 1906, Diaghilev also left Russia, later that year organizing in Paris the Russian section of the Salon d'Automne, the first step in what Benois described as the "export campaign of Russian art."[41] Diaghilev lived in the West from that time on, returning to Russia only occasionally, and increasingly devoting his time to what would become the real successor to *Mir Iskusstva,* the Ballets russes.

Others left Russia as well, but often for more pressing political and personal reasons. Merezhkovsky and Filosofov had written a book that, in Benois' words, was "a kind of personal indictment of the Tsar, a pamphlet obviously falling into the category of lèse-majesté." [42] Merezhkovsky's wife, Zinaida Gippius, had been widely known to have been associated with "parliamentary conspirators" at this time, and in the face of increasing governmental repression, she, Merezhkovsky, and Filosofov all left for France. Much of their fear may very well have been unfounded, however, and in fact, many of their friends felt they were only playing at revolution, achieving little with their activities.

Balmont left Russia under rather more directly threatening circumstances. Shocked at governmental reprisals in putting down the revolutionary uprisings, he had joined the Social Democrats and published his *Pesni mstitelia (Songs of an Avenger),* a collection of violent, noble, but poor poems in which he described Nicholas II as a "bloody hangman." Angry at the poet, the Tsar forced Balmont to emigrate in fear of arrest and did not allow him to return to Russia until 1913.

A new sense of social consciousness developed among many other artists and poets. Most of their actions, while significant in the development of their own psychological makeup, were ineffectual politically. Serov, for example,

always an independent spirit and fierce lover of social justice, had witnessed by chance the doings of that Black Sunday, from a friend's window; and, horrified, immediately sent in his resignation from the Academy, whose president was the Grand Duke Vladimir Aleksandrovich, commander of the troops that fired into the crowd.[43]

Lanseray and Dobuzhinsky were more active in the revolution, creating and contributing to such satirical revolutionary journals as *Zhupel (The Bugbear)* and *Adskaia Pochta (Hell's Post)*. Alexander Blok responded absolutely spontaneously to the excitement of events: "he even took part in one of the street processions and carried at its head a red flag, feeling himself one with the crowd."[44] Actually, Blok's reaction was essentially no different from that of most of those already mentioned. The times were so confused and uncertain, developments were taking place so rapidly and irrationally that purely emotional responses were almost all anyone, whether artist, poet, worker, or aristocrat was capable of producing.

A few men were less physically involved in the revolution, however, and devoted some time to an analysis of what they considered the situation in Russia to be. This was the case with Diaghilev before he finally decided to leave a Russia still embroiled in revolution. During the war months, he had been busily assembling and organizing the eighteenth-century paintings to be used in his "Historical Portrait Exhibition" in Petersburg's Tauride Palace. It opened in the midst of street demonstrations and battles, and at a banquet given in his honor, Diaghilev gave a fearful, reasoned, and sadly discouraged talk on himself, his activities, and the fate of Russia and its culture. His words deserve quotation at some length since his attitude was one widespread among his cultured and educated contemporaries:

> There is no doubt that every celebration [such as this] is a summation, and every summation is an ending. I am, of course, far from the thought that today's honor is in any way the end of those aspirations with which we have lived up until now, but I think that any will agree that the question of summations and endings forces itself more and more into one's thoughts these days. And it was with this question that I continually came into contact during the work I have just completed. Don't you feel that the long gallery of portraits of great and small people with which I attempted to populate the magnificent halls of the Tauride Palace is only a grandiose and convincing summing up of a brilliant, but alas, also dead period of our history? Saturated with an esthetic world-view, I am touched by the theatrical brilliance of the favoritism of the eighteenth century in the same way as before the legendary prestige of the sultans of the eighteenth year. But only old nurses remember these tales now, and the fruitful Tao with a note of imperceptible sarcasm brings us to the thought that we may no longer believe in the romantic heroism of terrifying helmets and invincible gestures. I have earned the right to say this loudly and definitively because with the last breath of the summer wind I finished my long travels far and wide across vast Russia. And immediately after these greedy wanderings I became convinced that the time of summation had come. I saw this not only in the brilliant images of those ancestors, so far from us, but more primarily in their descendants, still living out their lives. The end of a way of life is here at hand. The voiceless, boarded up, entailed estates, the palaces terrifying in their dead splendor, [are now] strangely inhabited by the present dear, mediocre people who could no longer stand the strain of earlier parades. Here are living out their lives not people, but a way of life. And this is where I became absolutely

convinced that we live in a terrible period of sudden change; we are doomed to die to give resurrection to a new culture which will take from us that which remains of our backward wisdom. This is the voice of history, and esthetics is exposed to it as well . . .
. . . We are witnesses to one of the greatest moments of summation and endings in history, in the name of a new unknown culture which will grow out of us, but which will brush us aside. And this is why, without fear and unbelief, I raise my glass to the destroyed walls of the beautiful palaces as well as to the new precepts of the new esthetic. And the only wish that I, as an incorrigible sensualist, may express, is that the battle confronting us does not insult the esthetics of life and that death would be as beautiful and as radiant as the Resurrection![45]

For a person as apolitical as Diaghilev to have described such an uncertain and politicized vision of the future of culture as he had known it in Russia was indicative of the change of attitude many Russians were making at the time of the revolution. For Blok, Lanseray, and Diaghilev, art (in its broadest sense) was clearly secondary to social and political necessity, to the demands of revolutionary change. Few would have dared to refute or disagree with such an idea in the midst of the confusion of the new surrounding reality. No one was certain how the transitional era would end, or whether his values or he himself would survive it.

Yet in January 1906, not long after Diaghilev's speech, a manifesto appeared on the first pages of the new magazine *Zolotoe Runo (The Golden Fleece)*. To emphasize its aspirations to universal relevance, it was printed in golden letters, and in French as well as in Russian:

> We embark on our journey at a formidable time.
> Around us life is renewing itself, seething like a raging whirlpool. In the crash of battle, in the midst of urgent questions that are put forward daily, and among the bloody answers given them by our Russian actuality, for many people that which is Eternal grows dim and retreats into the distance.
> We sympathize with all those who work for the renewal of life, we do not deny a single one of the problems of the present, but we firmly believe that it is impossible to live without Beauty . . . and together with free institutions . . . we must preserve for [our descendants] the eternal values forged over generations. And in the name of the life that is coming, we, the seekers for the golden fleece, unfold our banner:
> *Art* is eternal, for it is founded on the intransient; on that which is impossible to reject.
> *Art* is indivisible because its single source is the soul.
> *Art* is symbolic, for it carries in itself a symbol—the reflection of the Eternal in the temporal.
> *Art* is free for it is created by the free creative impulse.[46]

The new magazine was defending what in Russia had been considered an essentially "decadent" interpretation of the meaning of art, and which was still under attack from various directions at the beginning of 1906. While such people as Diaghilev and Benois had apparently abandoned hope for culture as they had known it in Russia, at least for the time being, the editors of *Zolotoe Runo* announced that they had not, and would not surrender their ideals to social and revolutionary exigencies.

But the goal of the preservation of the "Eternal values of Art," coupled with support for the ongoing "renewal of life" seemed contradictory to the manifesto's readers, whether they were symbolists or Socialist Revolutionaries. Such a combination simply did not correspond to a revolutionary situation which required one extreme attitude or another, not a mixture of what appeared to be opposing positions. Whether or not they were contradictory would become clear only later. The two themes were to be present not only in each issue of *Zolotoe Runo*, but were to flow throughout post-1905 Russian cultural life as well. Finally, the peculiar mixture of these two themes would define the nature of the years following the aborted revolution that would constitute a truly Russian *fin de siècle*.

The European *fin de siècle* as a whole grew out of the conditions of the second half of the nineteenth century: it was a response to the problem of materialism, to the threat of the machine and the masses who served the machine, and who wanted only material satisfaction from their lives. The term *fin de siècle* had its origin in a France disillusioned by the disaster of the Franco-Prussian War, the suppression of the Commune, and the continuing scandals and political crises of the Third Republic. A certain French elite, and other Europeans as well, came to envision an inevitable apocalypse, began to identify themselves with the last generation of Byzantium, on the eve of the city's fall to the Ottoman Turks. They believed that they and their world were repeating the Byzantine death agony. They rebelled against what in their eyes was an unstable society by attempting to escape into a world of dreams or illusions: for Ruskin, Morris, and the Pre-Raphaelites, the dream was the Middle Ages; for Yeats the world of the ancient Celts; for many Frenchmen, the mysteries of Baudelaire's *Les Fleurs du Mal,* one of "decadence" (the term was used first with its modern meaning in Théophile Gauthier's introduction to Baudelaire's book), of dandyism, exoticism, eroticism, and satanism. The *fin de siècle* feeling was one of unease becoming despair, often culminating in a cult of death and melancholy. Facing a world dominated by rampant materialism, the French symbolists wanted simply to escape: having concluded that the previously dominant European faith in realism had led only to systematic ugliness, they now considered it time for "beauty [to] be sought elsewhere, beyond facts, beyond life, beyond sense."[47] While disconsolate about the future, the major European *fin de siècle* cultural figures possessed tremendous talent, and in their searching for beauty, while attacked for their "decadence" by much of their society, they produced some of the greatest achievements of Western culture. At first consideration, this seems a dualistic paradox of this period, but in fact there is often an intimate connection between political and social disintegration (and the concomitant intellectual disillusionment), and esthetic rejuvenation, as Hilton Kramer has noted:

> The dialectic of culture is often fecund with paradox. A civilization may be dying, its social ethos drained of vitality and its political life driven to desperation and violence, and yet in the crucible of this extreme historical moment, when nearly all other signs point to dissolution and decay, an esthetic vision of great power and refinement may suddenly assert itself. Nor is it inevitably the case that such a vision draws its energy from a sense of partisanship with the most radical or forward-looking elements of society. Sometimes it does, and sometimes it does the very opposite. The greatest paradox may lie precisely there—in the fact that a great artistic accomplishment may derive its energy and focus from its sense of the distance, if not the outright opposition, that separates its own ideal of esthetic reconstruction from that of the political forces that are intent upon radical social reconstruction.[48]

It is in this paradoxical duality that the real essence of the European *fin de siècle* period lies.

Holbrook Jackson has pointed out that while discouragement may have been the initial cause of literary and artistic "searching" in Europe toward the end of the nineteenth century, the more general attitude of the time was one of change, struggle, and hope as much as one of despair, and that in fact the two were mixed in most of the age's major cultural figures. Max Nordau's remarkably influential *Entartung* (Berlin, 1892-93) described the 1890's as a period of decay, and contended that the "debased emotionalism" of the time had made every contemporary genius degenerate, that regressiveness was on a rampage. Jackson, on the other hand, described the 1890's, in Britain at least, as

> a renascent period, characterized by much mental activity and a quickening of the imagination, combined with pride of material prosperity, conquest and imperial expansion, as well as the desire for social service and a fuller communal and personal life.[49]

Unlike Nordau, Jackson saw the *fin de siècle* as an epoch of regeneration, within which the forces of decadence and renascence supplemented one another. On the one hand was the glorification of fine arts and artistic virtuosity alone, and on the other a militant commercial movement:

> The one produced *The Yellow Book* and the literature and art of "fine shades," with their persistent search for the "unique word" and the "brilliant" expression; the other produced the "Yellow Press," the boom in "Kaffirs," the Jameson Raid, the Boer War and the enthronement of the South African plutocrat in Park Lane.[50]

In most Western European countries there was a clear separation between "*The Yellow Book*" and the 'Yellow Press,' " between esthetes and materialists, modernists and traditionalists. The typical *fin de siècle* artist was more interested in the cultivation of his own emotions than in changing society so that it might appreciate his art. Yet John Ruskin felt that beauty was inseparable from a reformed society, and Oscar Wilde, the symbol of "decadent estheticism," wrote one of the most moving calls for the establishment of socialism. It often has been ignored or forgotten that while there was a duality within the age as a whole there was at the same time a surprising conflict between some of the esthetes who seemed best to represent the *fin de siècle* outlook.

In no case was the duality more noticeable than in Russia, however, where the government on the one hand, and the people on the other, the "small, victorious war" in Asia, and the spontaneous 1905 revolution provided the contrasts. Dualities abounded in turn-of-the-century Russia, particularly among the *fin de siècle* Russian modernists: the Russian decadents of the 1890's, the "first-generation symbolists," felt that art practised in isolation was still viable, and maintained this belief even after 1905; the younger poets, the symbolists of the "second generation,"[51] believed art could and should transform society, and that a theory of art was needed which could involve mankind as a whole. The typically *fin de siècle* theory of "art for art's sake" had some following among the Russian "decadents" up until the 1905 revolution. With that revolution's disillusioning failure, it was adopted wholeheartedly by large numbers of educated Russians, who carried to their extremes such "decadent" ideals as unfettered individualism, an indifference toward all ethical values, sensualism, amoralism, and eventually, narcissism. In the meantime, many of the former "esthetes" were rejecting their earlier, almost exclusive interest in Western culture, and were reexamining and newly appreciating Russian national poetic, literary, and artistic traditions, but selectively, and always from a modernist post-*fin de siècle* point of view. It is ironic that the *fin de siècle* traits of the "esthetes and decadents" of the 1890's received general public acceptance at a time when the Russian modernists themselves were already moving beyond them, when the "second generation symbolists" were combining German Idealism and the teaching of Vladimir Soloviev with the poetics of Mallarmé and Baudelaire. Yet an age's intellectual *avant-garde* often foreshadows the psychological development of society as a whole. The transition did not take place instantaneously, and as we shall see, was argued over and debated by all the modernists. Although Russia had experienced a cultural "decadence" similar to the Western European one in the decade immediately surrounding the turn of the century, there was no real Russian *fin de siècle* like that of Western

Europe's until after the 1905 revolution. At the center of this age was *Zolotoe Runo,* which although a continuation of developments begun earlier, and a strong indication of the directions Russian art and literature were to take after 1909, is the principal contemporary document for helping us understand the peculiar nature of the Russian *fin de siècle*. On its pages were represented and mirrored the successes, failures, enthusiasms and hatreds of its time in a way equalled by no other publication. It offers us a model of the hopes and disappointments of the revolutionary movement of 1905 among the modernists, of the period's popular preoccupation with such interests as sex and demonism, and of the beginnings of "realistic" modernism in literature and neo-primitivism in art. *Zolotoe Runo* provides us with what its editors would have called a "synthesized" example of the scope and significance of the cultural life of *fin de siècle* Russia, and the peculiarly Russian path away from "decadence" and toward a kind of modernist populism.

Part Two

Formation, Milieu, and Crisis:
Zolotoe Runo's First Two Years of Publication

V. Serov, *Portret M. Vrubelia (Portrait of M. Vrubel), ZR,* No. 11-12, 1909

II

APPEARANCE, RECEPTION, COMPETITION

...the pompous *Golden Fleece* of the disagreeable millionaire-snob Riabushinsky.
Johannes von Guenther, *Ein Leben im Ostwind,* p. 217

The first issue of *Zolotoe Runo,* with its (in the context of the times) decidedly apolitical esthetic manifesto, appeared during the greatest political and social upheaval Russia had experienced. Traces of the recent pitched battles of December 1905 could be seen throughout Moscow, and the magazine's first issue was itself being produced by the A.I. Mamontov print shop in the city's Presnia district at the same time the famous uprising was taking place. M.A. Mamontov, one of the shop's proprietors, assisted in the external mounting of *Zolotoe Runo,* and remarked later that it was strange to see on the presses the pages of a journal in which there was neither a reflection of the political events of the previous decade, nor of the more contemporary political and social troubles continually interfering with the magazine's printing.[1] Indeed, the only indication a reader unaware of the circumstances of the time might have of social unrest was the lines in the manifesto mentioning the "urgent questions and bloody answers of our Russian actuality," and a small insert facing the first issue's table of contents, apologizing for the typographical mistakes due to hurry and to the "conditions of the times through which we are living."[2]

The magazine's title itself, with its mystical associations, was representative of *Zolotoe Runo*'s rejection of social contemporaneity. It was in this way, in the tradition of other Russian and Western modernist journals, that *Zolotoe Runo* was in direct contrast to the previously dominant "thick journals." These other journals were clearly identifiable by their social and political positions: *Russkoe Bogatstvo (Russian Wealth), Nedelia (Week),* and *Russkaia Mysl (Russian Thought)* were populist journals; *Novoe Slovo (New Word), Zhizn (Life), Nachalo (The Beginning)* and *Mir Bozhii (God's World)* were Marxist; and *Vestnik Evropy (Messenger of Europe)* was considered independent of any organized group, but decidedly liberal. As its modernist predecessors had done, *Zolotoe Runo* dispensed with the political surveys and chronicles obligatory in these other journals, and despite the independent, apolitical position *Mir Iskusstva* had maintained, journals of literature and art were still expected to take definite political and social positions in early twentieth-century Russia.

The magazine's title caused something of a stir because it seemed to have a connection with a Moscow University circle to which Andrei Belyi (pseudonym of Boris Bugaev, 1880-1934) had belonged in 1901. Interested in poetry, esthetics, and modern cultural trends, the group had adopted the name Argonauts because they felt that the search for their (undefined) ultimate goal was similar to the mythological quest for the Golden Fleece.[3] Belyi had also published an "Argonautic" cycle in his book of poems *Zoloto v lazuri (Gold in Azure,* 1904), so the names had come to the symbolist public eye with some prominence by 1905. Belyi and his friends were certainly angry at what they considered *Zolotoe Runo*'s plagiarism, but felt there was no chance of legal action against the journal. And despite this apparent antagonism to the new magazine, Belyi became a prominent contributor to most of *Zolotoe Runo*'s early issues.

From the beginning, *Zolotoe Runo* proclaimed its aspiration to combine art and literature. The cover of the January 1906 inaugural issue was designed by the *miriskusnik* Evgeny Lanseray, and described the magazine as an "artistic, literary, and critical journal." While to some extent modeling the new magazine on *Mir Iskusstva,* the editors envisioned it as a successor that would nevertheless transcend the achievements of its Petersburg predecessor. Artistically, printed in quarto with remarkably fine reproductions, *Zolotoe Runo* surpassed *Mir Iskusstva.* Its programmatic manifesto was even printed in gold letters, in both Russian and French. Riabushinsky's personal wealth made such lavishness possible, and was a resource possessed by no other comparable Russian periodical (in 1906, for example, the magazine's revenue was only 12,000 rubles, while its expenses were 84,000 rubles; Riabushinsky made up the difference from his private fortune). The journal's artistic luxury was matched by the impressive list of contributors to the literary section, which included all the important Russian modernist writers.

Zolotoe Runo's publication in Russian with facing pages of French translation was an innovation among Russian periodicals. Undoubtedly, it was hoped that with what seemed inexhaustible financial resources, a technical competence equalling anything available in Western Europe, and the good will of so many important Russian modernist writers, "La Toison d'Or" might attract readers in France and elsewhere; in fact, subscription rates were quoted in both rubles and francs, and addresses throughout Europe were given where the magazine might be purchased. The first issues did not include translations of poetry into French, however, because a suitable "traducteur" had not as yet been found, and a notice had been inserted in the first issue promising that the translations of poetry into French would be of the highest quality. Ilya Ehrenburg was living in Paris at the time, and recalled that

> A stylist was required who was capable of correcting the translations. Riabushinsky stopped at no expense and ordered a real French poet. To fulfill this order proved difficult: no poet liked the idea of leaving Paris for a long time.[4]

In addition, the editors hoped to take advantage of the prospective translator's connections with Parisian cultural life in order to establish a wider exchange of ideas with France than had been the case in any previous Russian periodical.

During this early stage of *Zolotoe Runo*'s publication, it appears there was some interest in producing a German edition of the magazine as well. A German visitor to Moscow mentioned such an idea to Riabushinsky upon meeting him through friends of Belyi, "but [he] looked at me condescendingly, [saying] that he would not spend a single kopeck for such an endeavor."[5] Even though a German edition was not seriously contemplated in Moscow, the existence of such rumors does indicate a popular belief in the journal's enormous aspirations.

Zolotoe Runo's first issue fully expressed these hopes. To a great extent, the artistic section was devoted to Mikhail Vrubel (1856-1910), living at the time in a hospital for the insane in Moscow's Petrovsky Park.[6] As a creative artist, Vrubel had attained heroic stature among the Russian modernists, yet he was still ignored and rejected by the artistic establishment: it was only in 1908, for example, that the first (three) of his paintings were purchased by the Tretiakov Gallery,[7] although his work had always been popular with the Moscow merchant Maecenases. In this respect, it is significant to compare *Mir Iskusstva's* purely conventional selection of the considerably more traditional Viktor Vasnetsov as the major artistic subject for its first issue with *Zolotoe Runo*'s decision to dedicate its own to Vrubel: the choice indicated an (assumed) greater degree of sophistication on the part of the public, and a more outspoken, courageous support for modernist art by *Zolotoe Runo*. The section devoted to Vrubel included a poem by Valery Briusov set in a design by Riabushinsky. It was followed by several reproductions of Vrubel's works, including two self-portraits, costume and clothing designs, portraits, a panel later destroyed by the painter, and a colored drawing of the head of John the Baptist. While by no means a complete representation of Vrubel's oeuvre, the section did serve to give notice of what the magazine considered its artistic heritage.

Zolotoe Runo's second department, "Stikhi i belletristika" ("Poems and Prose"), began with the first installment of Merezhkovsky's long semi-autobiographical poem "Starinnye oktavy" ("Octaves of the Past"),[8] and

included a headpiece drawn by Lev Bakst. This was followed by four
Balmont poems under the general title "Ozherele" ("The Necklace") with
some remarkable drawings in the *Mir Iskusstva* tradition by Lanseray.
Accompanying the poems was Valentin Serov's full-page sketch of
Balmont, the first of a series of portraits of contemporary Russian writers
commissioned by Riabushinsky for the journal. The third major collection
of poems in the first issue was Briusov's "Voskresshie pesni" ("Resurrected
Songs"). An introductory note to the poems explained that they had been
written a few years earlier but could not be published because of prevailing
censorship conditions. Government censorship had only been relaxed
(under compulsion) toward the end of 1905,[9] and for the next year and a
half, until the Stolypin reaction reinstated it with a certain vengeance,
Zolotoe Runo and other Russian periodicals were to take advantage of the
new freedoms to publish what would never have been permitted previously.
The poetry section concluded with Blok's poem, "Vliublennost" ("In
Love"), and Belyi's "Goremyki" ("Poor Wretches").

The prose section consisted of three interesting works of a kind typical
in the magazine's later issues. Fedor Sologub (Fedor Teternikov, 1863-
1927) contributed his "Prizyvaiushchii zveria" ("The Summoner of the
Beast"), a chilling, psychological tale of irrational and inescapable
destruction set in a mystical past-present. It continued the tradition of
earlier "decadent" literature, had the type of theme particularly popular in
post-1905 Russia, and became an example of *Zolotoe Runo* fiction for the
non-modernist press.[10] The story was followed by Andrei Belyi's "Past
nochi" ("The Fall of Night"), described as a "fragment from an intended
mystery play" and the section concluded with Balmont's travelogue "Dva
slova ob Amerike" ("Two Tales About America," sent from El Paso,
Texas), the first of many such articles Balmont was to contribute to
Zolotoe Runo during the next few years of his enforced travel abroad.

Balmont began the journal's third section, "Khudozhestvennaia
kritika i stati kritiko-filosofskogo soderzhaniia" ("Artistic Criticism and
Articles of Critical-Philosophical Content"), with a product of his interest
in "exotic" subjects (one shared by the editors of *Zolotoe Runo*), a
translation of selections from the Mayan "holy book," the *Popul Vuh*.
Second was Merezhkovsky's "Vse protiv vsekh" ("All Against All"),
essentially a discussion of the new journal *Voprosy Zhizni (Questions of
Life),* which he called "one of the best of Russian journals."[11] Alexander
Blok contributed the final article, "Kraski i slova" ("Colors and Words"), a
theoretical examination of the problem of the artist's representation of the
real world of "living" nature and an article which would later prove an
important indication of Blok's changing attitudes toward literature and
reality, reflected in subsequent issues of *Zolotoe Runo.*[12]

The journal's fourth department, the "Khudozhestvennaia khronika"

("Art Chronicle"), opened with Filosofov's letter from the capital, "Khudozhestvennaia zhizn Peterburga" ("Petersburg Artistic Life"). The letter included one of the few clear indications in *Zolotoe Runo* of the impact revolutionary events were having on Russian writers and artists, Filosofov darkly wondering whether or not Russian cultural life would be able to survive contemporary social and political disruptions. He concluded more optimistically, and pointed out that a revolution such as the one through which Russia was living, with its increasing tempo of change, could only be represented in such satirical journals as *Zhupel,* with their political cartoons, and by implication, not in a magazine like *Zolotoe Runo,* entrusted with maintaining a Russian culture in danger of destruction.

Filosofov's article was followed by a series of art, theater, and music reviews. Nikolai Roerich, Sergei Makovsky, and V. Golubev wrote on a current exhibition of Japanese art; Nina Petrovskaia on Moscow theatrical life; Volfing (Emily Medtner) on two Rakhmaninov operas being performed at Moscow's Bolshoi Theater; and Nikolai Tarovaty on an exhibition of watercolors in Moscow. Konstantin Siunnerberg further emphasized the difference between the first issues of *Zolotoe Runo* and *Mir Iskusstva* in his "Sukhie listia" ("Dry Leaves"), a discussion of Viktor Vasnetsov's most recent works, which Siunnerberg described as "dry, uninspired, lifeless."[13] The notices concluded with an article by Mizgir (Boris Popov) on Mozart and a summary of the recent developments in Moscow's artistic life by A. K. (Alexander Kursinsky).

"Vesti otovsiudu" ("From Every Quarter"), a series of short news items, followed the section of artistic reviews and included a reprint of an open letter published in many of the Petersburg newspapers. Entitled "Golos khudozhnikov" ("The Voice of the Artists"), it was signed by Dobuzhinsky, Somov, Benois, and Lanseray, and was an attack on the St. Petersburg Academy of Arts, a call for the institution's radical reform. It was indicative of *Zolotoe Runo* that although the magazine itself was not directly involved with this protest, it was in complete agreement with it, and the letter's combative tone and anti-academism were to become fundamental features of the magazine's artistic program.

The final "Kritiko-bibliograficheskii otdel" ("Critical-bibliographical Department") consisted of brief reviews of recently published books. It included comments by Blok on Briusov's *Stefanos-Venok (Stephanos-Wreath),* Belyi on Balmont's *Feinye skazki (Fairy Tales),* Kursinsky on Sergei Rafalovich's *Svetlye pesni (Luminous Songs),* Khodasevich on the most recent *Znanie* collection and other reviews by Petrovskaia, Bachinsky, and Khodasevich. The issue concluded with instructions for the submission of manuscripts.

At the end of this and each succeeding issue of *Zolotoe Runo* was printed "Redaktor izdatel Nikolai Riabushinsky" ("Editor publisher Nikolai Riabushinsky"). The magazine's physical form and organization were officially the responsibility of five members of the editorial board, but Riabushinsky was the individual board member with whom the public was most familiar: *Zolotoe Runo* was recognized as being his journal. Riabushinsky reinforced this impression by making a point of riding ostentatiously to the magazine's offices in an ornate, elegant coach recognizable to everyone.[14]

As with Diaghilev and *Mir Iskusstva,* Riabushinsky's main contribution to his journal was in its organizational affairs. A.M. Mamontov remembered his company's dealings with Riabushinsky:

> We all . . . from the typesetter to the maker-up and owners of the print shop were sincerely fascinated with Riabushinsky's undertakings. He demanded only one thing from everyone: a bit smarter and a bit clearer. We, of course, tried as much as possible to fulfill the demands unhampered by [any limitations in] the customer's means, and it seemed that in such a way we succeeded in creating quite a good polygraphic publication.[15]

Despite his technical competence in putting together the magazine, as well as the fact that it was probably he who wrote the first issue's manifesto, Riabushinsky was not particularly interested in, nor did he take great part in the editorial work essential to each issue's publication. His own tastes in literature and art were inconsistent and not very discriminating, and although at times he was unyielding in his decisions, the real work of organizing and editing the magazine was carried on by the other editors. Fortunately, perhaps, Riabushinsky gave most of the editorial decision-making over to his secretaries and co-editors, and as a result, the majority of articles placed in *Zolotoe Runo* were read by him only after publication. It was not Riabushinsky who determined the "tvorcheskoe litso,"[16] the literary-artistic orientation of his publication.

The magazine's artistic section received most of Riabushinsky's interest and it was there he exerted the greatest influence. He appears to have been quite close to the art section's editor, Nikolai Tarovaty (1876-1906), who may even have been Riabushinsky's artistic mentor. Tarovaty had formerly edited his own magazine, *Iskusstvo (Art),* which appeared in Moscow beginning in January 1905 and ran for only eight monthly issues. Tarovaty's importance within *Zolotoe Runo* justifies considering his earlier journal the immediate predecessor and a model for the artistic section of Riabushinsky's publication. *Iskusstvo* adopted a positive attitude toward modernism and a negative one toward realism and impressionism. Viktor Hoffmann had stated *Iskusstvo*'s artistic position in the first number's "What Art Is," when he defined the "ideal" of symbolism (which he equated with the "ideal" of all contemporary art) as the science of the individual, of the subjective "I," of mystical intimism, and described symbolism as being valid both as an esthetic and theurgic force.[17] Not surprisingly, *Iskusstvo* was a firm supporter of the later *Golubaia roza (Blue Rose)* artists, and Tarovaty was known to have personal ties with these symbolist painters. Tarovaty did not reject all earlier artistic movements, however, and some *Mir Iskusstva* artists were included on his editorial staff, an expression of a certain artistic tolerance that would be adopted by *Zolotoe Runo*. *Iskusstvo* discontinued publication for a number of reasons: despite additional financial support from Sergei Krechetov (Sergei Sokolov, 1878-1936), the magazine's financial losses continued to mount; the problems arising from the disruptions of revolutionary activity were continually frustrating; and in addition, Tarovaty was incurably ill. He died in October 1906, "even while he was working,"[18] and was replaced as *Zolotoe Runo*'s art editor by Vasily Milioti (1875-1943), another close friend of Riabushinsky, and a member of *Golubaia roza*.

It was Tarovaty's friend and supporter Sergei Sokolov (co-editor of *Iskusstvo*'s last issue), who became *Zolotoe Runo*'s literary editor. Belyi wrote in his memoirs that Riabushinsky hoped Briusov would accept the position,[19] but Briusov was not anxious to do so because of his already time-consuming duties as editor of *Vesy*. Sokolov had been trained as a lawyer, but was also a poet, translator, and head of the modernist publishing house "Grif" ("Gryphon"). Sokolov and Riabushinsky did not get along well, however, and their mutual dissatisfaction with one another was only worsened by the publisher's at times dictatorial nature. Sokolov was competent as a literary editor, but when Tarovaty died, he saw no reason to remain with *Zolotoe Runo*. He resigned both as editor and contributor, and was replaced by Alexander Kursinsky (1873-1919). Sokolov then founded his own journal, *Pereval (The Pass)*, which was published in Moscow from autumn 1906 until autumn 1907. Describing itself as a journal of "volnye mysli" ("free thought"), it had to compete both with *Zolotoe Runo* and *Vesy*, the other major Russian modernist periodical, and never proved very successful. One important result of Sokolov's resignation was that Briusov, while not formally accepting the title of literary editor, did offer more help to *Zolotoe Runo*. Briusov wrote in his diary that

> In Sweden [Briusov had spent the summer of 1906 there] I learned that S. A. Sokolov had abandoned *Zolotoe Runo* and this encouraged me to become closer to the journal. Since autumn I have begun often to take part in the editing and to offer advice.[20]

Briusov's help could only have been appreciated in light of what appeared to be constant disorganization among the journal's editorial staff members.

Zolotoe Runo's initially small musical section was headed by Arseny Koreshchenko (1870-1921). Koreshchenko had attended the Moscow Conservatory of Music, where he had studied with Taneev and Arensky and had received gold medals for piano and theory. A conductor and pianist, he also composed a series of operas and music for plays, made adaptations of Armenian and Georgian folk songs for orchestra and voices, and was a musical contributor to the *Moskovskie Vedomosti (The Moscow Gazette)*. Koreshchenko's role in *Zolotoe Runo* was a small one, and he gave no original or critical work of his own to the magazine except for one short piece of music at the end of 1907; still, his name was an impressive one to have associated with the new journal. His influence was soon superseded by that of Emily Medtner (1871-1936), who took over official editorship of the musical section when the journal was reorganized in 1907.

Certainly the most significant editorial position was that of secretary and "manager of translations," held by Genrikh Tasteven (d. 1916). Tasteven was *Zolotoe Runo*'s managing editor, and his importance continually increased, especially with the journal's reorganization in 1907. Tasteven was an unusual man about whom not a great deal is known today.[21] Igor Grabar, an artist sympathetic to *Mir Iskusstva,* but who refused to collaborate with *Zolotoe Runo* (and who had wanted to create an art journal of his own in 1905 similar to *Mir Iskusstva*) wrote to Benois that he was unsure who was the greater boor, Riabushinsky or Tasteven.[22] Georgy Chulkov (1879-1939), on the other hand, was a close friend of Tasteven who thought very highly of him:

> No matter how significant Tasteven's cultural activity was, no matter how interesting the thoughts and judgements in [his] articles...one can't help forgetting it all when thinking about him. In his personality there was something more important than his literary experiences and public lectures. And to us, his friends, it seemed that in his articles he did not express the entirety of his spiritual life. For many he was only a dilettante, [even though he was the] possessor of a great deal of knowledge in the fields of painting, poetry, and philosophy. But there was not just dilettantism in Tasteven: in him there was a spiritual purity and greatness and a tense and disinterested thirst for truth. And these qualities combined in him with modesty and tenderness in his relations with people.[23]

Throughout his life, Tasteven was a strong supporter of modernism (expressed in *Zolotoe Runo* articles signed with his own name and his pseudonym "Empirik"), and in 1914 he published one of the first Russian books supporting Futurism.[24] Tasteven was a close friend of Riabushinsky, and was able to work as well with him as were Tarovaty and Milioti. He held the post of general secretary during the entire period of the magazine's publication, his influence and control growing as time went on, so that during its final year, *Zolotoe Runo*'s non-artistic section was more representative of Tasteven's tastes and judgments than of those of any other member of the magazine's staff.

The Russian public was at first little aware of the internal disagreements that faced *Zolotoe Runo* from its inception. Its impressions were based on the magazine's external appearance. Even the Tsar's attention was drawn by *Zolotoe Runo*'s brashness and luxury: Nicholas held a special audience to receive Riabushinsky and to accept the first nine issues of the magazine in a binding designed by the editor-publisher himself. Others were surprised at the fact of publication alone: Vladimir Giliarovsky and Savva Mamontov were enthusiastic about the magazine's polygraphic beauty, its extravagant paper, and the remarkable execution of the reproductions, noting that "all this seemed especially unusual and astonishing in that Moscow had not yet completely 'come to itself' and 'regained its senses' after the recent revolutionary storm."[25]

Others, however, refused to take the journal seriously, labeling it a "merchant's whim,"[26] a journal without direction, or a "vulgarly-ingenious publication."[27] A not atypical reaction was expressed by *Mir Bozhii*'s reviewer, Vladimir Kranikhfeld:

> The price of the folio seemed fit—two rubles for each issue. The thickness of the journal seems deceptive with detailed examination however. Not because the journal was lined with cotton [i.e, the thin semi-transparent dividers between some of the illustrations and preceding pages], but because the whole text, with the exception of the poems, was accompanied by a translation in French, while the text and translation was published in large type, the way books for the smallest children are usually published.[28]

Kranikhfeld was also critical of the quality of the French translations (done in this first issue by Tasteven), and used the Merezhkovsky article to point out some inconsistencies. Writing that few of the contributors to *Zolotoe Runo*, although talented, had any sense of measure in their work, he remarked that on every page the reader was plagued with "siurprizy" of "delirious ravings and nightmares" (Sologub's story), "ugly voluptuousness" (Briusov's "Voskresshie pesni"), and in general, "grimaces, grimaces without end . . . "[29] In his review's concluding lines, Kranikhfeld did admit that the quality of the illustrations was very high indeed, but countered that their organization seemed determined by chance and gave no clear indication of the individual physiognomy of the artist's work. Kranikhfeld's notice was a long one, and fairly typical not only of the Marxist view of *Zolotoe Runo*, but of that of the non-modernist press in general.

Such reactions to *Zolotoe Runo* must have been responses as much to Riabushinsky's promotional activities on behalf of the journal as to the magazine itself. The receptions in honor of *Zolotoe Runo*'s appearance had been especially notorious, as Briusov noted in a February 1906 letter:

> Every day *Zolotoe Runo* organizes solemn drunkenness (or "orgiastic festivals")—
> and this is all that our literary world talks about. The Metropol Restaurant has even
> invented a new parfait—the "Zolotoe Runo."[30]

Belyi's impression of the Metropol Hotel festivities celebrating the appearance of the magazine's first issue was one undoubtedly shared by a number of other observers:

> The evening on which [Riabushinsky] made his announcement terrified me; to be
> sure there were no longer [gun] shots being fired, but the hall resounded with the
> popping of corks; artists with arms around the sons of millionaires suddenly got drunk
> among the pile of cut-glass and golden-necked bottles; I was forced to deprive myself of
> this unappetizing spectacle, hurrying to go away—all the more so because a famous
> artist who had a salon in Paris, under the influence of alcoholic excitement suddenly
> sat down on my lap and did not want to get up.
> Getting her up, I left hurriedly; and in a day left: for Piter.[31]

Zolotoe Runo's initial impact was that of a *succès de scandale,* and there was considerable bewilderment (not least among the editors themselves) as to where the magazine's real focus lay.

Zolotoe Runo's debt to *Iskusstvo* was obvious, and Savva Mamontov remarked that in comparison with Diaghilev, who had started from scratch with *Mir Iskusstva,* Riabushinsky had simply taken as his basis *Iskusstvo,* a fact easily seen by reading the list of the new journal's contributors.[32] This uncertainty about the nature and goals of *Zolotoe Runo* was also present in a letter Vrubel wrote to his wife in January 1908, in which he mentioned that he recently had been visited by Tarovaty, "editor of *Iskusstvo* (now called *Zolotoe Runo*), and the head of the journal, Riabushinsky."[33] Vrubel was barely in control of his mind at this time, of course, but his confusion about the new magazine was not an uncommon attitude. *Iskusstvo* had been purely an art journal, however; *Zolotoe Runo* was not. Yet even today there is a tendency to describe *Zolotoe Runo* as being dedicated almost exclusively to fine arts.[34] Marcadé has pointed out that the preponderant place in the journal was given to literary works, and that this clearly distinguished it from its purely artistic competition and predecessor.[35] Its apparent emphasis on art seemed overwhelming only when compared with *Vesy.*

Vesy (The Balance) was also published in Moscow, but differed from *Zolotoe Runo* in its almost exclusive emphasis on literary concerns and in its modest, strict businesslike activity—a direct contrast to the disorderly, noisy chaos of *Zolotoe Runo.*[36] *Vesy* was published by Sergei Poliakov (1870-1938), who, although official editor, left the real day-to-day work of the journal to Briusov, rarely visiting the magazine's editorial office in the

Metropol Hotel. Unlike Riabushinsky, Poliakov had a retiring nature, and was respected by the Moscow intelligentsia for his wide cultural knowledge. Most importantly, building on his experience as director of the "Skorpion" ("Scorpio") publishing house (founded in 1900), Poliakov was able to reconcile contradictory points of view among contributors to *Vesy*, a talent Riabushinsky sorely lacked.

At Briusov's suggestion, *Vesy* had begun publication in 1903 as a forum for the expression of modernist opinions on literature. Briusov's programmatic article in *Vesy*'s first issue announced goals for the "new art": support for idealistic philosophy and esthetics in the battle for a pure, "higher" art, and opposition to the traditions of revolutionary-democratic criticism and the literature of critical realism.[37] *Vesy* was such a product of Briusov's activities and attitudes in the eyes of its contemporaries that Chulkov was able to write in 1910 that "for me the journal and the man merge into one."[38]

Vesy had been as much an innovation among Russian literary periodicals as had *Mir Iskusstva* in art publications. Its small format provided only one-third the number of pages of the thick journals, and was modeled to a great extent on the very influential *Mercure de France*. It remained aloof from political surveys and chronicles and even during the unrest of 1905 kept entirely to artistic and literary questions, ignoring social and political problems. The predominance of critical material over fiction or reportage was another new step for literary journals in Russia. While concerning itself primarily with literature, however, *Vesy* did include essays dealing with philosophy and art, and following the lead of *Mir Iskusstva,* considered individual issues independent artistic units, frequently devoting them to individual themes.

When *Zolotoe Runo* appeared, it was obvious that *Vesy* would be its principal competitor, since the two journals would be appealing to the same audience and drawing from essentially the same group of writers and critics. *Vesy*'s reception of the new magazine was undoubtedly more important than that of any other periodical to the editors of *Zolotoe Runo* and to the readers of both modernist journals. It was expressed initially in the review of Tovarishch German (Comrade Hermann, pseudonym of Zinaida Gippius) in the February 1906 issue of *Vesy*.

Gippius began by criticizing the pretentiousness of the journal's manifesto:

> I am absolutely sure that there is no reader of *Zolotoe Runo* who has not heard that beauty exists, that art exists, that beauty is eternal, and art as well. So why announce this on the nuptial announcement? This is really an innovation....[39]

Expanding this "nuptial" theme, Gippius compared the manifesto's golden letters to those of a wedding invitation and the images such a comparison conjures up of a carriage, church, and bridal veil. Returning to her criticism of *Zolotoe Runo*'s "pretension," Gippius wrote that "the 'invitation' is also repeated on the right—in a French dialect. Apparently it is also time for Frenchmen to find out that nothing can live without beauty and that it is eternal.... "[40] (*Vesy*'s criticisms of *Zolotoe Runo*'s French translations were to be a major reason for their eventual discontinuation). Gippius continued the determinedly superior, condescending tone of her review by discussing *Zolotoe Runo*'s position within the tradition established by *Mir Iskusstva,* warning the new magazine that it would have to do more than repeat the same mistakes *Mir Iskusstva* had made if it hoped to equal the Petersburg journal.

Having facetiously described the literary direction of *Zolotoe Runo* as being a "decadence that had fallen into decay," Gippius concluded with some guarded encouragement, and a warning:

> I judge only results, and am annoyed only by those who condemn nothing; on the other hand, I look forward with hope. If desires and attempts are true—there is always hope that desires will bear fruit sometime in the future. And, actually, one hopes with all his heart that they do bear fruit.[41]

Although *Zolotoe Runo* was uncertain of itself, in the eyes of *Vesy*'s reviewer, it was not a hopeless undertaking. But it must not only teach art, but learn it as well: " 'Beauty' is not copied, like a dress from Paris. And luxury is not beauty."[42]

Despite its sharp and cynical tone, German-Gippius' review did point out some of *Zolotoe Runo*'s problems and helped clarify its position at the beginning of 1906. The manifesto was indeed rather pretentious, and while much of its ostentatiousness could be attributed to Riabushinsky's own personal tastes, it was also the result of the journal's conscious vision of itself as the heir of *Mir Iskusstva.* There *were* great dangers in attempting to live up to the achievements of its enormously influential Petersburg predecessor. *Zolotoe Runo* hoped to accomplish this by combining the talents of the former *miriskusniki* with their Moscow associates and successors, and by promoting new, increasingly more modern schools of art.

One advantage *Mir Iskusstva*'s literary section had had over its successor's was that in the years immediately around the turn of the century, the Russian symbolists had possessed no real journal of their own and were consequently often forced to rely on *Mir Iskusstva* for their works' public exposure. With growing symbolist strength, *Vesy* and a number of other periodicals which would publish symbolist works came into existence. The resultant literary competition between *Zolotoe Runo* and *Vesy* intensified when it became clear that the number of talented symbolist writers was insufficient to fill both journals. One of the reasons pseudonyms were used so often by the Russian symbolists was that it made their number seem greater. Belyi warned about the problem in 1907, after returning to Russia from abroad: wondering where to concentrate his own activities (beyond *Vesy*, to which he felt he owed his first allegiance), he admitted that he and the other symbolists simply could not fill three journals.[43] Fortunately for *Zolotoe Runo*, it was *Pereval*, the third principal modernist periodical, that was unable to attract these writers.

Despite an uneven reception, *Zolotoe Runo* was assured some success by its optimism, enthusiasm (even its pretentiousness), and by Riabushinsky's financial resources. The timing of its appearance had been surprising at the least, and its life span was to cover an unsettled period in Russian history, one initially of almost unbridled freedom and license, and later one of increasing reaction and repression. The magazine began publication at a time when symbolism was becoming more popular with the general public than it had ever been before. Symbolist writers were able to demand higher salaries for their work, salaries that *Vesy* was unable to pay, but which *Zolotoe Runo* could. This popularity of symbolist literature was equalled by the unprecedented success of the former *miriskusniki*. No one (except Riabushinsky's brothers, perhaps) ever really expected *Zolotoe Runo* to be financially profitable, but at the beginning of 1906, and even in the face of a lukewarm reception of a nevertheless stunning debut, Russia seemed ready to support the new magazine, and its chances for success seemed undoubted.

III

THE ORGANIZATION AND CONTENT OF
ZOLOTOE RUNO: 1906-1907

The journal appears monthly, beginning in January 1906, with a fiction section, published simultaneously in two languages (Russian and French), in the format of large artistic publications, with drawings, illustrations, colored enclosures, original headpieces, vignettes, etc.

We plan to include in the journal, in the area of *belles-lettres,* a series of the latest works of the leading Russian writers and poets, and the editors intend at the same time to provide a place for the most interesting representatives of young literary talent.

A survey of the works of contemporary Russian artists.

A survey of the painting and sculpture of contemporary foreign artists.

Apart from the problems of pure art, the editors intend to give special attention to artistic industry and decorative art.

A series of portraits of contemporary Russian writers executed by well-known artists will appear in various issues of the journal.

Zolotoe Runo, 1906, No. 2, 136-7.

The tastes and interests of the real directors of *Zolotoe Runo*—its secretaries— were never really defined and the magazine never really determined what its "face" was to be.

V. Lobanov, *Kanuny,* p. 180.

I

Zolotoe Runo's Artistic Section

During its first two years of publication, *Zolotoe Runo's* principal interest was in art and art criticism, and this emphasis defined the magazine's nature and physical appearance. This was not an unexpected decision since *Iskusstvo* and *Mir Iskusstva,* upon which *Zolotoe Runo* modeled itself, were themselves concerned primarily with questions of art. In addition, the editors exercising initial control over the magazine were interested only secondarily in literature, and as a consequence, the large sums of money Riabushinsky intended to spend assured *Zolotoe Runo* a full and impressive artistic department.

The list of contributors to the artistic section was given in the February

1906 issue, and included most of the well-known Russian modernist painters of the time:

> Benois, Bakst, Vrubel, S. Vinogradov, Golovin, Golubkina, Grabar, Modest Durnov, Dobuzhinsky, Kuznetsov, Korovin, E. Kruglikova, E. Lanseray, Maliavin, V. Milioti, Nesterov, Roerich, Sabashnikova, Sapunov, Sredin, Serov, Somov, Feofilaktov, Vl. Fisher.[1]

With the addition of other names to the list in subsequent issues, *Zolotoe Runo's* artistic department soon included representatives from every modernist tendency within Russian art, from the St. Peterburg *miriskusniki* to the Moscow symbolist painters of *Golubaia roza*. Despite their heterogeneity, these contributors did share an enthusiasm for the works of the two almost legendary Russian modernist painters, Mikhail Vrubel (1856-1910) and Viktor Borisov-Musatov (1870-1905). It surprised no one that *Zolotoe Runo's* first issue was to a great extent devoted to Vrubel, and the March issue similarly to Musatov. The two artists' works were still controversial and (as we have noted particularly in Vrubel's case) even by 1906 had been purchased only by the merchant Maecenases and by a few members of the aristocracy. Their work was still rejected by such officially prestigious organizations as the St. Petersburg Academy of Arts. *Zolotoe Runo* announced its firm support for these artists, and for Russian artistic modernism, by naming them its artistic spiritual forebears.

It was Vrubel who held the predominant place as the true genius of modern Russian art, however, and his name and reproductions of his work appeared continually on *Zolotoe Runo's* pages, to an extent equalled by no other contemporary Russian periodical. Typical of the magazine's reverential attitude toward the painter was A. Vorotnikov's article in the April 1906 issue: "Tvoreniia Vrubelia v Kirillovskom khrame"[2] ("Vrubel's Work in the Cathedral of St. Cyril") described the eight-hundred-year-old Kiev church as a frame for the "immortal creations of Vrubel,"[3] and discussed in some detail the "glories" of Vrubel's mosaics.

Such enthusiastic praise was coupled with a continuing defense of Vrubel's works from the attacks of the more conservative Russian art critics, and *Zolotoe Runo's* editors even hoped to provide more direct financial and artistic support to the artist as well. Riabushinsky had written Vrubel in 1905, requesting that he do a portrait of Briusov as one in a series to be published in *Zolotoe Runo,* and offered the artist 200 rubles for the commission.[4] Briusov and Riabushinsky later visited Vrubel in the Usoltsev psychiatric hospital where he was living, and discovered that although the artist had accepted the commission, he had nothing with which to work. As a result, Vrubel wrote in a letter to his wife, "Riabushinsky gave me a good light easel and a complete, large collection not of pastels, but of colored pencils."[5] The work was finally begun, and continued for several sittings (although because of his failing memory, Vrubel was able to remember only three) and innumerable reworkings. It soon became clear to Riabushinsky and Briusov that although "through [Vrubel's] madness shown genius,"[6] completion of the portrait was physically and mentally impossible for the artist. Riabushinsky paid Vrubel and took the unfinished work, however, reproducing it in *Zolotoe Runo,* and later exhibiting it in Moscow, Petersburg, and Paris.[7]

Even in its only partially completed state (Vrubel's alterations in the background had left it a confusion of lines), the portrait remains one of the most remarkable in all Russian art, and Briusov commented later that "after this portrait, I need no others."[8] Briusov's evaluation was not exaggerated, for Vrubel had successfully captured the poet's psychological personality. In Maslenikov's words:

> It depicts Valery Briusov standing in his favorite pose, with his arms crossed over his chest; his broad face is stern; the high Mongolian cheekbones and the short, black, spade-like beard lend it an air of severity. Yet his black beady eyes suggest a feline slyness and belie a carefully studied solemn pose, calculated to impress his public. The portrait is a remarkable piece of interpretation: Briusov the poseur, shines through Briusov, the leader.[9]

This portrait was the last work Vrubel did before his death in 1910, and it was fitting that it was initiated and given public exposure by the magazine which esteemed him more highly than it did any other Russian artist and which propagated and defended his works throughout its publishing life.

Second in importance only to Vrubel for *Zolotoe Runo* was Borisov-Musatov. Musatov had lived in Paris and had been particularly influenced by such French symbolist painters as Puvis de Chavannes and Maurice Denis. After his return to Russia, in an attempt to depict an ulterior reality, he painted a series of "retrospective landscapes" which almost always included beautiful, and unattainable idealized women, two-dimensional representations of Vladimir Soloviev's "Eternal Feminine." Musatov had taught painting in Saratov and in Moscow and had been the primary artistic influence on the *Golubaia roza* artists, who were in turn of great significance in determining *Zolotoe Runo*'s artistic position.[10] The issue in Musatov's honor was similar to the one dealing with Vrubel of two months before. The pictorial section was introduced with a full-page design by Musatov's student Pavel Kuznetsov, and contained a photograph and self-portrait of Musatov, studies for frescoes, and drawings. Belyi's "Rozovye girliandy" ("Rosy Garlands"), a tribute written "on the death of Borisov-Musatov,"[11] followed, and was accompanied by vignettes designed by Vasily Milioti and by Bakst's drawing "Kolokolnyi zvon" ("The Sound of Bells"), dedicated to Musatov's memory. Finally, Alexander Sredin's "O Borisove-Musatove" ("On Borisov-Musatov") included a short biography on the artist's professional life, and discussed influences on, and themes in, Musatov's work.[12] Musatov's name appeared continually in *Zolotoe Runo*, and because of his close personal contacts with many of *Zolotoe Runo*'s contributors, he exerted an influence over the magazine's artistic section unequalled even by Vrubel. But because of his early death, it remained one more retrospective than continually active.

This esteem shown Vrubel and Musatov by *Zolotoe Runo*, in addition to the manifesto printed in the magazine's first issue, provides an indication of the initial artistic orientation *Zolotoe Runo* had determined for itself. Modern art would predominate in the new magazine, both because of *Zolotoe Runo*'s own esthetic position and because an important part of the magazine's artistic activity, the headpieces and decorations for all the issues' articles, were commissioned from the most progressive living Russian artists. Several special issues dealing with individual artists appeared during the first two years of publication. February 1906 was devoted to Somov's work, and was accompanied by Bakst's portrait of the artist. The same year's April issue was in turn devoted to the works of Bakst, and included his famous portrait of Zinaida Gippius (published for the first time), full-color reproductions of some of his costume designs, and a self-portrait. October 1906 dealt with Benois, and included reproductions of several of his works (some from his current Versailles series) and a biographical essay by Prince Alexander Shervashidze.[13] Three such issues devoted to modern artists appeared in 1907. The first, on Mikhail Nesterov (1862-1942), consisted of reproductions, a "spiritual" appreciation of the artist's works by Vasily Rozanov,[14] and a biographical sketch by Alexander Sredin.[15] The second dealt with Nikolai Roerich and featured a full-color reproduction of his painting "Boi" ("The Battle"), a portrait of Roerich by Golovin, a biographical essay by Sergei Makovsky,[16] and an article by Alexander Rostislavov on Roerich's "artistic individualism."[17] Much less encompassing was Maximilian Voloshin's article on Konstantin Bogaevsky (1872-1943) in October 1907.

While these attempts at a comprehensive examination of individual artists' works were of great value, equally important was the magazine's policy of publishing pictorial reviews of current Russian art exhibitions, usually accompanied by the comments of a well-known artist or critic. While at times an issue's entire pictorial section would deal with a single exhibition (as was the case with those sponsored by *Zolotoe Runo*), more common was the "obzor vystavok," a selection of works from several exhibitions. Certain prejudices were apparent, however, and reproductions from *peredvizhniki (The Wanderers)* exhibitions only rarely appeared, for example. There was a clear attempt at unity in the choices and organization of the "obzory": while the first part of the review of 1906 exhibitions appeared in May with the works of the symbolist artists Kuznetsov,

Milioti, Feofilaktov, Sapunov, Iavlensky, Krymov, and Larionov, the second installment (in the June issue) consisted of the similarly homogeneous works of the *miriskusniki* Golovin, Serov, Lanseray, Benois, Dobuzhinsky, Bakst, Bilibin, Iuon, and Grabar. By grouping the works together in such a way, and in fact, by reproducing paintings being shown at exhibition at all, *Zolotoe Runo* provided an important informational resource for anyone interested in current Russian artistic developments. No other Russian periodical made such a pictorial attempt at keeping its readers artistically informed.

The educative aim of the magazine's artistic section was expressed as well by a series of illustrated articles on historical subjects, usually directed toward the preservation of formerly unappreciated Russian artistic treasures. *Mir Iskusstva* and *Khudozhestvennye Sokrovishcha Rossii (Artistic Treasures of Russia)* had dealt with historical subjects, and the new *Starye Gody (Olden Times,* beginning publication in 1907) was dedicated entirely to eighteenth-century art, but such articles acquired special prominence by appearing in the "modernist" *Zolotoe Runo.* On the whole, in fact, the magazines proved complementary rather than competitive, since *Zolotoe Runo*'s choices for subjects (usually pre-Petrine art or specific aspects of more recent artists) were oriented more toward symbolist or neo-primitivist interests than was the case with the other magazines.

As early as March 1906, *Zolotoe Runo*'s entire illustrated section was devoted to eighteenth-century embroideries (with a comparative modern example by Pavel Kuznetsov). Later that year a triple issue dealt with Russian painting from the fifteenth to eighteenth centuries, and consisted of a five-part collection of reproductions, each with an interpretive essay by Alexander Uspensky (1873-1938), a highly-respected professor of art history at Kharkov University. The issue included lengthy discussions of icons, the frescos of the Moscow Kremlin's Annunciation Cathedral, foreign artistic influences during the seventeenth century (with a particularly fine article by Uspensky, an adaptation of a lecture given earlier in 1906), the painter Vasily of Poznan, and Russian genre painting in the seventeenth century.[18] Uspensky wrote a number of such essays for *Zolotoe Runo* and was a substantial asset to the magazine as its principal contributor on pre-Petrine Russian art. *Zolotoe Runo* proudly announced in its final 1906 issue that Uspensky had been received by Nicholas II at Peterhof and had presented the Tsar with a volume of his articles published in *Zolotoe Runo,* "which received the Tsar's special interest."[19]

Later issues featured articles on subjects similar to those Uspensky had written about. *Zolotoe Runo*'s special "Devil" issue of 1907 included Uspensky's fascinating essay on the esthetics of depicting Satan in ancient Russian painting. B. Dikovsky wrote in June 1907 about the tent-roofed wooden churches of northern Russia,[20] and in October "E. O." contributed an article on "pomor" (referring to the native Russian population of the White Sea-Arctic Ocean area) manuscripts, accompanied by a large number of illustrations.[21]

Two artists of primarily historical interest had issues devoted to them in 1906-7. The first dealt with Alexander Ivanov (1806-58) and included an article by Vasily Rozanov which emphasized Ivanov's religious significance, especially with regard to his painting "Iavlenie Khrista narodu" ("The Appearance of Christ to the People").[22] Rather more attention was given Alexei Venetsianov (1780-1847) in 1907, with frontis-pieces by Lanseray and Drittenpreis, Benois' "Khudozhestvennoe zna-chenie Venetsianova" ("The Artistic Significance of Venetsianov"), Uspensky's essay on the artist, and finally, Baron Nikolai Wrangell's "Vremia i shkola Venetsianova" ("The Times and School of Venetsianov").[23]

The third major interest of *Zolotoe Runo*'s artistic section was in the examination and discussion of private collections of historical art throughout the country. Benois wrote about the Miatlevaia collection of eighteenth-century art in Petersburg,[24] and Uspensky on Count A. V. Olsufiev's collection of furniture.[25] An indication of *Zolotoe Runo*'s attitude toward many of these private collections was found in Vasily Milioti's "Polskaia starina v Rumiantsevskom Muzee" ("Polish Antiquities in the Rumiantsev Museum"), appearing at the end of 1907.[26] Having described the collection itself, Milioti remarked in conclusion that it was time to return these works to Vilno, where they belonged, rather than having them remain in the Rumiantsev Museum. Like the majority of Russian artists at this time, *Zolotoe Runo* was interested in museum reform, and although the magazine naturally valued the preservation of artistic treasures by private collectors, it also felt that such collections should be accessible to the public, and in the Rumiantsev case, the Polish public, to whom the works had the greatest meaning.

Opinions such as Milioti's were expressed more often in the magazine's "khronika" and "vesti otovsiudu" departments, which consisted of collections of short articles, reviews, and personal comments. It was here that the real "face" of *Zolotoe Runo*'s artistic section could be found. Several writers contributed essays, but there were three whose articles were best representative of the magazine's artistic and esthetic position. Most prolific was Konstantin Siunnerberg (1871-1942), who wrote his continuing "Khudozhestvennaia zhizn Peterburga" ("Petersburg Artistic Life") throughout 1906 and for part of 1907, as well as a number of other essays and commentaries under his pseudonym, Erberg. He severely criticized Vasnetsov and the exhibitions of the *Soiuz russkikh khudozhnikov (Union of Russian Artists)*; he wrote of his concern for the loss of Russian art through its sale to foreign collectors; he was interested in foreign art publications and reported on such Western satirical periodicals as *Simplicissimus,* as well as on the French press's reception of Diaghilev's 1906 exhibition of Russian art in Paris; finally, he reviewed books, and in one case expressed his personal esthetic credo when he wrote that "Beauty has nothing to do with morality . . . nor with usefulness."[27] It was ironic, and perfectly reflective of *Zolotoe Runo'*s own conflicting nature, that at the same time this typically "decadent" attitude was expressed, Siunnerberg was the subject of the painting "Chelovek v ochkakh" ("The Man in the Eyeglasses") by Dobuzhinsky, one of the most politicized modernist artists.

Similarly outspoken attitudes and far-ranging interests were found in the "Zapisnye listki" ("Pages of a Notebook") of Nikolai Roerich (1874-1948), an artist earlier associated with *Mir Iskusstva.* Roerich was a prolific contributor to several magazines and newspapers, and participated in a number of publicistic debates of artistic questions. His articles in *Zolotoe Runo* had little relation to each other, and were concerned primarily with topics which happened to interest Roerich at any given time: on one occasion, for example, he wrote on Marées and Böcklin,[28] and on another, about the "strange museum" of the Academy of Arts.[29] Of special concern both to Roerich and to *Zolotoe Runo* was the "vandalism" taking place in certain old Russian churches, the result of incompetent over-restoration. Not dissimilar was Roerich's criticism of the attempted revival of past national styles in A. A. Parland's new cathedral in Petersburg, the "Spas na krovi" (The Church of Christ's Resurrection). He derided the building's exterior as a jumbled collection of parts of churches from all over Russia, and felt the interior mosaics in traditional style were especially poor, having been done by "second-rate, but [nevertheless] Orthodox artists." Roerich was most critical of Parland's own interior mosaic of marble, silver, and gold, and remarked that "through the luxury of the material there is visible spiritual poverty."[30] The derivativeness and lack of original inspiration in "official" Russian art was one of the principal *bêtes-noires* of all Russian modernists, and both Roerich and *Zolotoe Runo* never tired of pointing out the inadequacies of art commissioned and approved by the tsarist government. One of the best examples of what became continual sniping was Sergei Makovsky's comment in the April 1906 issue on a new monument to Glinka: "Poor Glinka, to have to be remembered by this statue."[31]

Such criticism of the government's artistic policy provided the basis for the third major series of articles in the "chronicle," Alexander Rostislavov's "Nabroski o khudozhestvennykh delakh" ("Sketches on Artistic Affairs"). Rostislavov was uncommonly fond of exposing official stupidity and ignorance, and in almost every essay he attacked what he called the "almost other-worldliness" of the Academy of Arts.

Rostislavov's attitude was echoed in the unsigned notices inserted at the end of each issue in the "vesti otovsiudu" section: in March 1906, it was mentioned that the Academy had given the annual 1000 ruble Kuindzhi Prize to an artist named Kulikov "for a portrait, boringly enough painted."[32] Rostislavov attacked the continuing police censorship of art exhibitions and outright confiscation of works, and was again supported by the magazine's unsigned accounts of "censorship scandals": *Zolotoe Runo* gleefully reported that on one occasion, the confiscated works were reproduced in the illustrated supplements of a number of periodicals, as a result reaching many more people than they might, had the confiscation never taken place. Finally, Rostislavov repeatedly noted that as long as the Alexander III Museum in Petersburg continued to ignore modern Russian art, enormous opportunities for its popularization were being lost. Both Rostislavov and *Zolotoe Runo*'s editors considered such official bias inexcusable. The "vandalism" of official stupidity, ignorance, and above all, poor taste, was continually criticized and exposed by Rostislavov, Roerich, and Siunnerberg on the pages of *Zolotoe Runo*.

Although these three men's comments dealt primarily with contemporary Russian art, some reports on foreign artistic developments did appear in *Zolotoe Runo* as well. Both Alexandre Benois and Maximilian Voloshin were Paris correspondents of *Zolotoe Runo*, as was Prince Alexander Shervashidze, who sent the magazine a glowing description of Diaghilev's 1906 exhibition of Russian art there. Voloshin wrote an appreciation of Carrière on the artist's death in 1906. In addition, two letters from Esmer Valdor (a pseudonym of Alexandre Mercereau) were also sent from Paris, one about the Créteil artistic settlement of which Mercereau was a member, and the other dealing with the Russian sections of the 1907 Salon d'Automne. With few exceptions, these contributions from abroad dealt not with indigenous foreign developments themselves, however, but with the foreign reception of Russian art and artists. During the second two years of *Zolotoe Runo*'s publication, this would change fundamentally.

Despite the emphasis placed on educative articles and opinionated reportage in its artistic section, the magazine did provide space for several long essays concerned with theoretical esthetic problems of current interest. One notably reflective of contemporary conditions was D. Imgardt's "Zhivopis i revoliutsiia" ("Painting and Revolution").[33] Imgardt wrote that traditional, previously understood artistic aims were no longer viable, and that new artistic criteria were necessary in order to apply "new colors" and "musical tones" to figurative art. He conceived a kind of visual music, a synthetic and abstract art much like that being developed by the little-known Lithuanian artist Mikolajus Čiurlionis (1875-1911).[34] Surprisingly, Imgardt's prescient description of an as yet undeveloped abstract art received little reaction either in *Zolotoe Runo* or elsewhere, although his ideas would certainly have enjoyed enthusiastic support from most symbolist painters and poets.

Somewhat less theoretical, and more typical in tone of contemporary artistic discussions, was Filosofov's confused and at times mystical "Iskusstvo i gosudarstvo" ("Art and Government").[35] The article was preceded by a note from the editors explaining that although they did not agree with all of Filosofov's ideas, they had agreed to print the essay because of the general public interest in the question. Filosofov began by attempting to democratize the artist's position in society, defining him as having the same dependence on the "ruling-classes" as did the "workers and proletariat." He then expanded this point:

> The artist strives above all for freedom—not only material freedom, but spiritual freedom. In modern bourgeois society he frequently finds himself in a poverty that is not only material, but spiritual as well. Socialism frees him from material poverty, but does it insure his spiritual freedom? And if it does insure it, does it then save him from the main suffering of every genius—from loneliness? That is the whole question.[36]

Filosofov envisioned the imminent end of artistic self-containment, and wrote that even the "decadents" had begun to feel closer to society, that many literary and artistic circles were now discussing "sobornost." He considered this trend positive and irreversible, and concluded his essay with hope for a better future: that the resurrection of Russia would grow not from any empirical or rational strength, but from a mystical one, out of which would arise a national religious rebirth. Filosofov's analysis of the Russian artistic situation in mid-1907 included much that was true, but his mystical predictions for the future could be accepted by only a small segment of the Russian artistic intelligentsia. It was none the less indicative of *Zolotoe Runo*'s generally tolerant editorial position at this time that such essays could appear.

As had Imgardt's, Filosofov's essay received little response within *Zolotoe Runo*. His vision of the end of artistic self-containment was relevant to a controversy which developed in the magazine during 1906-7, however: "individualism in art" became a major issue among the contributors to *Zolotoe Runo*'s theoretical section, and the question itself became the principal problem of post-1905 Russian art. The argument was initiated by Benois' lengthy "Khudozhestvennye eresi" ("Artistic Heresies") in the magazine's February 1906 issue.[37] Written at Versailles between October 1905 and January 1906, the article gave a summary of Benois' view of recent cultural developments in Russia. Once again, the editors inserted a note stating that Benois' point of view was not their own and that the article was included "only because we consider it interesting to give a complete picture of the artistic beliefs of A. Benois."[38] Such

disavowals became common in *Zolotoe Runo,* and permitted the magazine
to print conceivably unpopular or inflamatory opinions from a standpoint
of intellectual curiosity rather than advocacy.

The most widespread "heresy" Benois found in contemporary art was
individualism, heretical because it denied the possibility of individuals
joining together, and because it was a striving for an "I" which only
separated people from one another. He considered such a separation the
greatest weakness of modern art:

> In former times, the artist lived in unity with the whole society and was the clearest
> representative of the ideals of his time.... Vigorously carried out individualism is
> absurd, it leads not to the development of human personality, but to its running wild.[39]

Benois continued that the artists of his time were confused, were not
serving God, but on the contrary the Caesar of the "narod-gosudarstvo"
(the "people-state"), that they were "giving away their sacred gifts to the
utilitarian goals of the battle against the existing worthless order."[40] Benois
warned that when the upheavals subsided and life returned to normal
(which he now felt it soon would), artists would have to discontinue serving
"Caesar" and return to God and to Apollo.

Stressing Apollonianism as the artist's ideal, Benois wrote that
"Beauty" was the only absolute and that its enemy was the now rampant,
omnipresent philistinism. Benois asserted that all earlier art had had a
purpose, was based on definite canons and formulas, whereas
contemporary art rejected all such restrictions. He admitted that the old
established artistic forms (in which progressive artists no longer believed)
deserved to be rejected, but stressed that "the art of our time was absolutely
wrong, it became 'heretical' when it came out against the very principle of
canons and formulas."[41] To Benois, such individualism could lead only to
emptiness, and was "driving humanity into the dark, blind alley of
complete brutalism."[42] In conclusion, he stated that he would not presume
to suggest new formulas, but warned that they must be found if a truly
viable new art was to be created.

"Khudozhestvennye eresi" was representative of Benois' fear of
artistic anarchy leading to the eventual destruction of art, and he felt this
anarchistic tendency all about him (and especially in the works of the
Moscow symbolist painters). Benois was uncomfortably aware of the
serious lack of cohesion in Russian society that had become apparent in
1905, and he saw uncontrolled individualism as encouraging further
disintegration. Significantly, however, Benois did not demand that any
particular form or theory be used, just *a* form, not preconceived formulas,
but formulas nonetheless.

Benois' opinions in this article were not inconsistent with those he had formerly expressed,[43] but these ideas fell on more sensitized ears after 1905. The first of a series of responses to Benois' article appeared in *Zolotoe Runo*'s June issue. Alexander Shervashidze (1867-1968), one of Benois' friends, sent his "Individualizm i traditsiia: Aleksandru Benua i Morisu Denisu" ("Individualism and Tradition: To Alexandre Benois and Maurice Denis") to *Zolotoe Runo* from Paris, where he was a correspondent for a number of Russian periodicals.[44] Shervashidze first summarized the positions of Benois and Denis (Denis had written that most new artists were interested only in personal artistic satisfaction and gratification), describing the two as artists who were now attacking the path of individualism along which they themselves had developed. To Shervashidze, the real problem was not individualism, but what Benois had called "servileism," and gave as proof the yearly Paris Salons, filled with copies of Gauguin, Cézanne, and Puvis de Chavannes. But since to Shervashidze, art was a reflection of society, as society continued to develop, so must art move on to new forms, ideals, doctrines.[45] The great artist, as a consequence, must oppose the demands of his individuality to the demands of formula:

> The whole history of our art is the struggle of the personality, that is the principle of individualism, with a falsely understood tradition, genius with mediocrity, the principle of renewal with the intolerant conservatism of collectivism.[46]

Shervashidze believed in the need to combine individualism and tradition, but warned that traditional formulas should not be allowed to predominate over individualism. Shervashidze feared that Benois and Denis wanted artists to look at life through museum windows, whereas in fact new forms of life demanded new forms of art, and although such forms were created on the basis of past artistic experiences, they could not be limited by them:

> No, let art grow freely, going where it will ... What it will be we do not know, but we believe in the inexhaustible force of Life. And if in the course of this journey painting dies, then it will not be because it traveled on the slippery path of individualism, but because life demanded different forms from a different art.[47]

Shervashidze, Benois, and Denis all shared a concern for the future of art; their disagreement arose on where the source of the danger to art lay.

Rather than as an attack on Benois' position, Shervashidze clearly intended his article as a clarification to Benois of the real nature of artistic individualism. With a not dissimilar aim, Filosofov entered the controversy late in 1906 in an article devoted primarily to attacking Chulkov's "mystical anarchism."[48] Filosofov admitted his own surprise at Benois' rejection of the individualism which he had always "served," and attempted to explain such apparent inconsistency:

> Benois believed in free personality and its self-sufficiency, but seeing that this cult leads to the greatest *poshlost,* to the weakening of that very personality, he became frightened.[49]

Filosofov wrote that for Benois, the artist's stress on his own individual vision caused him to lose touch with the objective world, as a result making such an artist and his work shallow. Considering Benois' argument unclear and illogical, Filosofov felt it his duty to his friend to protect Benois from misinterpretation,[50] and he used the most immediate means available to him, a somewhat irrelevant article in *Zolotoe Runo.*

More to the point was Maximilian Voloshin's "Individualizm v iskusstve" ("Individualism in Art") in *Zolotoe Runo*'s October 1906 issue (with vignettes and drawings by Benois, interestingly enough).[51] Echoing Ruskin and Morris (and Shervashidze), Voloshin summarized his position on Benois' ideas in four theses:

> 1. Tradition and canons are not dead mechanical forms, but the living and eternally growing language of symbols and images. And only upon them can individualistic art arise.
> 2. Individualism arises from the instinct of self-preservation, but only when it reaches the most extreme point of its development; it finds its highest self-assertion when it voluntarily gives up of itself.
> 3. Modern artists, in order to reach this most extreme and highest point of individualism, must withdraw from their names and from their earthly visage, in order to pour completely all personality into artistic work and to die away in them as the spirit dies in the heap of matter.
> 4. The final goal of art is found in the fact that everyone should be a creator of the nature surrounding him, whether he be a creator who has become obscured and limited in his artistic work or one at the stage of consciousness of artistic works.[52]

Again, however, Voloshin's article too was more an attempt at pointing Benois in the right direction, of explaining to him the consequences of his position, than it was a personal attack.

By 1907, this somewhat unfocused debate on artistic individualism was no longer related to Benois' seminal essay, and the question had become an independent problem of its own to *Zolotoe Runo*'s contributors. Rather peripheral was Rostislavov's article on Roerich (which praised the artist's "fantastic individualism"[53]), while the main thrust of the discussion was continued in Tasteven's late-1907 article concerned ostensibly with Nietzsche and the "contemporary world cultural crisis."[54] Tasteven conceptualized the present dilemma of Russian artistic life in Nietzschean terms:

And look, mankind is once again standing before one of the most agonizing and fatal problems on whose solutions may depend the future of our culture. Is the overcoming of individualism possible now, is a new creative synthesis possible? That same striving of the soul, which compelled us to overcome "idealism" and "moralism" compels us to strive for the overcoming of individualism, which must, together with it, be its final confirmation. Is such a new synthesis possible now, may individualism from its negative phases (atheism, amoralism, egoism, illusionism) turn to its opposite? May the "irreconcilable No" turn into the "blinding Yes?"[55]

Tasteven's conclusion was that only when art returned to real life, and no longer dwelled on dead symbols, would the artist be united with the creative poetry of the "national soul" and "become simultaneously a creator and a spokesman for culture."[56] Tasteven's synthesis of populist, mystical, modernist, and realist ideals moved the magazine's earlier discussion of artistic individualism considerably beyond Benois' more straightforward misgivings of over a year before. But because of his importance within *Zolotoe Runo,* Tasteven's essay provided a clear indication of some of the fundamental esthetic and ideological positions the magazine was to adopt during its second period of publication (discussed in more detail in Part III).

Pavel Muratov's long essay "O vysokom khudozhestve" ("On High Art") in *Zolotoe Runo's* last issue of 1907[57] was the final contribution to the debate on artistic individualism, and was particularly anti-climactic, appearing as it did both after Tasteven's article and after *Zolotoe Runo's* official change of direction. Essentially, Muratov supported Benois' position, criticizing many new artists' striving for purely external dramatic effects, and warning that only by building on both native and Western artistic traditions would Russian artists be able to achieve the "higher art" to which they must aspire.[58]

Muratov's essay was not a satisfactory conclusion to the debate on artistic individualism, and in fact, much of it read as an apologia for academism. In some ways, however, and like Tasteven's essay, it was indicative of the position *Zolotoe Runo* was cautiously adopting, a turn away from pure individualism and toward an emphasis on the recognition of former traditions, but significantly, of national or primitivist traditions. Although the editors of the magazine's artistic section seem to have had an intuitive understanding of what was meant by this combination of individualism and national traditions, it remained much less clear there than in *Zolotoe Runo's* literary section. The actual outcome of what appeared at the time a confused, frequently mystical and obscure debate would not be seen until at least a year later (a year and a half after *Zolotoe Runo's* theoretical reorganization), when the magazine printed special issues on Gauguin and Matisse, and important theoretical works by the latter.

Despite the unclear resolution to this discussion on artistic individualism, it is not difficult to summarize *Zolotoe Runo*'s artistic position
during 1906-7. Its official policy was one of permissiveness, and as has been
seen, the editors felt no compunction against publishing opinions with
which they personally disagreed. "Whatever is interesting" to modernist
Russian artists was the magazine's principal criterion of judgment.
Zolotoe Runo was itself a modernist magazine as much because it
published reproductions of works by Kuznetsov, Milioti, Larionov, and
Dobuzhinsky as it was for refusing to promote "academic" or "proletarian"
art, for not publishing reproductions of Semiradsky's or Arkhipov's works,
for example. The historical artistic figures discussed were always safely far
enough in the past that selective "rediscovery" could be considered the real
purpose for including them. Even these excellent reflective, historical
articles were combined with the magazine's strong support for modernist
Russian artists in that their headpieces, titles, and decorations were done
by the best contemporary Russian graphic artists. As a result, no other
Russian periodical, including *Mir Iskusstva,* attained such quality in
combining art and prose as *Zolotoe Runo* did in its first two years of
publication.

Of importance equal to *Zolotoe Runo*'s support for artistic
modernism was its dedication to the goal of public enlightenment, the
spreading of artistic knowledge and the exposure of the educated Russian
public to the latest developments in Russian art. Although its success was
more than questionable in 1906-7, it was undoubtedly this aim that the
editors would have considered their single most important goal. Yet,
despite this emphasis on "popularizing" art, *Zolotoe Runo* did not
vulgarize itself or lower what it considered high standards to a mediocre
level for popular consumption. It consistently supported unpopular artists
and groups, and continued doing so throughout its existence. At a time
when *Vesy* alone offered some aid to the *Golubaia roza* artists or (later) to
the neo-primitivists, *Zolotoe Runo* gave them firm, enthusiastic support
that they found nowhere else. If *Zolotoe Runo* was at times uncertain of its
own fundamental esthetic position, its artistic section did represent the
most progressive aspects of the artistic life of its time.

II

Zolotoe Runo's Literary Section

It has been mentioned that one of *Zolotoe Runo*'s major achievements
was the high quality of the decorative art accompanying the magazine's
prose and poetry, continuing throughout 1906 and 1907, and deteriorating

immediately thereafter. Interestingly, the November-December issue of 1907, the last before the magazine's reduction in format, was one of the most impressive in its attempt at "synthesizing" works of art and literature. The presentation of Balmont's poem "Khorovod vremen" ("The Circle Dance of Time") in this issue was certainly the single best example of such a union. The poem consisted of thirteen parts, twelve representing the months of the year, with a thirteenth added after "December." Each was illustrated with some of the best and most representative work of Arapov, Drittenpreis, Iuon, Sudeikin, Krymov, Utkin, Dobuzhinsky, Bilibin, and Masiutin.[59] This attempt at strict relevance between illustration and text was a continuing feature of *Zolotoe Runo,* and its consistent success was not a negligible accomplishment. In *Mir Iskusstva,* there often had been no correspondence between artistic and literary subject matter: Merezhkovsky's long article on Tolstoy and Dostoevsky was illustrated with completely irrelevant drawings by Hiroshige and Beardsley for example.[60] Such esthetic inconsistency (even if deliberate as it probably was in the Merezhkovsky case) was rarely present in *Zolotoe Runo.*

*Zolotoe Runo'*s interest in promoting the union of art and literature also may be seen in the portraits Riabushinsky commissioned for the magazine, the majority of which had writers as their subjects, and in the magazine's non-figurative aspects, especially in the essays by well-known literary figures on artistic or musical topics. In an attempt to uncover the basic unity of artistic experience, *Zolotoe Runo* accepted articles such as Belyi's on Borisov-Musatov and on Nikolai Medtner's newly-composed music for nine of Goethe's lyrics.[61] The second article is particularly interesting, for in it Belyi attempted to unite Medtner with his greatest contemporaries in literature (Briusov and Merezhkovsky) and art (Vrubel), whom Belyi considered the true innovators within modern Russian artistic life. Discussing Medtner as a "tragedian" in music, Belyi then praised him as the only Russian composer who affirmed rather than denied life. After again examining Medtner in the context of Russian artistic life, Belyi concluded that Goethe's lyrics, put to Medtner's music, formed one of the few manifestations of true culture.

While Belyi's essay was generally representative of *Zolotoe Runo'*s "synthetic" approach to culture, a number of longer, more purely theoretical articles appeared in the magazine as well. The most interesting of these was Blok's "Kraski i slova," printed in *Zolotoe Runo'*s inaugural issue.[62] It was the first of a series of speculative and interpretive essays on esthetics to be published in the magazine. Written at the end of 1905, the article was Blok's initial theoretical examination of the artist's representation of the objective, real world, and the first of a series of works that would define Blok's "transitional period" (most of these appeared in *Zolotoe Runo* and will be discussed in more detail in Chapter 5). In "Kraski i slova," Blok described poetry as being not the art of sounds alone, but as a combination of "color and line." Stressing poetry's closeness to nature, he warned the writer not to be caught up in any all-inclusive theory from which there was no escape. Blok considered painting an object lesson for writers: painting teaches "looking and seeing," keeps alive the feelings of children, where "the word" is secondary to "the line," to drawing. Noting that the artist was able to preserve a childlike susceptibility through the use of pure and distinct color, Blok saw the success of such new works as Sergei Gorodetsky's "Znoi" ("Heat") as deriving from their aspiration to color and to a concrete, simple vocabulary. Blok mused that writers had spoiled their souls by insisting on an analysis of everything, and warned again that the "clever and beautiful" words of symbolism were quite possibly leading them in a false direction.

Blok moved on to an examination of "living nature," which in his eyes was best reflected in painting—a painting that teaches childhood and that laughs in the face of "profound" criticism. Such painting says "I am nature itself," a nature populated by innumerable kinds of beings, one that is neither symbolist nor mystical, a nature amazing in its simplicity.[63] Finally, Blok warned that modern writers did not know the other beings inhabiting the forests, fields, marshes and that only *by* knowing them could the writer's soul be freed, as the artist's is, to give birth to the "prekrasnaia mysl" ("the beautiful thought").[64]

Blok's ramblings on the nature of painting and literature were firmly based in the revolutionary events of present-day reality, of course. Foreseeing the impending defeat of the revolution in which he himself had been so ineffectually involved, Blok felt he had to reject the "lifelessness and abstractness of formula"[65] in which writers (and critics) were holding themselves prisoner. "Having grown sad in the laboratory of words,"[66] Blok discovered an alternative in nature, away from "symbols" and abstractions. This new appreciation for nature and its simplicity, for what was before one's eyes rather than for the superplanal reality behind appearances, was the first step toward Blok's appreciation of the *Znanie* realists, expressed in his review articles beginning in mid-1907. "Kraski i slova" was therefore interesting not only in its attempt at finding a common means for understanding art and literature; it was prophetic as well: its emphasis on a "childlike" way of looking at nature unconsciously indicated a move toward primitivism in art, and its reexamination of symbolism led soon thereafter to a considerable debate, and eventually to the decline and demise of the popularity of symbolist technique.

While Blok's "Kraski i slova" was typical of the kind of "synthetic" articles published in *Zolotoe Runo,* it was not representative of the magazine's literary section as a whole during the first year and a half of publication, in the ideas expressed, its technique, or its prejudices. As a result, the article elicited little response either in the magazine's literary or artistic sections. As has been noted, *Zolotoe Runo*'s literary section was not the editors' primary interest, even though a considerable proportion of each issue was given over to fiction and to critical articles on literature. Despite this editorial indifference, the magazine was able to attract almost all the prominent Russian modernists to its list of contributors. Their names were pubished in *Zolotoe Runo*'s February 1906 issue:

> Andreev, Balmont, Blok, Belyi, A. Bachinsky, Briusov, Maks Voloshin, L. Vilkina, Vorotnikov, Gippius, Dymov, Zaitsev, V. Ivanov, Krechetov (S. A. Sokolov), Kondratiev, Kursinsky, S. Makovsky, Minsky, Merezhkovsky, Miropolsky, W. R. Morfill, N. Petrovskaia, B. Popov, S. Rafalovich, V. Rebikov, Remizov, Sats, Sologub, Siunnerberg, [A.] Struve, Tarovaty, Khodasevich, Shervashidze, Iarkov, Filosofov.[67]

Many of these contributed little to the literary section, of course, and some of them wrote almost exclusively on music, but the list did indicate that *Zolotoe Runo*'s ability to attract modernist writers was at least equal to that of any of its competitors. This list remained much the same until mid-1907, when a substantial change took place in response to the magazine's esthetic redirection and because of personal conflicts between *Zolotoe Runo* and members of the Belyi-Briusov circle. Up until that time *Zolotoe Runo* was able to maintain a fairly continual reflection of the current work being done by all the Russian modernists, and it is this first year and a half that will be discussed in this chapter.

Noticeably absent from the literary section's list of contributors were any foreign names, and since the magazine was published in both Russian and French, especially French names. It is instructive in this regard to compare *Zolotoe Runo* with its major competitor, *Vesy*.[68] While *Vesy* had several foreign correspondents, *Zolotoe Runo* had only a very few, and these were obtained almost by chance. W. R. Morfill, *Vesy's* Oxford correspondent, was also mentioned as a *Zolotoe Runo* contributor, but he sent nothing to the magazine, and his name was removed almost immediately. Except for Alexandre Mercereau, it was solely on Russians abroad that *Zolotoe Runo* relied to send it reports on foreign cultural life. Similarly, while fiction and poetry by foreign writers received considerable exposure in *Vesy*, which printed translations of Verhaeren, Maeterlinck, Moréas, and others, *Zolotoe Runo* included no original work by foreign writers during this first period (Przybyszewski was an exception, of course, but his was a special case). This nationalist orientation carried over into reproductions of foreign artists' works, almost nonexistent in *Zolotoe Runo*'s first two years of publication, yet quite prominent in *Vesy*. Finally, *Vesy*'s close scrutiny of foreign periodicals was in direct contrast to *Zolotoe Runo*'s unenthusiastic and somewhat haphazard interest in the opinions of foreign writers and journals.

The reason for *Zolotoe Runo*'s lack of concern for foreign cultural developments is not readily apparent, but most likely it arose from the magazine's editorial difficulties. Certainly *Zolotoe Runo* did hope to achieve some distribution outside Russia, and perhaps the fact that it initially considered itself as aiding the spread of Russian art and literature abroad rather than vice-versa explains why foreign contributions were not more actively solicited. The one feature of *Zolotoe Runo* that did tie it with the West, of course, was its parallel publication in French and Russian. In the magazine's very first issue, the editors announced that they would take all steps possible to attract the attention of the best French poets for *Zolotoe Runo*'s poetry translations, but as was noted in the previous chapter, it was difficult to find a French translator for the poetry. In February 1906, it was announced that Tasteven had been made "manager of translations," but it was unclear whether he translated the articles himself or merely supervised their translation. Finally, the March 1906 issue stated that Esmer Valdor (Mercereau) had been put in charge of the poetry section's translations. Mercereau, whom Ilya Ehrenburg remembered as an "unremarkable poet, but an amiable man," had settled with some other poets in an old abbey on the outskirts of Paris, but since "life at the poets' phalanstery was monotonous," Mercereau decided to take Riabushinsky's offer, and traveled to Moscow to supervise the new magazine's French translations of poetry.[69]

Mercereau was never really successful either at understanding the Russian language or Russian life, as one of Voloshin's favorite stories about the French poet indicates; when Mercereau returned to Paris, he described his Russian mistress' house to his friends: "At their house they served red caviar! Black caviar is eaten everywhere in Russia, but they had red, they were very rich people.... "[70] Red caviar was of course much cheaper than black. Mercereau's translations were rarely more subtle than his taste in caviar, and they frequently were ridiculed in *Vesy* (particularly by Gippius) for misunderstanding the nuances of the poetry.

Technical problems with the Russian typesetters, who were unable to read Latin characters, and difficulties in having contributors meet the earlier deadlines necessitated by the extra time demanded for translation, led to discontinuation of the French text after the June 1906 issue. The official announcement stated that this decision had been made in order "to expand the literary section"[71] and this probably had some basis in fact, although it was not the major reason for the change. Publication in both French and Russian had proved much too ambitious for *Zolotoe Runo*, and when it became clear that there would be little circulation of the magazine abroad, it seemed pointless to include the superfluous French text. It should be noted, however, that this decision was reached not for any reason reflective of the future changes in *Zolotoe Runo*'s official esthetic program, but was based purely on technical and logistic problems.

In each issue the magazine's literary section began with poetry. While there was a large number of poets represented (more than were listed as official contributors, in fact), by far the most frequent appearances were made by Balmont, Viacheslav Ivanov, Briusov, Sologub, Belyi, and Blok, although poems by Remizov, Voloshin, Bunin, Gorodetsky, Chulkov, and Kuzmin were also often printed on the magazine's pages. On the whole, the poetry was symbolist-modernist, but with very little emphasis on any particular themes or currents within symbolism. In general, *Zolotoe Runo* seemed ready to print the works of any writer well-known to the public who showed talent and was not associated with the realists of Gorky's *Znanie* school (Andreev's is a special case which will be discussed later).

Only somewhat less heterogeneous was the prose fiction section which followed the poetry, and again, the works published were generally symbolist or decadent. The magazine did publish a number of important and interesting stories and plays: Sologub was the most frequent contributor, and especially notable was his play "Dar mudrykh pchel" ("The Gift of the Wise Bees"), a "tragedy with a classical theme."[72] Alexei Remizov's story "Pozhar" ("Fire") appeared in April 1906,[73] and his famous collection of stylized folklore and impressionistic nature studies, "Posolon" ("Follow the Sun"), was first printed in *Zolotoe Runo*.[74] Another interesting work was Blok's unproduced play "Korol na ploshchadi" ("The King on the Square," accompanied by a stage design and set for the play by Nikolai Sapunov), an allegory dealing with a popular uprising and the conflict between authority and the crowd, between traditional and modern poetry.[75] Finally, and of particular interest both because of the subject of the story itself, and because of the author's equivocal position within Russian modernism, was Leonid Andreev's "Eleazar" ("Lazarus").[76] Written in a biblical, rhetorical tone, the story dealt with abstractions, and in its preoccupation with Lazarus' infection of life with death, it was similar to the themes and techniques of many modernists. Nevertheless, Andreev remained closely connected with Gorky, and the publication of the story was considered a questionable move on the part of *Zolotoe Runo*'s editors by several symbolist writers, who were still skeptical of the literary value of any of Andreev's works. In any case, although Andreev's name continued to be linked with *Zolotoe Runo*, "Eleazar" was the single contribution he was to make to the magazine.

Unlike the poetry and fiction published in *Zolotoe Runo*, its critical and speculative articles fall into more easily defined categories expressive of the magazine's current concerns. Not surprising was a special interest in exotica, often expressed in straightforward travelogues. The most prominent author of such reports was Balmont, whose enforced wandering abroad produced a number of sketches sent to the magazine, so many that they helped make Balmont the single most prolific contributor to *Zolotoe Runo*. His "Dva slova ob Amerike" and his retelling of Maya legends in the first issue of 1906 have already been mentioned. For the May issue he sent another, not dissimilar article, "Fleity iz chelovecheskikh kostei" ("Flutes from Human Bones"), in which he used a lengthy examination of the musical instruments of Pacific islanders as a pretext for a discussion of the relative merits of Polish and Russian as two currents of Slavic language, a logical and stylistic jump of rather dubious validity.[77] Other writers contributed similar essays: Vasily Rozanov wrote an article on Egypt that defies any short description,[78] while Belyi sent a letter from Munich in which he discussed beer, the city's architectural heritage, the Oktoberfest, *Simplicissimus,* and the simple Bavarian life, remarking in passing that Viacheslav Ivanov could "calm himself down" in Munich simply by considering the mystery surrounding the beer stein.[79]

Belyi's almost whimsical letter from Munich was not typical of his work in *Zolotoe Runo,* which consisted more often of critical articles on literature or the theater. In the third issue of 1906 he contributed a long essay dealing with Merezhkovsky's *Trilogiia (Trilogy)*. Written at a time when Belyi was strongly under the Merezhkovskys' influence, the essay praised Merezhkovsky as "the first [person] since Nietzsche to unite the forms of Christianity with the images of true paganism"[80] (the precise aim of Merezhkovsky's three novels, of course). Belyi wrote another long article, on Briusov, describing him as the "first among contemporary Russian poets," one whose name should be put alongside those of Pushkin, Lermontov, and Tiutchev in the history of Russian poetry.[81] His final critical contribution of this type was written on the death of Henrik Ibsen. Belyi repeated the not uncommon view of Ibsen as one of history's great anarchists, and characterized the playwright as being at the same time a realist, idealist, symbolist, and mystic. Rather effusively, he wrote: "Ibsen, Nietzsche, Wagner—these are our brave Vikings, our only ones,"[82] and concluded with the consolation for Ibsen's admirers that the playwright had gone to join the other heroes of the nineteenth century in Valhalla. All this outpouring of praise by Belyi was to prove a direct contrast to the cynical and virulent attacks he made on writers and critics after his return to Russia from abroad in mid-1907, and after his break with *Zolotoe Runo.*

Critical essays by other writers as well appeared during this first year and a half of the magazine's publication, of course: Balmont wrote on Oscar Wilde's socialism,[83] Rozanov on Dostoevsky's "Grand Inquisitor"[84] and Boris Sadovskoi on the poetry of Ia. P. Polonsky.[85] Still, it was Andrei Belyi who was the most prolific contributor of articles of considerable merit to *Zolotoe Runo.* As was the case with several others, Belyi's reason for joining *Zolotoe Runo*'s staff had been purely financial; he explained this in a letter to Blok in December 1905:

> I told *Vesy* and *Zolotoe Runo* that I would sell my soul and from S. A. Sokolov I
> received an answer that they would pay me 50-75 rubles a month for it. From *Vesy,* no
> answer, so I sold myself to *Zolotoe Runo.* I will work mainly on *Runo* and secondarily
> on *Vesy.*[86]

He came to resent this dependence on *Zolotoe Runo's* financial support, however, and was never satisfied working with Riabushinsky. Undergoing a personal crisis beginning in August 1906, he soon left Russia and discontinued his contributions to *Zolotoe Runo.* During the winter of 1906-7, he lived with Merezhkovsky and Gippius in Paris, and they supported his growing antagonism to Riabushinsky and his magazine. Belyi returned to Moscow in March 1907, and when *Vesy's* editorial board was reorganized that spring, he became head of its "theoretical section" and soon abandoned *Zolotoe Runo* entirely. Despite this uneven record of participation, Belyi's large number of contributions to *Zolotoe Runo* assured him an importance in the magazine's critical section that would be equalled only by Blok's between mid-1907 and the end of 1908.

While Belyi's work was predominant in *Zolotoe Runo's* critical section, no one held such a position in the series of speculative articles on philosophy and esthetics also printed in the magazine. One article by Belyi, "Printsip formy v estetike" ("The Principle of Form in Esthetics"),[87] appeared in this section, but its attempt at defining esthetics by means of mathematical formulas was not notably successful. A great deal less obscure was Briusov's essay on realism in art, a transparent allegory contrasting the "esthetic" and newly-emerging "realist" schools of symbolism.[88]

Essays on mystical and philosophical themes outnumbered those dealing with pure esthetics: Rozanov wrote two such articles, one on Minsky's "poetic-philosophical conceptions,"[89] and another discussing letters he had received from Vladimir Soloviev,[90] while Siunnerberg contributed his long and obscure "Bezvlastie" ("Anarchy"),[91] divided into sections devoted to "pride," "God," "miracle," "hatred," and "antitheism."

Finally, there were two writers who published essays on concepts which would later initiate considerable discussion both within *Zolotoe Runo* and Russian symbolism as a whole. The first was Viacheslav Ivanov, whose "Predchuvstvie i predvestie" ("Presentiment and Portent," a discussion of the "new organic epoch" and the art of the future)[92] and "O veselom remesle i umnom veseli" ("On Joyful Trade and Clever Fun," ostensibly on the contrast between Hellenism and barbarism)[93] were to raise questions basic to the theory of "mystical anarchism" for which he and Georgy Chulkov were responsible. The second was Alexander Blok, who wrote two essays indicative of the direction his thoughts would follow over the next few years. "Bezvremene" ("Hard Times")[94] continued Blok's theme of the writer's alienation from nature, but in a more desperate tone. Such alienation was given substantial political form in the second article, "Devushka rozovoi kalitki i muravinyi tsar" ("The Girl of the Rosy Wicket and the Ant King"),[95] in which Blok for the first time brought up the problem of the "intelligentsia and the people," a theme that was to prove of primary importance both to Blok and to *Zolotoe Runo* in the succeeding years. Although neither Ivanov nor Blok realized it in 1906-7, these articles put forward the first arguments in the two most significant debates that would define the years of symbolism's decline in Russia.

Considerably less theoretical than these speculative esays were the book reviews and notes which concluded each issue of the magazine. Unlike reviews in other Russian periodicals, frequently used as excuses for long dissertations on irrelevant topics, those in *Zolotoe Runo* were usually short and concise, and more often than not, critically negative. The reviewers included Blok, Belyi, Boris Sadovskoi, Kursinsky, Iarkov, Bachinsky, Nina Petrovskaia, Khodasevich, Briusov, and Sergei Soloviev. Belyi and Kursinsky wrote the greatest number of notices by far, however, and only Bachinsky, who contributed nothing else to *Zolotoe Runo,* came near equalling them. Some books by foreign writers in new Russian translations were reviewed (works by Fichte, Wilde, Hamsun, Verhaeren, Hofmannsthal, and Huysmans were noted, for example), but most of those chosen for review were either about or by Russian cultural figures. While reviews of critical studies of such authors as Dostoevsky, Gogol, and Saltykov-Shchedrin appeared, it was usually the new works of Gorodetsky, Sologub, Przybyszewski, Chulkov, Balmont, Gippius, Briusov, or Blok that were given primary attention. In general, *Zolotoe Runo*'s critics seemed to delight in dismissing new books with as much venom as possible:

> One of these books appeared in Batum, the other in Moscow. This is a large enough distance. But the authors have one thing in common: they are both absolutely lacking in talent.[96]

> [the] article is a boring and untalented account of the polemic between the old-liberal and Black-Hundred clique of Orthodox clergy, written with an impossible style.[97]

> [this book] belongs to those colorless, mediocre, and primarily unnecessary books about which absolutely nothing can be said.[98]

Chosen for special opprobrium were *Znanie* publications, particularly their *Sborniki.* Two such miscellanies were discussed in some detail, in one the reviewer considering Gorky's play "Varvary" ("Enemies") proof of his lack of talent as a playwright. Summarizing the works in the other collection, the critic mentioned that "there are also poems in the collection—all bad, although Mr. Rukavishnikov's 'Three Banners' is especially unbearable."[99] This distaste for the realists was shared by all the Russian modernist writers until mid-1907, and such strongly expressed opinions were fairly common in the modernist press as a whole. Not all the reviews were negative, however, and while the new "third generation" symbolists were criticized unmercifully, works by such writers as Blok, Briusov, and Sologub received positive, if somewhat lifeless, notices from *Zolotoe Runo*'s critics. The magazine's critical section was not a great success, and in April 1907 it was replaced by a series of survey articles on recent literature, written by Blok. The first of these, "O realistakh" ("On the Realists"), appeared in May 1907 and not only attempted a complete change of direction for symbolist literary criticism, but also indicated the reconsideration of literary policy being made by *Zolotoe Runo*'s editors.

Although some literary news appeared in it, the magazine's "chronicle" had no articles specifically devoted to literary developments in Russia or abroad, as was the case with art and music. It did include a series of interesting reports on contemporary Russian theatrical life in Moscow and Petersburg, however. A monthly letter, "Peterburgskie teatry" ("Petersburg Theaters"), was sent by Osip Dymov (pseudonym of Osip Perelman, 1878-1959), beginning in February 1906 and continuing throughout that year. Dymov reviewed new plays, especially those performed at the Komissarzhevskaia Theater, and discussed theatrical developments in the capital. One article was devoted almost entirely to a criticism of the lack of attention given the 150th aniversary of the founding of the Imperial Theaters, and another gave a lengthy and detailed report on the meeting of the recently organized "Pervyi vserossiiskii sezd dramaticheskikh pisatelei" ("First All-Russian Congress of Authors of Drama").[100] Dymov's articles had no lasting individual literary value in themselves, but they were useful in their relating and summarizing of theatrical events.

A similar series on the contemporary Moscow theater was begun early in 1906 by Nina Petrovskaia [the eccentric wife of Sergei Sokolov whose affair with Belyi and Briusov became the subject of Briusov's novel, *Ognennyi angel (The Fiery Angel)*].[101] Petrovskaia produced only two nondescript essays, however, and the reports were discontinued after March 1906. During the next few months, theater in Moscow was given only anonymous attention in *Zolotoe Runo*'s "vesti otovsiudu" section. Beginning with the October issue, Kursinsky began writing his "Moskovskie dramaticheskie teatry" ("Moscow Drama Theaters"), under the pseudonym A. Kursky, and continued on through part of 1907.

Other attempts at theatrical criticism and reportage were made in *Zolotoe Runo* during this early period as well. Dymov discontinued his letters with the last issue of 1906, and two essays by Kornei Chukovsky on the Petersburg theater were published early in 1907. The editors apparently hoped Chukovsky would continue Dymov's work, but Chukovsky seemed unable to accept the "decadent modernism" he felt the magazine represented. Believing that his defenses of traditional writers and artists would not be welcome in the Moscow journal, Chukovsky soon resigned from *Zolotoe Runo* to work regularly for the newspaper *Rech (Speech).*[102] These constant changes in contributors for the magazine's theatrical reports were reflective of the general turmoil in *Zolotoe Runo,* and resulted eventually in the discontinuation of any articles devoted purely to theater, and appearing on a regular basis. Instead, "vesti otovsiudu" absorbed theatrical reflections and opinions after mid-1907, and usually they were expressed either anonymously, or in the case of particularly sharp criticism, were signed by one of the editors with a single letter, Riabushinsky's "R" or Kursinsky's "K" appearing most often.

The confusion within *Zolotoe Runo*'s "chronicle" proved endemic during the entire period of the magazine's existence. Although the literary department's list of contributors became even more impressive throughout 1906, personal conflicts between the editors and Riabushinsky, and disagreements and misunderstandings between the editorial staff and the contributors, continued with little abatement until mid-1907. Two decisions by the editors marked an end to this first period of impressive, yet anarchically organized publication. The first was a change in the magazine's approach to literary criticism: individual reviews were discontinued, and a series of survey articles by Blok were initiated that would deal with specific aspects of contemporary Russian literature and would include authors and works previously castigated in modernist publications. The second decision affected the magazine's entire esthetic policy: announcing the "end of decadence," the June 1907 issue stated that *Zolotoe Runo* was redirecting its interest toward the new "national" element in Russian modernist art and literature. The change in program was less extensive than it first appeared, but considerable reorganization both in editorial and contributional staff did take place.

Until this official change of direction, there was little on the surface from a literary point of view to distinguish *Zolotoe Runo* from *Vesy.* The two shared a firm support for modernism and published poems, stories, and articles by many of the same writers. Although chance must have played an important role in determining who published what where, with few exceptions the quality of literature published in *Vesy* was superior to that in *Zolotoe Runo,* a reflection of the higher esteem held by modernist writers for *Vesy.* One of the major differences between the two was personality conflicts: while having a relatively minor influence within *Vesy,* they were a significant contributing factor to *Zolotoe Runo*'s reorganization and redirection. The second difference, and more to

Zolotoe Runo's credit, was its attempt at creating a magazine that was a complete work of art within itself, a combination of art and literature on a scale, and with a quality unequalled by any previous or (it was hoped) subsequent Russian periodical. This was no longer true after the magazine's reduction in size and format at the beginning of 1908, but during its first two years of existence, *Zolotoe Runo's* editors and contributors produced an extraordinarily fine example of a periodical *Gesamtkunstwerk,* one that was the equal of any foreign publication.

III

Zolotoe Runo's Musical Section

While *Zolotoe Runo's* editors always intended to devote a significant part of the magazine to musical criticism and esthetics, a separate musical section was never created. Throughout 1906 and 1907, *Zolotoe Runo's* musical interests remained disorganized, and were expressed primarily in reports from a few correspondents dealing with musical events in Petersburg and Moscow, and published in the magazine's "chronicle."

Zolotoe Runo did attempt to secure the cooperation of some of the most prominent Russian modernist musical figures during its first year. Emily Medtner, who from the beginning took over many of Koreshchenko's duties as official musical editor, asked Alexander Scriabin to be a regular contributor to the magazine, and although Scriabin promised intermittent contributions,[103] he published nothing in *Zolotoe Runo.* Nonetheless, Medtner's proposal, and Scriabin's favorable attitude to *Zolotoe Runo,* do indicate that the musical section was expected to be a significant department of the magazine, and was intended to be forthrightly modernist.

Zolotoe Runo's February 1906 issue included a list of the magazine's contributors, and for the musical section the names "B. Popov, V. Rebikov, Sats, [and A.] Struve" were given. [104] This list was misleading, however, since the well-known composer Rebikov wrote nothing for the magazine, and because most of the articles on music published in *Zolotoe Runo* during its first two years were written by people whose names were not included as official contributors.

Characteristically, the magazine's early "musical letters" and "notes" consisted primarily of reportage on the musical life of the two capitals, with some reference to events abroad. Appearing most frequently was the "Peterburgskaia muzykalnaia khronika" ("Petersburg Musical Chronicle") of Viacheslav Karatygin (1875-1925), who usually signed his work for *Zolotoe Runo* with the intials "V. K." A persistent and uncompromising

modernist, Karatygin ensured that Scriabin was almost the only Russian
composer played regularly at St. Petersburg's "Evenings of Contemporary
Music," and in what later became almost daily writings in the press, he
supported modernism in any form, condemned enthusiasm for
Chaikovsky as a sign of poor taste, and despised Rakhmaninov as a
reactionary sentimentalist. Highly regarded by modernist musicians, he
became a strong supporter of Prokofiev, who wrote that "later on
[Karatygin was] one of our best music critics."[105]

With his unequivocal modernist attitude, Karatygin was precisely the
kind of musical correspondent *Zolotoe Runo* had hoped to find in
Petersburg. Best representative of his contributions to *Zolotoe Runo,* and
of the magazine's musical position itself during this first year, was the initial
paragraph of his June 1906 letter:

> Summer has begun in full force. In the capital it is dusty and stuffy. The pavement is
> being repaired, once again there is lime dust from the houses being built, the fumes of the
> steamships and of the asphalt furnaces—everything blocks up the "average"
> Petersburgian who finds it impossible to force himself to migrate beyond the boundaries
> of the city atmosphere, intensely abandoning himself to evening attendance at such
> places around the capital as the "Bouffe" or the Krestovsky Garden. There, among
> dozens of stunted trees and a pair of flower beds with mirror globes on dirty columns, in
> the *entre'acte* between a mug of beer and a couple of sandwiches, one can try either
> exotic illusions (achieved with the benevolent assistance of the director Tumpakov and
> the music of the elder Suppé), a harmless "Journey to Africa," or breathing the cool
> humidity of the luminous Petersburg night, delight in the "singing" of international
> "étoiles," Rumanian waltzes, Hungarian dances, gypsy choruses, Russian singers, cake-
> walks, balalaikas, "coupletists," or other representatives of animate or inanimate
> eccentricities—the subjects and forms of "summer art." Summer music is no more than
> one of these forms.[106]

Karatygin clearly enjoyed his sophistication (and his sense of superiority to
the *petit-bourgeois* tastes of the Petersburg public) immensely, and his
contributions to *Zolotoe Runo* were highly literate and amusing, if usually
snobbish. The style of none of the magazine's other musical correspondents
approached Karatygin's fluid, readable, and entertaining prose.

Karatygin's Petersburg articles were paralleled for Moscow by Ilia
Sats' "Moskovskaia muzykalnaia zhizn" ("Moscow Musical Life"). Sats
(1875-1912) had studied at the Moscow Conservatory under Taneev, and in
1907 graduated as a conductor from the Moscow Philharmonic School.
Stanislavsky was particularly impressed with Sats' work, and in 1906
appointed him head of the Moscow Art Theater's musical section, where he
attempted to create an "organic synthesis" of music and drama, composing
music for productions of Maeterlinck's "Blue Bird" and "The Death of
Tintagiles," Hamsun's "Drama of Life,"[107] and other modernist plays.
Sats' articles were not unlike Karatygin's, and were as merciless toward
Moscow's musical tastes as Karatygin's were toward those of the capital.

Firmly supporting modernist musical experimentation, Sats' essays seemed doomed from the beginning by the reality that "the musical life of Moscow is little by little falling into its usual (unfortunately, all too usual) rut."[108] In addition to such musical reportage, Sats wrote one longer article, "Satana v muzyke" ("Satan in Music"),[109] and another in two parts discussing the "theory and practise" of contemporary Russian opera.[110]

Two other men contributed a certain amount of material to the magazine's musical section, in general using the same format as did Karatygin and Sats. Alexander Struve wrote two "Muzykalnye pisma (Moskva)" ["Musical Letters (Moscow)"] in February and March 1906. The second letter, in pointing out that "there was no concert season this year and apparently there will be none,"[111] indicated one important reason why *Zolotoe Runo*'s musical section was slow in organizing: since the revolutionary upheavals of the previous two years had not as yet subsided, audiences were not assured of their safety in crowded theaters, and musical performances suffered accordingly. Boris Popov (who at times wrote under the pseudonym "Mizgir") contributed a review of a book on Wagner, in which he compared the composer to a biblical prophet; a reappreciation of Mozart; and, in the spirit of the time, a reevaluation of Musorgsky, "this artist of musical truth, one of the most passionate and persistent 'seekers.'"[112]

Having depended primarily on musical reports, reviews, and short notices for its first year of publication, *Zolotoe Runo* announced at the beginning of 1907 that the "musical section will be significantly expanded,"[113] and a number of considerably more analytical articles began to be printed in the magazine. K(onstantin?) Eiges had provided a model for these speculative articles with his "Muzyka i estetika" ("Music and Esthetics") of June 1906, and his "Osnovnaia antinomiia muzykalnoi estetiki" ("The Principal Antinomy of Musical Esthetics") of December 1906. In the second article, Eiges envisioned music as the "incarnation of the spiritually high," and glorified it as spiritually beautiful action.[114] He expanded this theme in his June 1907 "Muzyka, kak odno iz vysshikh misticheskikh perezhivanii" ("Music as One of the Highest Mystical Experiences"), in which he described music's independence from any other kind of art or science:

> Music is super-empirical. It unites in itself "subject and object," "I" and "non-I," idea and will. In an ontological relation, music is will to sounds. This, it seems, is sufficient to consider music outside of any encroachments of scientific explanations.[115]

At times bordering on mystical nonsense, Eiges' essays did repeat questions being argued in early twentieth-century Russia, even though Eiges himself appears to have been unable to reach any convincing conclusions of his own.

Considerably more significant than Eiges' speculations were the increasingly prominent articles by "Volfing" (Emily Medtner). Although Medtner had written two short pieces for the magazine in 1906 (including one directed at proving the importance of form in Schumann's works[116]), it was his February 1907 article sent from Munich that was the first major step toward a significant change in *Zolotoe Runo*'s musical posture. "Sixtus Beckmesser Redivivus ('etude' o 'novoi' muzyke)" ["Sixtus Beckmesser Redivivus (An 'Étude' about the 'New' Music)"] was accompanied by a note from Koreshchenko recommending the special attention of the magazine's readers to the article: "We believe this article will produce objections from many admirers of Reger's music, and that it will provide the basis for a highly interesting musical-scientific polemic."[117]

Medtner wrote that he had recently seen Reger in Munich, and felt that despite the praise Reger had received as "the new Bach," he was in fact fairly typical of modernist musicians in general:

> Modernist composers have renounced the essence of music and only masquerade as musicians; besides this, in their pseudo-music there is no trace of even the most subjective regularity; this absence of traits of autonomy of any kind, invariably inherent in every true talent, overturns the objective value of the modernists' novelties, novelties of daring to genius or to...! Here in a nutshell is the risk of their position—either they are geniuses or charlatans; *tertium non datur....* [118]

Medtner then attacked Reger as a "dilettante and a Philistine, pretending to be a genius; an *Alltagskopf* with an awkwardly-pulled-on mask of the highest individualism."[119] He wrote that Reger's lack of inspiration made his compositions "remind one of carelessly created piano arrangements,"[120] and he wondered how Reger had become so popular and successful, and why it was that more people had not opposed him publicly.

Max Reger (1873-1916) was enormously successful among European modernists in the first decade of this century, both as a composer and pianist. While Russian classicist composers reacted unfavorably to what they considered Reger's contrived neo-classicism, his December 1906 performance in Petersburg had reinforced his popularity among such Russian admirers as Karatygin, who had already written about Reger twice for *Zolotoe Runo,* wishing him a great triumph,[121] and remarking that "among [his] works are some of the most original pearls of romantic musical literature."[122] It would have been difficult for *Zolotoe Runo* to have found anyone with an opinion on Reger as directly opposed to Karatygin's as was Medtner's, and Koreshchenko's belief that a polemic might result from "Volfing's" article was not an unfounded one.

Despite his antipathy to such modern composers as Reger and Richard Strauss, Medtner's house in Moscow was described by Belyi as being the "center of the fertilization of chaotic Muscovites by

Germanism,"[123] although by a very particular variety of "Germanism."
Belyi wrote that it originated in Goethe and Weimar, not with Nietzsche or
Wagner, and Medtner's pseudonym undoubtedly was derived directly
from the medieval *Nibelungenlied* rather than from Wagner's operatic
cycle. The strongest musical influence on Medtner was his brother, the
well-known composer Nikolai Medtner (l880-1951), who considered his
life's mission the preservation of the great musical traditions of the past.
Emily Karlovich was convinced of his brother's genius, and in this light, his
opposition to the modernists is not surprising.

It became clear to *Zolotoe Runo*'s other music critics that Medtner
enjoyed the editors' special confidence when two more articles attacking
musical modernism appeared during the course of 1907. The second of
these, again sent from Munich, continued Medtner's earlier criticism of
Reger. As a footnote to "Cagliostro v iskusstve (*Étude* o 'novoi' muzyke)"
["Cagliostro in Music (An *Étude* on 'New' Music)'] the editors remarked
that in the interests of fairness, they retained the right to provide a place for
other evaluations of Strauss' works, since Medtner's was so negative.
Medtner peremptorily dispatched Reger, then began with Richard Strauss:
"Reger counterpoints absurdities; Strauss instrumentalizes them."[124]
Recounting Strauss' background, Medtner dismissed the Berlin Imperial
Opera (of which Strauss was director) as a "musical army."[125] Ridiculing
the "Sinfonia Demestica" and "Salomé," Medtner admitted that he had
liked "Till Eulenspiegel," although he qualified his praise by commenting
that "when Eulenspiegel wished to become Zarathustra, he could only
become Cagliostro."[126] Medtner concluded resignedly, observing that it
was unfortunate that in an age of prophets, the Germans could only
produce false prophets and "Cagliostros."

Medtner had attempted to synthesize many of these ideas in his earlier
"Modernizm v muzyke" ("Modernism in Music"), published in *Zolotoe
Runo* in March 1907, and to a certain extent reminiscent of some of Benois'
criticisms of the "new art" in his "Khudozhestvennye eresi." Medtner
defined modernism as an aspect of an eternally recurring romanticism, and
noted that while the best literary modernists were living rejections of the
principle of "fashion" (he gave Stefan George and Valery Briusov as
examples), this was not the case with musicians or music critics, who had
fallen together into "seasonal fashions" which changed from moment to
moment:

> The typical modernist...is incapable either of comprehending the past, or of
> understanding its greatness; for this reason he sees everything together, as transient, one
> only as a step to the next; e.g., Mozart as a stage toward Rebikov (I do not exaggerate:
> there was such an article!).[127]

Medtner felt that in comparison with modernist poets, modernist composers were illiterate, that they were unable to create a new art (as Mozart had done, in creating new conventions based on older ones), and that their critical suporters had failed them by being "infirm theoretically."[128]

It was clear that it was to Karatygin among others that Medtner's criticisms referred, and Karatygin replied with his "Maskarad (Po povodu etiudov g. Volfinga o novoi muzyke)" ["Masquerade (On the Studies of Mr. Volfing on New Music)"], which appeared in *Zolotoe Runo* toward the end of 1907.[129] Karatygin's anger burned through his point-by-point criticism of Medtner's position, and reexamining the works of Reger and Strauss, he gave his own enthusiastic evaluation of the composers' works. The irreconcilability of the two critics' positions became obvious from Karatygin's admission that "For me, Strauss is one of the most talented musicians of the present, but he is not a genius. Genius can only be found in the younger 'modernist' of the twentieth century—in Reger."[130]

It was probably accidental that it was Reger who provided the stimulus for the conflict among the musical contributors to *Zolotoe Runo,* especially since his "modernism" is open to question today. The disagreement over Reger was the cause of a significant change in the journal's musical orientation, however. Medtner was being given considerably more exposure in the magazine than was any other musical contributor, and despite his being abroad, his influence within the editorial board was growing (this was seen particularly in the context of Belyi's argument with *Zolotoe Runo,* discussed below). Above all, it undoubtedly appeared to such critics as Karatygin and Sats that they had been mistaken in believing that *Zolotoe Runo* was dedicated to the support of musical modernism. Admittedly, the magazine had never given an official direction to its musical section, but no one expected Medtner's "traditionalist" positions to become as prevalent in *Zolotoe Runo* as they did.

The unofficial changes in esthetic position becoming apparent in *Zolotoe Runo*'s musical department were to be reflected in the magazine's official redirection as a whole in mid-1907. The editors' naive attempt at attracting modernist contributors to the musical section while initiating polemics with them proved a failure. Although Karatygin continued to contribute short notices to *Zolotoe Runo* until the end of 1907, he then abandoned it and began writing reviews for *Rech,* and later also for *Severnye Zapiski (Northern Notes).* Sats and Popov also left, probably for similar reasons. *Zolotoe Runo* never did establish a definite musical esthetic position, but with the magazine's reorientation in 1907, and based on Medtner's known prejudices and increasing influence, it was clear that after that year, while *Zolotoe Runo* would not officially oppose the newest forms of musical modernism, neither would it support them.

Viktor Lobanov's criticism of *Zolotoe Runo* as being a journal without a "face" has some justification with regard to its first two years of publication. *Zolotoe Runo*'s initial manifesto was equivocal in meaning, and the significance of what seemed contradictory positions never became clear during 1906 and 1907. In many ways, *Zolotoe Runo* was a catch-all for all modernist tendencies in Russia. If it gave space at times to such "non-progressive" opinions as those of Benois and Medtner, at others it just as indiscriminately gave its support to those attacked by such "non-progressives." Fortunately for *Zolotoe Runo,* no serious editorial and contributional disagreements flared into open conflict until mid-1907. The magazine's non-committal "face" was forced into change both by internal and external developments after that date. Serious adjustments had taken place in *Zolotoe Runo,* in its competition, in Russian symbolism and modernism as a whole, and in Russia itself, above all. The personal, ideological, and programmatic changes occurring in *Zolotoe Runo* will be discussed in the following chapter, and their product, a *Zolotoe Runo* with a new "face," more specifically defined, but often still contradictory, will be discussed in the second half of this work.

IV

CONFLICT AND REDIRECTION:
ZOLOTOE RUNO IN MID-1907

At this conference it was finally made entirely clear that Riabushinsky's relations with his collaborators and to writers in general were such that they excluded the possibility of any self-respecting person's taking part in his journal. I do not want to relate everything he said, but here are two phrases which he repeated several times with emphasis: "Really, I can't even deny my own cook something without *Vesy* sticking its nose in the affair." "I am completely certain that writers are the same as prostitutes: they give themselves to him who pays, and if a great deal is paid, one can do with the writer what one likes."

> Briusov letter to Sologub, August 31, 1907, quoted in A. A. Volkov, *Russkaia literatura XX veka,* p. 409.

Striving to be a high-principled expression of Russian creativity, *Zolotoe Runo* will illuminate the crisis through which Russian symbolism is now living, and in a series of articles subject to examination the basic questions of esthetic world-view.

> Notice from the editors, *ZR,* 1907, No. 10, 86.

Although during the first year and a half of its publication *Zolotoe Runo* expressed a nominally symbolist, but undoubtedly modernist esthetic position, by mid-1907 the editors felt it necessary to announce a change of program. The first indication of what circumstances were to prove a fundamental official reorientation for *Zolotoe Runo* was given with the reorganization of the magazine's critical section. In April 1907, the following announcement from the editors, with an accompanying note by Alexander Blok, appeared:

> Instead of the bibliographic section abolished with #3, the editors of *Zolotoe Runo* will introduce in the next issue a critical survey giving a systematic evaluation of literary developments.
>
> The editors have secured the consent of our collaborator Alexander Blok as author of these evaluations, a statement from whom, in accordance with his wishes, will be found below:
>
> "The editors of *Zolotoe Runo* have entrusted me with a difficult and responsible task—a critical review of current literature. In order to note everything valuable while still current, I intend to consider the maximum possible in each of my first surveys. In

such a way, I think, it will be possible to discuss contemporary realism [and] include a wide range of very diverse writers. In the same way it will be possible to [deal with] recent drama, lyric poetry, criticism, [and] the religious-philosophical movement of our day. My task will be facilitated by the fact that I will deal mainly with fiction, in accordance with the nature of this journal.

I will devote my first article in the next issue of *Zolotoe Runo* to realist fiction appearing during the last few months. Finishing with these "combined" articles as soon as possible, I will attempt to give monthly accounts of the principal literary occurrences with all possible completeness."

Al. Blok[1]

The editors' decision to discontinue the former practice of short critical notices for new works was primarily a logistical and esthetic one, since the reviews never approached a high literary level. Blok's announcement that he would deal with the realist writers created some consternation among modernists, however, since they were held in almost universal disrepute by modernist writers, even those earlier associated with *Zolotoe Runo*. It soon became apparent that a serious reevaluation of esthetic position was being undertaken by *Zolotoe Runo,* reflected in Blok's initial review article on contemporary Russian realist literature.

The implications of this redirection received some clarification in an announcement from the editors in June 1907:

> In the period of general crisis through which we are living today, when in the depths of consciousness work of enormous importance is taking place—the revision of the theoretical and practical bases of the individualist world-view—criticism must be of fundamental importance. Perhaps we will find ourselves on the eve of a new creative synthesis and a new blossoming of art, but what is coming is still indicated darkly: only one thing is clear, "decadence," appearing as a unitary and artistically complete world-view, has already been finished with by our modern consciousness.
>
> In such an epoch, one feels in particular the need for retrospection, in order to take in at a glance that which has already been lived through, and to try to see signs of the coming path. The editors of *Zolotoe Runo* will give primary consideration to the question of criticism, having in mind the dual nature of the problem: on one hand—an examination of the theoretical and practical questions of an esthetic world-view; on the other—the as objective as possible analysis of the art of recent years and of new developments in painting and literature, in conjuction with the goal of clarifying the perspectives of the future. The editors will give special consideration to an examination of questions about the national element in art and about "neo-realism"...
>
> In connection with the journal's new goals, there will be a slight change in the composition of the contributors as a series of writers connected with new, young searching in art are gradually attracted.[2]

A summary of related notices and prospective contributors follow: two articles by Gorodetsky and Makovsky on the national element in art, and others by Blok, Viacheslav Ivanov, and Voloshin were promised; the artistic section was to be enlarged, as was the "chronicle," which would include more reports on cultural developments in the West. *Zolotoe Runo*'s public recognition of the "period of crisis" through which the whole of Russia was living reflected an attitude common to both symbolists and realists; its announcement that "decadence" was dead as a viable approach to art might have drawn some qualification from the Russian modernists, but in the end they probably would have agreed in principle with the magazine's evaluation. Most considered "decadence" thoroughly outdated in Russia, something associated with *Mir Iskusstva*'s early years and the first works of Merezhkovsky, Briusov, and Balmont in the 1890's. *Zolotoe Runo*'s promise to give special attention to the examination of "national art" and "neo-realism" was a prospect in no way appealing to large numbers of modernist writers and artists, however. Some of *Zolotoe Runo*'s readers must have felt the magazine's editors had become slightly addled. Yet *Zolotoe Runo*'s new orientation was not entirely a surprise, since Blok's article on the realists, appearing the month before the June notice, had expressed opinions and judgments no one would have expected either in a modernist publication or from the symbolist poet Blok.

As Blok had announced earlier, his survey "O realistakh" ("On the Realists")[3] dealt with the full range of contemporary realist literature. Certainly of most interest to his modernist readers was Blok's evaluation of the *Znanie* writers and in particular, his judgment of Maxim Gorky. Blok challenged the widely-accepted positions of Belyi and Merezhkovsky, considered the chief theoreticians of symbolism, and defended Gorky from their criticisms. Only two years before, in the midst of revolutionary upheaval, *Vesy* had expressed in print the general modernist position that all those who loved Russian literature must fight the influence of Gorky and his *Znanie* collections.[4] Blok's position was decidedly different. He began his essay with a discussion of two recent criticisms of Gorky, dwelling primarily on Filosofov's "Konets Gorkogo" ("The End of Gorky"), which had appeared in *Russkaia Mysl* the month before. Blok wrote that Gorky was not necessarily at the end of his creative path (as Filosofov alleged), but described him as undergoing a crisis, and he faulted Filosofov for judging Gorky from social, scientific, and religious points of view rather than on the basis of purely artistic standards. Blok admitted that Gorky had lost much of his earlier literary strength, that some of his most recent *Znanie* contributions were filled with "banal epithets" and "naive sentimentality," and that most of the principal figures in his recent novel *Mat (Mother),* for example, were only shadows of earlier Gorky characters. Although Blok agreed that Gorky's writing had reached a nadir, he felt that even through this present weakness Gorky possessed a contrasting strength not present in his modernist critics:

> Gorky has "spat" all his life, and has only recently become banal. But behind all his spitting and banality hides that enormous melancholy, "which has no name and no measure." And great sincerity—the kind that is simply impossible for people of great culture, like Merezhkovsky and Filosofov, to have. Impossible because that very culture is a great and fatal dream.[5]

The personal nature of this attack on the Merezhkovsky group was intensified by Blok's aside that the realists at least were not so pretentious as to write "Christ-Antichrist novels." "O realistakh" was Blok's first such sharp criticism of the Merezhkovsky-Filosofov position, and the not unexpected rift between him and his former friends which soon appeared was not to be bridged until the end of 1908.

The remainder of Blok's essay dealt with several other realist writers. His discussion of Andreev's story "Iuda Iskariot i drugie" ("Judas Iscariot and the Others") was a lyrical exposition and description of the psychological characteristics of Judas, Christ, and the Apostles. Describing Andreev admiringly as the "voice of the national soul,"[6] Blok again mentioned Filosofov, writing that his earlier objections to Andreev no longer had any foundation after the appearance of this story.

Blok was less kind to the other realist writers, whose themes dealt mainly with the recent revolution. He called the works of "Skitalets" and Serafimovich "business-like" literature which nevertheless had some value in that they were the type of literature needed by the masses, and by some of the intelligentsia—works in which the riot of the revolution sometimes entirely concealed the riot of the soul, and the voice of the crowd drowned out the individual's voice.[7] He contrasted the superior skill of Artsybashev to that of the *Znanie* writers, whose literary talents, he wrote, were directed toward a single, all-consuming goal—the destruction of the capitalist order.

"O realistakh" concluded with positive statements on the work of Boris Zaitsev and great praise for Sologub's *Melkii Bes (The Petty Demon)*, which Blok analyzed in some detail. Blok ended the essay with an anticipation of the attacks he expected from his former literary allies, and returned to a theme that was at the basis of his new-found appreciation for realism:

> Let them say that my words are *blasphemous*, those who feel they have the right to castigate and judge. I admit that my words are blasphemous. But let them not forget to answer me: are not all words blasphemous with which man dares to investigate nature, when put next to the age-old and prophetic silence of the earth—always simple and spring-like?[8]

Blok's appreciation for the simplicity and purity of nature had already been expressed in his first *Zolotoe Runo* article, "Kraski i slova,"[9] and he used this theme throughout the next year and a half to justify his own personal esthetic "searchings" and to provide a strong counterpoint to the "melée symboliste" of the post-1905 years in Russia.

Blok's direct personal attacks on writers with whom he had previously been close, in addition to his "heretical" views on realism, created an uproar of their own in conjunction with the official announcements *Zolotoe Runo*'s editors had made. The final result was the withdrawal of a number of prominent symbolists from collaboration with *Zolotoe Runo,* announced in the August 1907 issue of *Vesy:*

"Zolotoe Runo"

In the August numbers of the majority of Moscow and Petersburg papers, and in some of the provincial ones, the following two "letters to the editor" were published.

I

Permit us through the means of your esteemed newspaper to announce to our readers that we no longer consider it possible to contribute to Mr. N. Riabushinsky's *Zolotoe Runo* and that we will no longer take any part in it.

D. Merezhkovsky, Z. Gippius, Valery Briusov, Andrei Belyi

II

Completely agreeing with the letter of D. Merezhkovsky, Z. Gippius, Valery Briusov, and Andrei Belyi, we also no longer consider it possible to contribute to Mr. N. Riabushinsky's *Zolotoe Runo* and we will no longer take any part in it.

M. Kuzmin, Iu. Baltrushaitis, M. Likiardopulo.[10]

It is important to note that all these writers were closely associated with *Vesy* at this time, a clear indication that relations between the two magazines had reached a serious point of tension. It should also be mentioned that Merezhkovsky and Gippius had published little in *Zolotoe Runo,* that Likiardopulo and Baltrushaitis had each published only one book review in the magazine, and that Kuzmin continued publishing in *Zolotoe Runo* after a short absence.

The loss of Belyi and Briusov was considerably more significant, however, and was the culmination of a two-fold development. While *Zolotoe Runo*'s change of program provided the initial reason for the writers' withdrawal, and Blok's "O realistakh" inflamed the decision, there were other equally compelling factors. Fundamental were the arguments and polemics between *Zolotoe Runo* and *Vesy* which had become increasingly caustic at the beginning of 1907, alienating former contributors to both magazines and forcing them into different camps. This intensified division of loyalties between the two major Russian modernist magazines was recognized by *Zolotoe Runo*'s editors, who described the withdrawn writers as being "close collaborators" of *Vesy*.[11] Of equal importance were the ongoing personal conflicts among *Zolotoe Runo*'s editors and contributors, an important source of which was Riabushinsky's insistence on having final authority in all editorial decisions. The significance of this difficulty was emphasized by the withdrawal notices' direct mention of Riabushinsky along with *Zolotoe Runo*, and it was the personal antipathy which developed between Briusov and Belyi on one hand, and Riabushinsky on the other which was the fundamental reason for the break. Both these developments, publicistic and personal, came to a climax in mid-1907, and each deserves some background examination in order to clarify the reasons for the very serious division between the two modernist groups.

A minor argument between *Vesy* and *Zolotoe Runo* erupted soon after the initial review of the new magazine by "Tovarishch German" (Zinaida Gippius) appeared in *Vesy* in February 1906.[12] Sergei Sokolov's "Apologety kultury" ("The Apologists of Culture"),[13] written under his pseudonym, Sergei Krechetov, appeared the very next month in *Zolotoe Runo*, and was written in a tone of distress in response to *Vesy*'s "uncharitable" review. Sokolov wrote that since the article was signed with a pseudonym, it must be taken as an expression of the views of *Vesy*'s editors, yet in its argument and tone, Krechetov felt, the review showed no sense of the literary decency one would expect from such an esteemed journal.[14] Defending *Zolotoe Runo* from Gippius' charges, Sokolov felt it necessary to summarize the Russian artistic situation of the previous few years. He remembered that it was not long before that only utilitarian art was permissible in Russia, and that it was only recently possible to dream not of lowering art to the masses, since such an act would ruin art, but of raising the masses to the level of pure art. A sufficient number of people to accomplish this task had only just arisen in Russia, and when *Zolotoe Runo* began publication, Sokolov wrote, one would have thought that true lovers of art would have greeted the new journal enthusiastically:

> From whom then would one expect more sympathy than from *Vesy*, which had so long and vigorously championed ... the interests of true art?
> Now I see that we were mistaken.
> We thought that to *Vesy*, as to *Zolotoe Runo*, art itself was important, but it has now become clear that to *Vesy* only its role in Art is important. ... [15]

Sokolov wrote that *Zolotoe Runo* welcomed honest criticism, but from *Vesy* it had received only "mud-slinging" and "market abuse," in no way relevant to questions of "Art." Finally, Sokolov attempted to raise *Zolotoe Runo* above the level of criticism in Gippius' review:

No . . . streams of mockery will prevent *Zolotoe Runo* from proceeding on its way, alone. We believe that art is eternal, even though this seems a humorous and outmoded truth to *Vesy,* and we do not want to profane it in the name of vain and petty inducements. We will not answer invectives with invectives. "The service of the muses does not tolerate vanity."[16]

Sokolov's righteous indignation was shared by *Zolotoe Runo'*s staff, who were undoubtedly surprised and deeply disappointed at what they considered a less than friendly reception from a magazine for which most of them had the greatest respect. It soon became clear to them that *Vesy* considered itself *the* Russian symbolist journal, whose opinions and judgments were beyond reproach. Sokolov understood this, and the combative nature of both his and Gippius' articles set the tone for what developed over the next year into a full debate.

Gippius replied in May,[17] expressing surprise that Sokolov had not understood the review's criticisms of the *Zolotoe Runo* manifesto's "banal" truths, although noting that Sokolov's reaction itself could be seen as an indication of the "naive judgments" which abounded in the new magazine. Gippius wrote that Sokolov (the two maintained the use of pseudonyms throughout their argument), like the author of *Zolotoe Runo'*s manifesto, had "shown himself to be below that cultural level demanded of the editor of a European artistic publication."[18] Gippius' short reply was aimed at pointing out how "pathetic" Sokolov's article was, however, that his anger had caused him to confuse both his grammar and the elementary rules of logic. She described Sokolov's style as pretentious, and wrote that "some phrases were almost classical in their incoherence,"[19] and that in general the response was reminiscent of some of the worst sections of Sumarokov's tragedies. Gippius concluded that it was humorous for a magazine whose contributors included some of the greatest stylists of the Russian language to have an editorial answer "given in the language of Sergei Krechetov!"[20] Gippius' riposte to Sokolov was certainly written with a polemical intent. Repeating earlier criticism of the new magazine's pretensions, Gippius dealt primarily with Sokolov's choice of words, using them to ridicule both him and *Zolotoe Runo.* The article included nothing new, and was directed not toward Sokolov's opinions themselves, but to how they were expressed, in the process becoming a literary exercise, an exposition on the stylistic flaws of Sokolov's writing.

Sokolov's answer appeared almost immediately.[21] Calling Gippius' article pure polemic, Sokolov wrote that it was directed not at *Zolotoe Runo* as a journal, but towards him personally. Annoyed at such anonymous criticism, Sokolov wrote that he saw no point in analyzing the base personal motives for the attack. He called "Tovarishch German" "almost a coward" for hiding behind a false name that permitted the use of "bitter abuse, where feelings of decency and measure are lost,"[22] and wrote that from then on he would no longer reply to works signed with pseudoynms. In any case, with Sokolov's leaving the magazine in mid-1906, no one else on *Zolotoe Runo's* staff cared to initiate or carry on any arguments with *Vesy* until almost a year later.

There was sufficient reason for continuing the polemic, however, since a long unsigned evaluation of *Zolotoe Runo's* first four issues appeared in *Vesy* in June 1906.[23] Criticizing what he called *Zolotoe Runo's* lack of coherence and unity, *Vesy's* reviewer wrote that after four issues, the magazine could be expected to have found its own physiognomy, but that instead, "*Runo* remains as before a storeroom for poems, articles, and drawings, without any kind of program, and no one knows what may be printed in it tomorrow."[24] *Vesy* saw in *Zolotoe Runo* no group of similarly-thinking individuals necessary for a clearly-expressed program, and by implication predicted the new magazine's imminent demise from sheer disorganization.

The central point of *Vesy's* evaluation of *Zolotoe Runo* was directed at the new magazine's "individualist" position: the *Vesy* reviewer noted that since *Zolotoe Runo's* editors had stated that they disagreed with Benois' attack on individualism published in their magazine, they must consider themselves to be "individualists." This seemed an inconsistency to *Vesy's* critic, however: he wondered why half of each issue of *Zolotoe Runo* consisted of anonymous "chronicles" which had no real individuality of their own, reports which belonged in a newspaper, not in a magazine "pretending to artistry." *Vesy* asked that if the editors were individualists, why was it that their translations into French were so mundane as to cause the works translated to lose all individuality, Belyi sounding in *Zolotoe Runo's* French translation like Minsky, for example, and Remizov like Blok. *Vesy* found the transparency of such "individuality" in the magazine's artistic reproductions as well: it was in color that the distinctiveness of Vrubel's and Borisov-Musatov's works lay, yet the majority of *Zolotoe Runo's* reproductions of their works were in black and white, causing *Vesy's* reviewer to enquire whether the magazine considered the number of illustrations more important than the inherent value of each one.

Finally, *Vesy* asked, if the French text were to be removed from *Zolotoe Runo*, along with the "chronicles," which could be found in any Petersburg or Moscow newspaper, as well as the black and white illustrations, what would remain?

> ...three or four well-executed drawings, a few interesting vignettes and then some poems and "leading" articles by people who usually are contributors to *Vesy, Severnye Tsvety, Mir Iskusstva* [*Mir Iskusstva* was no longer being published, of course]. This then comprises the true value of *Zolotoe Runo:* everything else is just a husk.[25]

Summarizing his position, and by implication, *Vesy's* expectation for *Zolotoe Runo,* the review's author concluded:

> It is clear that it is not enough for a magazine to attract the services of leading writers, graphic artists, typographers, and photoengravers: it still needs literarily- and artistically-educated directors. Such a presence is indiscernable in *Runo.* In individual issues there is much that is interesting and good; as a whole, there is no soul, no sense. And this Argo (*Runo's* emblem is the ship of the argonauts) seems to us to be a vessel without a captain and a helmsman.[26]

Many of *Vesy's* criticisms of *Zolotoe Runo* were justified, although the belabored discussion of individualism was carried out on very flimsy grounds. The review did not depart from what had been said in earlier *Vesy* notices, and it is probable that it was written by either Gippius or Briusov, but in a style much less personal and polemical than that used previously. Above all, it was clear from this review that *Vesy* did indeed intend to be the established modernist periodical in Russia, the one which should pass judgment on new modernist endeavors, and whose opinions should be overwhelmingly influential. *Vesy* was unprepared to accept enthusiastically any competitor, but none the less felt it necessary to justify its negative attitude with convincing criticism.

There were a number of reasons for the reticence of *Zolotoe Runo's* editors to reply to this long, serious attack. Of primary importance was Sokolov's withdrawal from the magazine in June, his replacement Kursinsky seeing little cause for beginning anew the polemic with Gippius that had already reached an impasse. Kursinsky also undoubtedly did not want to subject himself to the personal attacks Gippius had made on Sokolov. In addition, *Zolotoe Runo's* editorial staff must have felt that there was little advantage in irritating writers who were closely tied to *Vesy,* and who owed it their primary loyalty. Briusov was the most significant of these, and since he increased his private, unofficial aid to *Zolotoe Runo* after Sokolov's departure, it was obviously in *Zolotoe Runo's* interest not to antagonize him by attacking his journal. In fact, it was Briusov himself who broke the truce between the two magazines by publishing a devastating criticism of *Zolotoe Runo's* first two issues of 1907 in March of that year in *Vesy.*[27]

Using his well-known pseudonym "Pentaur," Briusov repeated several earlier *Vesy* charges: because of the "innumerable" mistakes and contradictions of the first two issues of 1907, Briusov wrote that he was forced to ask if anyone was in charge in *Zolotoe Runo's* editorial office. Briusov called "Maestro" (Vasily Rozanov) "sick" in his criticisms (published in *Zolotoe Runo's* January 1907 issue) of Kuzmin's *Krylia (Wings)* and of a collection of Briusov's poems. Worse, in Briusov's eyes, was that in the

February issue, *Zolotoe Runo*'s editors had to explain that "Maestro" had meant his criticisms for some poems of Viacheslav Ivanov, and not those of Briusov at all. Rereading the review, Briusov wrote, he found similar incompetencies in "Maestro's" discussion and citation of some of the characters in *Krylia,* and confronting both the editors and the reviewer, asked:

> Do the editors of *Zolotoe Runo* read their own journal or do they consider this superfluous, as some of *Zolotoe Runo*'s critics consider it superfluous to read the books they criticize?[28]

Briusov concluded that such accidents were commonplace in the magazine, and gave further examples of what he considered *Zolotoe Runo*'s anarchical editing. Most serious of his criticisms was Briusov's discussion of Sats' "Satana v muzyke," which appeared in January 1907. Briusov wrote that he had found several ridiculous errors in the article, and that it was undoubtedly written by an uneducated person, completely ignorant of history, who nevertheless had the presumption to call his article an "historical note."[29] In an added comment, "Pisat ili spisyvat" ("To Write or to Copy"),[30] signed with his own name, Briusov remarked on these mistakes: they were not the result of editorial or typographical misreadings, but derived from the author's use of an "illiterate" book by E. Nauman as a direct source for almost half the article. Briusov supported his plagiarism charge by a textual comparison of parts of Nauman's book with the essay, and found similarities of style, concept, and most damaging, even of spelling and translation errors. Briusov could no longer consider *Zolotoe Runo* a reputable, responsible magazine: "It is simply a pity that *Zolotoe Runo,* having at the end of 1906 several excellent issues, has again turned into a storehouse for chance articles."[31]

Despite the fact that Briusov, *Vesy,* and the readers of both magazines undoubtedly expected a necessarily defensive response from what must have been an embarrassed *Zolotoe Runo,* what appeared instead were two strong counterattacks in the magazine's April issue which indicated a newly-determined, officially tendentious attitude toward *Vesy.* Written under the pseudonym "Empirik," Tasteven's "Prichiny odnoi literaturnoi metamorfozy" ("Causes of One Literary Metamorphosis")[32] was in its own way as significant in its attack on *Vesy* as was the editors' subsequent announcement that "decadence" was dead within the modernist movement as a whole. Tasteven began by asking if this really were the same *Vesy* that had fought so fiercely for the new art in the struggle with esthetic realism and positivism, since it now appeared to have taken as its major task the "evaluation of all values." He described what he considered *Vesy*'s very noticeable deterioration: its critical sensitivity had become progressively less acute and frequently contradictory, he wrote, as the contrast between Belyi's "manifestoes" and Kuzmin's neo-Hellenism proved, for example. Other indications of decline were the magazine's "narrow and analytical" bibliographic section, filled with "niggardly" articles, the large number of translations from foreign journals, and the incomplete "chronicle." Tasteven concluded that *Vesy* had become too old and decrepit, and that it was undergoing an irreversible metamorphosis: "The individualism of which *Vesy*'s ideological skeleton is made has completed its logical development, and is becoming fixed and conservative."[33]

A short attack on *Vesy*'s artistic section by "Z" immediately followed Tasteven's more general discussion of the journal. The ostensible reason for the notice was that with Sudeikin's decorations for *Vesy*'s third issue of 1907, the magazine's artistic section ("if one can give this title to such an unsystematic collection of illustrations"[34]) apparently had been given its own independent position. "Z" felt that this section relied heavily on previously unpublished works with no merit in themselves: a poem by Pushkin was accompanied by an "insignificant and uncharacteristic" drawing by Levitan, both of which were valuable to *Vesy* only in that they were "unpublished." "Z" concluded that even considering *Vesy*'s special issues devoted to the works of new young artists, its artistic section was representative of the magazine's general tastelessness and a candid expression of its motto: "cheap [because of its 'pitifully-colored repro- ductions'] but good" ("deshevo i serdito").[35]

These two criticisms indicated that *Zolotoe Runo* no longer con- sidered it necessary to remain on the defensive. Tasteven and "Z" attacked with much the same tone and outrage as had *Vesy*'s critics, and like them, used their own magazine as a standard against which its competition should be measured; the extent of either's "chronicle" or the number of translations from foreign journals of course had no implicit significance in themselves, however, but were simply expressions of different journalistic approaches. As the gap between the two groups of contributors allied to *Vesy* and *Zolotoe Runo* became increasingly apparent, *Zolotoe Runo*'s editors no longer considered it necessary to avoid alienating Briusov and his principal aides on *Vesy*'s staff. This was especially true since it had become clear in early 1907 that *Vesy*'s official position was now directly opposed to *Zolotoe Runo*'s continued existence as an independent, competitive magazine.

The wrangling between the two reached a climax in June 1907 with *Vesy*'s "Zolotomu Runu" ("To *Zolotoe Runo*"), signed by "R."[36] For the first time, *Vesy* felt obliged to defend itself from *Zolotoe Runo*'s criticisms. *Vesy* protested what it called *Zolotoe Runo*'s distortion of the facts, and attempted to answer the charges that *Vesy*'s artistic section relied mainly on republications and curiosities, in passing accusing *Zolotoe Runo* of the

same practice. Adopting what earlier had been *Zolotoe Runo*'s tone, "R"
concluded his reply to *Zolotoe Runo*'s statements:

> Confining ourselves to only one of *Runo*'s assertions, we have shown all its
> unfoundedness; but in the two notices directed against us, there is a whole series of such
> factual inaccuracies and distortions, which give rise to only a feeling of pity in us.
> Argument must be honest, this is an ancient truth. With no kind of polemical passion is
> it possible to excuse an opponent who knowingly speaks falsehoods.[37]

The ties of good will which earlier had existed between the two magazines
were completely broken by the necessary defensiveness of the *Vesy* reply.
Briusov simply would not tolerate such attacks on his magazine by fellow
modernists. Throughout the next two and a half years of publication,
Zolotoe Runo and *Vesy* would quarrel continually and become havens for
opposing factions within Russian symbolism. Their polemics would
become an important feature of subsequent Russian literary-artistic life,
but after June 1907 would deal with esthetic and philosophical questions
rather than purely journalistic concerns. The sources for this later mutual
abuse were found in the publicistic debates and criticisms already
discussed. An important contributing factor to the exodus of a number of
Zolotoe Runo's collaborators (clearly marking the break between the two
magazines), however, was the personal conflicts which developed between
the two groups that were to unite around *Vesy* and *Zolotoe Runo*.

The best-known source of information on these personal conflicts
resulting in the break is Andrei Belyi. Although frequently misleading,
Belyi's summary of the events leading up to the exodus is worth repeating:

> When I returned to Moscow [from Petersburg], these three journals—*Vesy, Zolotoe
> Runo, Pereval*—could have become the organs for the expression of the ideas of our
> group (Petersburg did not have its own organs); and I dreamed of creating a block of
> three journals against the destructive Petersburg, and from these three batteries to place
> under fire the malicious "tower" of Ivanov; but there was competition among the
> journals (*Vesy* continually tried to "pin-up" *Pereval, Pereval* offendedly looked askance
> at *Vesy,* however, and had long been in a fury at *Zolotoe Runo*); the three journals each
> wished that I would take a closer part in each, but my partisan duty connected me
> indissolubly with *Vesy*: it was there that we had hoisted the banner of symbolism; later
> on I succeeded in softening the discord between Briusov and S. A. Sokolov (editor of
> *Pereval*); and a secret agreement took place: not to allow the ideology of the
> Petersburgians in *Pereval*...I broke with *Runo,* the pretext for the break was the
> tactless action of the editor-publisher N. P. Riabushinsky regarding one of his
> collaborators, but also my refusal to be the head of the literary section; I laid down
> conditions to Riabushinsky—his quitting as head of the journal; this was motivated by
> the impossibility of working with him, a person incapable of being competent in
> questions of literature; Briusov and a number of artists (as I recall: Sapunov, Sudeikin,
> Feofilaktov, and others) joined with me; the motives for the struggle of the corporation
> of writers with those Maecenas-publishers who had little understanding in art
> (ideological motives).[38]

Belyi related essentially the same account in various places, but each included a number of discrepancies and inconsistencies.[39] Most conspicuously absent in Belyi's summary is any real discussion of Briusov's role in the affair. As we have seen, Briusov had always wanted to ensure *Vesy*'s position as the foremost Russian symbolist organ, and hoped to move *Zolotoe Runo* in a direction sympathetic with the predominance of *Vesy*. Eventually, however, Briusov and Riabushinsky argued over who should direct *Zolotoe Runo* (Belyi wrote that Riabushinsky "stuck his nose into the area of Briusov's competence"[40]), and he left the staff of contributors to *Zolotoe Runo* soon thereafter. In his *Mezhdu dvukh revoliutsii (Between Two Revolutions),* Belyi recounted that Briusov insisted in secret that Belyi remain on as a close collaborator to the new journal "so that enemies would not take root there."[41] Belyi agreed, but presented Riabushinsky with an ultimatum of "non-intervention" in the literary "tactics" of the journal, and moreover, demanded for himself and the now absent Briusov the right of veto in the selection of contributors and location of literary materials in *Zolotoe Runo*. The negotiations dragged on, and during them Riabushinsky quarrelled with his current literary editor Kursinsky, who then left the magazine as well. Finally, Belyi wrote a letter to Riabushinsky "with a challenge: for him there is sufficient honor in subsidizing the journal; he, a petty tyrant and lacking any talent, should not take part in the journal."[42] Belyi enjoyed good relations with none of the Moscow Maecenas-patrons at this time, and as we have seen, had never liked Riabushinsky.[43] Belyi had stated that his letter was the reason for the final break with *Zolotoe Runo,* but as the Soviet literary historian Vladimir Orlov has pointed out, Belyi had another reason for his decision: he wanted *Zolotoe Runo* to publish a letter to the editors in answer to Volfing's "polemicizing" with Belyi's article "Protiv muzyki" ("Against Music").[44]

> The misunderstanding with *Runo* was even harder for me in that Medtner, living in Munich, was also involved in it; he was sent a short article of mine, "Protiv muzyki," and [this] lover of music burst out with an article, published in *Runo* with delight, against me . . . Tasteven set Medtner on me in a way that he began to turn out letters by the half-*pud*—one after another; above my little article a Himalaya was set up; we were barely reconciled, this battle with a friend affected me more than the argument with Riabushinsky; I wanted to cry out "Et tu, Brute!"[45]

Riabushinsky at first denied Belyi's request, then agreed on condition Belyi return to *Zolotoe Runo*. Belyi's letter soon thereafter appeared in *Pereval*[46] (this seems a corroboration of Belyi's statement that the break between Sokolov, himself, and Briusov had been healed), Riabushinsky published what Belyi called a "slanderous" reply in *Stolichnoe Utro (Capital Morning),*[47] and the August announcement of withdrawal by Belyi and Briusov was confirmed.

An important contributing factor to this confused sequence of events was Blok's appearance as the author of *Zolotoe Runo's* literary surveys: his new opinions and his refusal to join the *Vesy* boycott worsened the situation, especially since he was a member of those Belyi called the "Petersburgians":

> The Petersburg group had now received its organ in Moscow. I was furious; it seemed to me that the appearance of the Petersburgians in *Runo,* their knowing that our reason was not wanting to work with a "petty-tyrant editor"—that the appearance of these Petersburgians in *Runo* seemed to me to be strikebreaking; from then on there began to appear there the literary surveys of A. A. [Blok], dedicated to the realist writers (in our opinion at the time—the reactionaries in art) and to attacks against us, his former companions.[48]

Belyi's expression of personal disappointment over Blok's (and the other Petersburgians') "strikebreaking" was deceitful, since he later admitted that he had done all he could to keep the Petersburg writers from gaining a position of importance on any of the major Moscow symbolist journals, including the now despised *Zolotoe Runo.* Belyi's anger at Blok climaxed in a letter he wrote Blok on the fifth or sixth of August 1907. Directing himself toward Blok's "O realistakh," Belyi charged his former friend with ingratiating himself from tactical considerations before the "anti-symbolist," realist group of writers and "severed for all time" his relations with Blok.[49]

Belyi's letter resulted in a challenge to a duel from Blok, but a short reconciliation between the two was reached at the end of August in Moscow, where they discussed the circumstances of the argument with Riabushinsky. Blok told Belyi that he had been deceived by Briusov, that Belyi and the *Vesy* writers had "left *Runo* at the same time Briusov had his argument with Riabushinsky; up until the quarrel he (Briusov) had actually been the editor, having made peace with Riabushinsky."[50] Belyi refused to believe in Briusov's duplicity, even if it had been only partial, because he was strongly under Briusov's influence at the time, in Maslenikov's words, revering him "both as a teacher and a wizard."[51] Blok was able to examine the situation more objectively than was Belyi, and it is clear today that Briusov was the determining factor in the exodus. When Briusov saw the new factions arising within symbolism in 1907 which threatened the supremacy of *Vesy,* he set out to convince his colleagues and admirers that such new groups as the "mystical anarchists" were undermining the ideals for which symbolism and *Vesy* stood. Finally, it was Briusov's status that attracted the other writers away from *Zolotoe Runo,* and not Belyi's, as it may appear from the latter's memoirs. Briusov was active in attempting to lure away *Zolotoe Runo's* collaborators, and although little effort was necessary in the case of Gippius, for example, the letter to Sologub quoted at the beginning of this chapter was intended as much to gain the writer's support for Briusov's position as it was to be informative.

As we have seen, then, there were several reasons for the exodus of writers from *Zolotoe Runo*. The initial stimulus for the withdrawal came from the new magazine's official change of policy, especially the new tolerant attitude it expressed toward realism. Second was the division within symbolism between two competing groups, the "mystical anarchists" and the "esthetic" symbolists, Belyi's "Petersburgians" and his own group in Moscow. Although Belyi overemphasized the geographical nature of these differences, since at the beginning of 1907 he had been made the chief theoretician of *Vesy* and felt it his duty to keep symbolism "pure," there was a division within symbolist theory that grew increasingly stronger after 1907, and played an important role in mutually alienating the *Vesy* and *Zolotoe Runo* contributors. Third, and of equal importance, was the disagreement between Briusov, Belyi, and Riabushinsky on how *Zolotoe Runo* was to be edited, a personal argument which aggravated the other problems. Since Belyi could barely tolerate Riabushinsky, he was relieved to find support among other symbolists for rejecting both him and his magazine. The chronology of Briusov's changing attitude toward *Zolotoe Runo* is confusing, since although one of his strongest criticisms of the magazine appeared in *Vesy* in March, and he contributed nothing to *Zolotoe Runo* after January, his final break with Riabushinsky did not take place until after the middle of the year. Briusov was disgusted at Riabushinsky's well-known lack of respect for those on his payroll, and saw a danger of Riabushinsky's wealth attracting writers away from *Vesy*, because of the older magazine's comparatively smaller monetary resources. Last of all, Riabushinsky himself played a major role in the exodus because of his insistence on final editorial approval (more formal than actual) and his notorious lack of tact in dealing with the literary and artistic contributors to his journal. By mid-1907 he had alienated most of *Zolotoe Runo*'s closest collaborators with the exception of Vasily Milioti and Genrikh Tasteven. Milioti was to direct *Zolotoe Runo*'s artistic section toward the adoption of a neo-primitivist emphasis, and Tasteven was to be responsible for the journal's redirection toward the realist aspects of symbolist literature and criticism.

Although *Zolotoe Runo* was not altered physically after the loss of the *Vesy* group, the list of the magazine's contributors and the works printed did change considerably. In the July-August-September issue the editors announced they had received the following letter:

As a result of the change of program of the journal *Zolotoe Runo* and of its editorial declaration, appearing in numbers 3 [sic] and 6, and also in view of the

reorganization of the editorial board, we will [rededicate our efforts as] contributors to
the journal.

Leonid Andreev
Ivan Bunin
Boris Zaitsev
Georgy Chulkov[52]

The magazine needed such support and the editors emphasized that these
four writers were "among" the new contributors, and that *Zolotoe Runo*
would welcome enthusiastically "new young talent." Interestingly enough,
while Chulkov contributed a great deal to the magazine over the next two
years, Zaitsev sent only two short travel sketches, Bunin one poem, and
Andreev nothing. Their names as possible, if not actual, contributors did
add a welcome luster to the somewhat smaller list of collaborators of which
Zolotoe Runo could now boast, however.

Despite such encouraging signs, and after the loss of Belyi and
Kursinsky, Riabushinsky's difficulties finding a full time literary editor for
Zolotoe Runo became more acute, primarily because he still would not
relinquish the complete editorial control that most of the prospective
editors desired. Accounts of his search had even reached the newspapers.[53]
In the summer of 1907 Andreev, having broken with *Znanie,* was offered
the literary section's editorship. He seemed a good choice, and most
symbolists recognized his talent, although they considered him culturally
unsophisticated. Andreev hoped to maintain an independent position,
however, and even though *Zolotoe Runo's* program was not a restrictive
one, and certainly not antithetical to his own beliefs, Andreev refused the
offer, instead accepting an editorial position with "Shipovnik" in Petersburg. His subsequent letter did indicate an interest in maintaining
significant contacts with *Zolotoe Runo,* however.[54]

With Andreev's refusal, Riabushinsky continued his search. Zaitsev
was asked, and he refused. Blok wrote to Ivanov in September:

> I promised *Zolotoe Runo* to ask you to be its editor, that is to take the whole journal into
> your hands internally. Internally because Riabushinsky will for nothing give up the
> official editorship.[55]

Ivanov declined, and once again, the reason was probably Riabushinsky's
insistence on official control over editorial decisions. In the end, it was
decided to offer the editorship to Chulkov, whose own position vis-a-vis his
modernist contemporaries was unclear at this time.[56] Chulkov sent
Riabushinsky and Tasteven an equivocal reply; in his own words:

> I refused the direct editorship of *Zolotoe Runo,* not wanting to move to Moscow,
> but gave my consent to the direction of the journal while remaining in Petersburg.[57]

Chulkov's offer was accepted, and he and Tasteven became the major shapers of *Zolotoe Runo*'s literary section for the remainder of the magazine's publication. Chulkov's position with regard to Blok was a nebulous one, since Blok had been assigned the magazine's review articles and a certain amount of other editorial work, as well (Blok wrote to Kuzmin during this period, for example, that he was "frightfully tired and over-worked with the boring 'chronicle' of *Runo*"[58]). Belyi's confusion over Blok's role in the magazine is understandable since until Chulkov took over officially as literary editor, Blok must have done most of *Zolotoe Runo*'s editorial work, both at the magazine's office and at his family's country estate. Nevertheless, it should be made clear that Blok never agreed to be official editor, was never satisfied with what he considered *Zolotoe Runo*'s generally inconsistent and contradictory editorial and programmatic policies, and although he did do editorial work when necessary, he directed most of his activity for *Zolotoe Runo* toward his surveys and speculative essays.

Although the arguments between the *Vesy* and *Zolotoe Runo* groups primarily involved literary figures, some artists also joined the *Vesy* boycott. One important loss was that of Pavel Kuznetsov, who withdrew because of what he called "the discrepancy between the journal and the literary-artistic goals of today."[59] Despite his theoretical reservations about the magazine's new aims, however, Kuznetsov continued to allow the reproduction of his works in *Zolotoe Runo* throughout 1908 and 1909, and he helped organize and contributed to the "Salon *Zolotoe Runo*" exhibitions. His withdrawal from the magazine was probably due to personal difficulties and to arguments he had with Riabushinsky, since he reestablished his connections with both Riabushinsky and *Zolotoe Runo* when his own work began moving toward the artistic neo-primitivism the magazine soon began to sponsor. Kuznetsov's withdrawal was followed in 1908 by those of Anatoly Arapov and V. Drittenpreis, who announced in *Vesy* that they "no longer consider it possible to be considered among the contributors to the journal *Zolotoe Runo*."[60] In this case, the reason was almost certainly personal conflicts between them and Riabushinsky.

While the rancor surrounding these artists' leaving *Zolotoe Runo* did have a certain effect on the magazine's artistic production (notable especially in the real decline in number and quality of vignettes and headpieces after the beginning of 1908), the change was not as great as that in the magazine's non-artistic sections after mid-1907. The prose section was dominated by the articles and essays of Blok, Chulkov, Ivanov, and Sergei Gorodetsky, and frequently included discussions of problems related to "mystical anarchism." They were direct expressions of the serious examination both of the meaning of the 1905 revolution and its failure, and of the new popularity of symbolism which had produced the symbolist "third generation." All the "older" symbolists considered these two developments as contributing to a "crisis" within Russian life in general, but more specifically, within symbolism itself; *Zolotoe Runo*'s promise to examine and deal with this "crisis of symbolism" was to define its subsequent period of publication.

Zolotoe Runo had made several promises of projected articles in its June 1907 notice,[61] but few found any expression in the magazine, many of them undoubtedly deriving from the editors' bravura intent at inspiring a sense of expectation and confidence among the magazine's readers. It was soon clear that *Zolotoe Runo* would no longer be a mirror of all the currents of Russian modernism, as had been the case previously. Instead, it came to represent the ideas of a select group of individuals who were united in their opposition to *Vesy*, Belyi's theorizing, and Briusov's authoritarianism.

One notable exception was Mikhail Kuzmin (1875-1935). Kuzmin had signed the letter supporting the *Vesy* group's break with *Zolotoe Runo*, and *Zolotoe Runo*'s editors noted in the July-August-September 1907 issue that the works by Kuzmin appearing in that issue had been received before his official withdrawal from the list of contributors. Yet Kuzmin published a number of poems and a story in *Zolotoe Runo* later in 1908, and his important novella *Nezhnyi Iosif (Gentle Joseph)* appeared serially in the magazine throughout 1909. Whether Kuzmin continued participation because of the high fees *Zolotoe Runo* was able to pay,[62] because of a previous commitment, or because of his friendly relations with Blok, his position remains an indication that the Belyi-Briusov "boycott" was not as effective as it first appeared, and that works of writers with disparate esthetic positions could still appear in *Zolotoe Runo*.

One final indirect result of the discord and upheaval taking place within *Zolotoe Runo* during 1907 was the magazine's reduction in size to octo at the beginning of 1908.[63] The smaller format itself was forced on Riabushinsky by his financial situation, which had worsened considerably because of unwise investments and because of the heavy subsidies required by the magazine. The economizing was reflected even in the magazine's use of the same cover design for its final two years: executed by Lanseray and incorporating a drawing by Vrubel, each issue differed externally from the next only in the colors chosen for the covers.

Zolotoe Runo's diminished size and format was an indication of a general reorganization taking place in Russian modernism: while its popularity increased tremendously, symbolism itself broke up into warring factions, each with its own literary mouthpiece. It seems almost contradictory that *Zolotoe Runo* would have to reduce its size at a time when its audience was conceivably increasing. Yet when we consider that the number of first-rate symbolist writers had not increased, but merely the number of pseudo-symbolist writers, Riabushinsky's decision is not surprising. Symbolism had gained enormous support from Russian educated society, and the former "decadents" were now leading figures within Russian literature. From a school, symbolism had grown into a movement. The predicament in which the "first" and "second generation" symbolists found themselves has been aptly described by F. D. Reeve:

> The sense of ethical unity of purpose, of opposition to reactionary politics and to perversely traditional art, that had held the symbolists together despite their wide differences of esthetic theory and practise had been lost once there had come about political liberalization and general acceptance of the principles which the symbolists had reintroduced to literature and which, in the period 1895-1905, had seemed extremely avant-garde...The common agreement among the symbolists to reject the appeal to a majority was subverted by majority acceptance of their principles.[64]

The "vulgarization" of symbolism, which Belyi had feared and against which he was to rail for the next few years, appeared inevitable. Renato Poggioli has pointed out that success is fatal to any *avant-garde* movement, and the frustrations of symbolism's break-up and its search for new esthetic foundations were to provide the setting for the second period of *Zolotoe Runo*'s publication. It was fitting that since *Zolotoe Runo* had come to represent a smaller group of Russian symbolists and modernists, it should adopt a smaller format, symbolism's growth in public popularity notwithstanding.

One question remains unanswered: what was it that brought about *Zolotoe Runo*'s change of program, thereby causing the magazine's complete restructuring? Reeve's general explanation of the symbolists' situation is important as a background cause, as were the personal arguments already discussed. Both these developments undoubtedly helped reaffirm what initially must have been a tentative decision on the part of *Zolotoe Runo*'s editors. Other contributing factors were the results of the 1905 revolution, the discussion of individualism initiated by Benois' essay, and the personal esthetic preferences of Tasteven, among others. With the loss of those writers who disagreed with what appeared a "neo-populist" approach to art and literature, *Zolotoe Runo* was compelled to adopt its new position wholeheartedly and without reservation, having lost hope of reconciliation with the opposing *Vesy* writers. Still, a complete solution to the problem will be found only when the positions, ideas, and theories expressed in the articles published in *Zolotoe Runo* in 1908 and 1909 are considered. The later essays of Blok, Chulkov, Ivanov, Gorodetsky, and Tasteven will help provide answers to why the change of direction was decided upon, and where that change would lead.

Part Three

Polemics, Neo-Primitivism, and Decline:
Zolotoe Runo's Final Two Years of Publication

Pavel Kuznetsov, *Nevesta (La Fiancée), ZR,* No. 1, 1909

V

ALEXANDER BLOK: LITERARY CRITIC AND SOCIOLOGICAL THEORIST FOR *ZOLOTOE RUNO*

> Strange journal! They [*Zolotoe Runo's* editors] have long had the tendency to combine "refinement" with the "intelligentsia and the people."
>
> Alexander Blok, *Pisma k rodnym*, p. 248.

From a historical standpoint, surely the single most important contributor to *Zolotoe Runo's* literary section during 1907 and 1908 was Alexander Blok (1880-1921). Blok's essays and articles dealt with a number of literary, theoretical, esthetic, and sociological subjects, but they have a unity of their own in style and recurring themes. Although some of them were considered expressions of the "mystical anarchist" position associated with *Zolotoe Runo* (discussed in the following chapter), Blok denied any such connection. Indeed, the articles may be seen more justifiably as an independent entity, representative not only of Blok's work for *Zolotoe Runo,* but of his general esthetic philosophy as well, since almost all his important essays written at this time were published in *Zolotoe Runo.*

Blok's articles have often been divided into three categories. The first, and largest, consisted of his critical literary surveys, the main task entrusted him by *Zolotoe Runo's* editors. Along with his earlier reviews of individual works, his articles "O realistakh," "O lirike" ("On Lyric Poetry"), "O drame" ("On Drama"), "Literaturnye itogi 1907 g." ("A Literary Review of 1907"), and "O teatre" ("On Theater") provide a full picture of his opinions on contemporary literature. Second are Blok's "lyrical essays," and although consisting essentially only of "Kraski i slova" and "Bezvremene," their lyrical style strongly influenced his literary surveys.[1] Finally, the third category is comprised of his writings on "the people and the intelligentsia": "Devushka rozovoi kalitki i muravinyi Tsar," "Voprosy, voprosy, voprosy" ("Questions, Questions, Questions"), and "Rossiia i intelligentsiia" ("Russia and the Intelligentsia"). Again, this was a theme present to varying extents in a number of his other essays, developing through all of them to a point of crisis, after which Blok left both *Zolotoe Runo* and Russia. Since there was such intermingling of themes within the articles, they necessitate a discussion both individually and in conjunction with one another.

While Blok's "Kraski i slova" is usually considered his earliest "lyrical essay," he himself reserved the first use of that term for his "Bezvremene," published at the end of 1906.[2] The latter article repeated much already expressed in "Kraski i slova," but was written in a more esoteric, "melodic" style. Blok wrote that "earlier it was felt that life must be free, beautiful, religious, creative. Nature, art, literature were in the foreground."[3] He considered this no longer to be the case, however. A change had taken place and people had lost all contact with nature, man had fallen into a mechanical circle of life: "This circle, drawn beforehand, began to be called the life of a normal man."[4] Men's passions had died and nature had become "alien and incomprehensible."

Blok found the solution to such separation in the simplicity of rural solitude; he advised his readers to leave their houses in order to find their true home, the soul. Blok offered hope to all, writing that even behind all the outer artificial appearance of the "decadents" the beat of a healthy pulse could be heard, a desire to live a beautiful life could be discovered. Blok was optimistic because he believed some disinterested seekers of truth and happiness had appeared who were possessed by the "melancholy of unfulfilled desires," and who were compelled to leave their "spider-like dwellings" to set out on a journey to the "green meadow," to the "endless plain of Russia," to the people. Written in a prose style rivaling Belyi's for incoherence, Blok's lyrical essays expressed his sense of isolation and his desire to reestablish lost connections with nature and "the people." The ideas were important ones to him, and they found a more direct expression in his later analysis of the relationship between the intelligentsia and the people, his principal intellectual concern toward the end of 1908.

An uncertain intermediate period followed Blok's publication of these two "lyrical" essays, but while visiting Moscow in April 1907, he accepted regular work as *Zolotoe Runo*'s literary critic. Blok's first survey article, "O realistakh," was a bombshell: modernist writers had always considered it *de rigueur* to despise this "gray" realist literature, and to defend Gorky from Merezhkovsky's criticisms was quite scandalous. His second survey, "O lirike,"[5] seemed much less the work of a *provocateur*, and discussed "lirika" as a theoretical problem of art, a question which especially interested and troubled Blok at that time. Blok conceived "lirika" as being more than simply a poetic genre, and although he never precisely defined its meaning, in essence he undoubtedly considered it an esthetic world-view. He used the survey as a means for approaching the real meaning of "lirika" and began by discussing the complete autonomy of lyric creative work. Calling Vrubel's fallen angel (Lermontov's "demon") the first lyric poet, Blok wrote that while lyric poets give nothing to people "except for the distant song, except for the stupefying drink," they also "are unable to give and need not give anything if they maintain the purity of their element."[6] Blok wrote that the lyric poet was especially independent in his singular raptures and despairs, that he was poetically free:

> "Lirika" is "I," a macrocosm, and the whole world of the lyric poet lies in his manner of perception. This is a vicious circle, magical. The lyric poet is buried alive in a rich grave, where everything necessary—food, drink, and weapons—accompanies him.[7]

Reaffirming the individualist ideal, Blok defended and separated himself from what he considered the narrow arguments and criticisms growing up within Russian symbolism, and wrote that a true poet was free from any "tendencies," that it was pointless to classify poets into poetic "schools" or "trends."[8] To Blok, the true lyric poet was profoundly individualistic by his very nature, and independent of any adjectival qualifications, either self-applied or given by others. Blok's comments make it clear that he hoped to maintain a nonaligned position outside the ever more vicious wrangling within Russian symbolism. To a certain extent his attempt was successful, since he was the only major symbolist writer during this period who published in all three of the feuding major Russian modernist periodicals.

Blok's desire for independence encouraged him to criticize his colleagues, and he concluded the theoretical section of "O lirike" with a discussion of contemporary poets and their attempts at criticism:

> A poet may be a good critic (like Valery Briusov) or a bad one (like Andrei Belyi, who reviles Sergei Gorodetsky and [yet] praises Sergei Soloviev to the skies). A poet is absolutely free in his work and no one has the right to demand of him that green meadows should please him more than houses of prostitution.[9]

Despite his profession of devotion to poetic autonomy, Blok concurrently was pondering seriously the problem of the poet's relation to his native land and people, and would conclude within a year that without such connections poets would be doomed. The inconsistencies of Blok's thought at this time are readily seen by comparing his positions in "O realistakh" with those of "O lirike."

The major section of "O lirike" followed Blok's theoretical discussion, and was devoted to an examination of recent poetic works. Blok praised Balmont's "spring-like poetry" but admitted that he was somewhat disappointed with Balmont's recent *Zhar-ptitsa (The Fire-Bird)*. He described Bunin as occupying a major position among contemporary Russian poets, and was enthusiastic about Sergei Gorodetsky's recent books of verse.[10] Sergei Soloviev's *Tsvety i ladan (Flowers and Incense)* was dismissed as "frightful banality" however, and Blok gave a number of examples of Soloviev's poetry, each in Blok's opinion worse than the one preceding it. He then moved on to discuss a number of minor poets and their works, but in the end gave no real general evaluation of contemporary Russian lyric poetry.

Blok's approach in "O lirike" was typical of most of his survey articles: beginning with a theoretical section, it then dealt with specific works and writers by means of a long and rigorous criticism. In none of the surveys do polemical arguments supercede the intended purpose (as was the case with Belyi's articles), rather they remain peripheral to the main concern.

While poetry was naturally one of Blok's major interests throughout this period, 1906 and 1907 also witnessed his emergence as a major theatrical figure. In fact, much of Blok's fame at this time derived from his turning to the theater, where, he felt, art and life met. His "Balaganchik" ("The Puppet Show"), for example, performed under Meyerhold's direction at the Komissarzhevskaia Theater, has been recognized as one of the most important works of twentieth-century Russian drama, and the resultant noisy uproar over the play made Blok's name widely known in Russian dramatic circles. Blok's interest in the theater was reflected specifically in two of his articles for *Zolotoe Runo,* "O drame" and "O teatre."

"O drame"[11] began by bemoaning the present condition of Russian drama: Blok wrote that, unfortunately, contemporary Russian dramatists were not leaders in modern theatrical techniques, that they had been paralyzed by lyricism. Yet he went on to praise a number of contemporary Russian dramatists and their works. He discussed plays by Dymov, Scholom Asch, Sergei Rafalovich, and Chulkov, and in rather more detail, Kuzmin. Blok called Kuzmin a writer who was at present "singularly original for his type," a writer with no predecessors and no successors, and was especially pleased with his "playful prose and airy verses."[12] Of particular interest, of course, was Blok's evaluation of the *Znanie* dramatists. Although he was generally negative toward naturalist trends in contemporary drama, Blok gave a great deal of praise to Gorky's "Na dne" ("The Lower Depths"). But on the whole, Blok was critical of Gorky's dramas, contending that while Gorky was capable of writing effective scenes with lively dialogue, he was not really a dramatist.[13] With the exception of Andreev [Blok called his "Zhizn cheloveka" ("The Life of a Man") his very best work], the other *Znanie* dramatists received much stronger criticism than had Gorky, Blok's major observation being that they were unable to make their plays work without a hero.

"O teatre"[14] was considerably more theoretical and was based on a lecture he had given in the Petersburg Theatrical Club in March 1908, his first in public. It dealt essentially with modern theater and included a considerable amount of specific criticism. Describing theater as the "flesh of art," Blok discussed the relationship between the actor, the director, and the dramatist during the nineteenth century, and the ways in which that relationship had changed in the present day. Characterizing the modern period as one of transition in theater, the article's conclusion looked toward possible future developments, and expressed hope for a new "narodnyi" theater, although what Blok meant precisely by this term remained unclear.

A strong indication of the direction in which Blok's "populism" was to take him was seen in his "Literaturnye itogi 1907 g.," published at the end of that year.[15] Blok wrote to his mother in November that he had been studying contemporary literature a great deal, and that he had made some conclusions: that translated literature predominated over original work in Russia (a charge *Zolotoe Runo* had made against *Vesy,* it should be remembered), and that criticism and commentary prevailed over creative work.[16] Blok supported these observations in "Literaturnye itogi" with numerous examples, and added further conclusions. He noted that the formerly dominant Russian thick journals had been superceded by the *almanakh* and *sbornik* collections so prevalent in his day. Somewhat related to this, Blok wrote, was the enormous growth in the number of lyric poets appearing in Russia, poets with no particular talent who inevitably "vulgarized" symbolism (an idea that was, of course, a major theme in Belyi's writings).

Certainly the most interesting point in the article, however, was Blok's indignant, angry outburst against what he saw as the intelligentsia's isolation from the people. Writing that they had a "world-misunderstanding," Blok demanded from the "writer-esthetes" that their lives be continual martyrdoms, and from the lyric poets that they recognize their responsibility to the worker and the *muzhik*—a requirement almost entirely contradictory to his definition of the true lyric poet in "O lirike" as being profoundly individualistic and independent from any social responsibility or role. Blok wrote with special distaste in this regard about the Merezhkovsky-Filosofov-Gippius Religious-Philosophical Society. He warned that the Society was typical of such Russian sectarianism and psychological extremism as that of the Old Believers, and that the idea prevalent among some members of the intelligentsia that the common man would come to talk to them about God was ridiculous; in fact, Blok felt, this common man would probably only laugh at them. Calling the Society's discussions a *"café-chantant* of words,"[17] Blok wrote that the intelligentsia and the people would only be united in a union of "holy love and steel knives," inevitably destructive to such religious-philosophical societies. He concluded the article with a retrospective discussion of developments in Russian literature during 1907, mentioning the numerous almanacs that had appeared over the course of the year, and the newest works of Lidia Zinovieva-Annibal (posthumous, since Zinovieva-Annibal had died in 1906), Remizov, Sologub, and Artsybashev (whose novel *Sanin* Blok called "this writer's most remarkable work"[18]).

A major source of Blok's new interest in the relationship between the artist, nature, and the people was his recently-begun correspondence with Nikolai Kliuev (1855-1937), a poet from the region north of Petersburg whose principal theme was a mystical faith in the Russian peasantry. For Blok, Kliuev became a special symbol of the desires and destructive potential of the Russian people. Their correspondence gave Blok added assurance in corroborating his views by a source close to the people,[19] and throughout 1908, Blok would increasingly value Kliuev's poetry and ideas.

Blok's essay "Tri voprosa" ("Three Questions")[20] continued this intellectual-populist theme, but on a considerably more theoretical plane, entirely excluding any bibliographic criticism. To a certain extent, "Tri voprosa" was intended as an answer to Filosofov's "Tozhe tendentsiia" ("Also Tendentiousness"), which had appeared in *Zolotoe Runo* in January 1908. Filosofov had accused Blok of deliberately escaping from life by means of, and into, art. He asked if the title "man" were not more important than the title "poet" since it appeared to Filosofov that Blok did not believe this to be the case. "Tri voprosa" was Blok's attempt to explain his position on this question, particularly since it was no longer the same as it had been in "O lirike," to which Filosofov's questioning referred.

Blok's article was organized around a division of the history of the "new art" into three periods. In the first, Blok wrote, the question "how" was asked about the forms of art, and it became a "fighting word" in the face of the opposition of the rest of society. Blok gave Briusov as an example of the enormous achievements of those who had asked "how." With the success of the new art, Blok continued, a number of talentless imitators arose, and during this second period the question "what" predominated. Blok felt this question was considerably more significant than the "how" which had been determinant for the older generation of symbolists, because it dealt with the artist's spiritual content. The issue of content had been raised by imitators who lacked the talent to handle symbolist forms adequately, and had to be answered by those who were the true artists. Blok rejected the contemporary relevance of both these approaches, however, and envisioned a new and more important problem as yet considered by no other Russian symbolist. In the third period, the "most dangerous, most Russian" question arose—"why."[21]

Blok's "why" related to the need for, and use of artistic works, and the artist's duty to society. With his third question, Blok began to examine skeptically the theory of art for art's sake. He wrote that the true artist need not fear the publicistic question "why" because he knew he could deal with the question successfully. Blok chose Ibsen as the ideal example of such an artist's success. Ibsen was "the banner of our epoch, the last writer of world significance, necessary for the people, and now especially—for the Russian people."[22] To Blok, Ibsen's works were closely related to this question "why": Ibsen received his powers from the people, and "did not for one minute break his connections with society";[23] moreover, behind the principal character of Ibsen's play "Catiline" could be seen a "conspirator with a socialist soul."[24]

The question of utility brought up by Ibsen's plays was an important one for Russian artists, Blok wrote, but was "a question asked not by us, but by Russian society."[25] To Blok, the issue of the artist's responsibility and duty gained increasing importance: "To the eternal concern of the artist with form and content there is added a new concern *about duty,* about what is required and not required in art."[26] Blok asserted that this question was a touchstone for art, that an artist who is too abstract-minded to grasp it might find himself smashed against it. Beyond this problem of duty Blok saw another "how": how the apparently useless and the obviously useful could be meaningfully combined. He found an answer in folk art and folk song, which combined the two: "Thus the connecting link between art and work, between beauty and usefulness, was rhythm."[27] Again, Ibsen's plays provided a model, an indication that the "rhythm" for Blok's time was duty, an acceptance of the responsibility of defining the meaning of all social activity. Blok warned that it was a treacherous but direct route between the "Scylla" of the beautiful and the "Charybdis" of the obligatory, that a miracle was necessary to put together the "soul of the beautiful butterfly and the body of the useful camel," to show the world "a new kind of free necessity [and] the consciousness of the beautiful duty, in order to make the world flesh, the artist a man."[28]

Blok's "Tri voprosa" was a significant step beyond what he had written earlier on the relationship between the artist and society. Its call for the artist to recognize and to carry out his duty to society was not unlike the demands made of artists and writers by the Russian populists of the 1860's and 1870's—or at least that was how it appeared to most of the symbolists not associated with *Zolotoe Runo.* Blok's expressive style was essentially symbolist, mixed with some Nietzschean terminology, which must have made the ideas themselves appear all the more strange to whoever read them, a symbolist such as Belyi or a realist such as Gorky. In the end, "Tri voprosa" gave no specific suggestions as to what the artist should do once he had recognized this "duty," and although Blok felt competent to point art in the right direction, he was unable to describe clearly, or move in that direction himself. "Tri voprosa" recognized and brought to the surface an important problem within Russian symbolism, but the article's unsatisfactory conclusion proved Blok ineffectual as a "spiritual leader," much as his carrying a red banner on a single occasion during the 1905 revolution had proved him ineffectual as a revolutionary.

Blok wrote two more essays for *Zolotoe Runo* before moving on to the question that would be his primary concern during his final months of work for the magazine. The first was a rather indifferent survey of poetry, dealing with the latest work of Minsky, Sologub, Kuzmin, Bunin, and Sergei Soloviev.[29] The second essay, "Solntse nad Rossiei" ("A Sun over Russia"),[30] was written for Tolstoy's eightieth birthday. In it, Blok called the novelist the "great and singular genius of contemporary Europe, the greatest pride of Russia," and discussed him in the context of the reaction prevailing in Russia.

After this short interlude, Blok's publicistic activities reached their peak: at the end of 1908 and beginning of 1909, he delivered a number of public lectures and published several articles dealing directly with the question of "the intelligentsia and the people," a theme present to one extent or another in all his *Zolotoe Runo* articles. Blok again raised the question of the "abyss" lying between the intelligentsia and the people, and attempted to find some point of agreement between "150 million on one side, and a few hundred thousand on the other, people who mutually do not understand one another on the whole."[31] In his February 1907 "Devushka rozovoi kalitki i muravinyi Tsar,"[32] Blok expressed a lyrical admiration for the Russian people and a gloomy uncertainty about the future of the Russian intelligentsia. Blok discussed Russia's lack of the beautiful legends and romantic medieval history which were important traditions in Germany, and asserted that consequently the real power and beauty of Russian history lay in popular life and superstitions. Blok felt the Russian peasant had always been "down to earth" and concerned with the fundamentals of life and death. As had Viacheslav Ivanov, Blok insisted that it was wrong to reject popular traditions and beliefs as being mere superstitions, since in fact they were the true strength of the Russian people. Blok doubted that the intelligentsia could accept and understand that strength. He believed they were incapable of overcoming the academic conceit of considering the people "primitives," of examining them through the eyes of "ethnographers," and were unable to see them as "real people, with human astonishment in their eyes."

Considering the isolation of the intelligentsia a serious problem, Blok decided he had to support those who had more contact with popular life, who were directly interested in the people, in the revolution, in the future of Russia, than were his symbolist friends in Petersburg and Moscow. It was for this reason that he was so positive toward Gorky, whose seriousness and sincerity seemed so unlike the love of esoterics Blok saw among the poets, critics, and philosophers of Russian intellectual society. On one occasion, in fact, Blok wrote that of all the people present at one of the gatherings at Ivanov's "tower," he had liked Gorky the best,[33] and in "O realistakh," he described Gorky as the embodiment of "Rus . . . this great, boundless, expansive, sad, promised land."[34] Blok considered Gorky, alone among contemporary Russian writers, capable of understanding the people, and able to act as an intermediary between them and the intelligentsia. Blok warned the intelligentsia that instead of ridiculing the lack of literary grace of such realist writers as "Skitalets" and Serafimovich (Blok had remarked in "O realistakh" that the masses needed such writers to speak to them of their problems in their own language[35]), they should listen to what the realists had to say; otherwise, isolated within the confines of "cultured society," the intelligentsia would remain unaware of the forces transforming Russia, which might very possibly sweep them away.

Blok developed his position further in his "Literaturnye itogi 1907 g." He described the weakness of Russian literature as arising from the intelligentsia's isolation from "real life." He contrasted the Petersburg intelligentsia, broken into "fifty" bickering groups unable to find a satisfying way of looking at the world, with the people, who had for centuries held to the same unchanging and fundamental concept of God.[36] One day, Blok predicted, a great writer from the people would extinguish the memory of all the modernists and their experiments. Blok's play "Pesnia sudby" ("Song of Fate"), written at much the same time as "Literaturnye itogi," expressed a similar doubt that the intelligentsia could survive in the coming new world. Both the article and the play were indications of the sense of apocalypticism recurrent throughout Russian symbolism, but especially noticeable in the years of reaction following 1905.[37]

Blok found some hope for change within the intelligentsia at the end of 1908 with the renewal of the previously ineffectual religious-philosophical meetings in Petersburg. The Society's radical reform and turn toward a discussion of the role of the intelligentsia in Russian life resulted in Blok's favorable reception of the reorganized group in his "Voprosy, voprosy, voprosy."[38] Despite his previously negative attitude toward the Society, Blok believed that it was there that the best members of the Russian intelligentsia were now to be found and perhaps influenced.[39] Fired with this hope, on November 12, 1908 Blok read his "Rossiia i intelligentsiia"[40] at a private gathering in the Merezhkovsky apartment, and the next day repeated it at a meeting of the Religious-Philosophical Society itself.

Blok began the lecture somewhat peripherally by defending Gorky from criticism made at an earlier meeting of the Society, but soon moved on to his central point; noting a series of forebodings, Blok asked if the intelligentsia deserved, or indeed wanted to survive. It seemed possible that the intellectuals, with their "individualism, demonism, esthetics, and despair," were infected with the will to die, in contrast to the people's will to live. Blok said that what love for the people there was among the intelligentsia was a love born of abstract idealism and curiosity that lacked any true understanding of its object; moreover, the people recognized this and were hostile and contemptuous in return. Blok warned that the people had reached the limit of endurance of the starvation and brutality brought about by the post-1905 reaction, and were on the verge of a mighty upheaval, which, when unleashed, would obliterate the intelligentsia. Blok could discern a "thin line" of contact alone between the two groups: only a minority of the intelligentsia's writers, social workers, officials, and revolutionaries were facing this actuality by meeting with a minority of workers, sectarians, tramps, and peasants in an attempt to establish a basis for mutual understanding. Blok believed that a focus of emotional attachment was needed to tie the two groups together. Certain great Russian intellectuals (Blok gave Gogol, Dostoevsky, Tolstoy, Mendeleev, and Gorky as examples) had been close to the people and estranged from the intelligentsia because they shared this necessary common ground—a love of Russia. Blok concluded with a question that was also an implicit warning: "Are these words comprehensible to the intelligentsia?"[41]

Not surprisingly, Blok's speech was followed by lively discussion, and when he repeated the lecture a month later, in his own words, "the old men from *Russkoe Bogatstvo* fed me sweets, applauded, and treated me as a favorite grandson."[42] Blok had expected considerable opposition to the speech, but even Merezhkovsky was enthusiastic, and promised Blok he would publish it as an article in the first issue of *Russkaia Mysl* for 1909. Not everyone was so favorable, however, and despite Merezhkovsky's promise, Peter Struve refused to publish the article in his journal, pointing to Blok's unscientific approach, and his failure to consider sociological and political facts and theories (it was for this reason that Blok published the article in the more sympathetic *Zolotoe Runo*). Other opposition to Blok's position soon appeared as well: Chulkov wrote (also in *Zolotoe Runo*) that Blok's description of the intelligentsia as being isolated in its literary coteries from the people and national life was accurate as a description of the "decadent" wing of Russian writers, but not of the intelligentsia as a whole.[43] Even Merezhkovsky, despite his praise for Blok's speech, had continually maintained that there was no gulf between the intelligentsia and the people.[44]

The finale to the minor uproar following the speech was Blok's public rejoinder to his critics, a second paper delivered at the Religious-Philosophical Society on December 30, 1908, "Stikhiia i kultura" ["Elements and Culture," published by chance not in *Zolotoe Runo* but in *Nasha Gazeta (Our Newspaper)*]. Using a discussion of a recent Italian earthquake as a point of departure, Blok's talk was a lyrical expression of his fears of impending disaster, and a corroboration of a statement in his diary that in this article he could only announce his theme, not examine it systematically or sociologically. The discussion begun with the March 1909 publication of *Vekhi (Signposts),* whose principal concern was also· the relation between the intelligentsia and the people,[45] drew attention away from Blok's views. For those interested in the question, Blok's ideas seemed much too esoteric, non-symbolist ideas expressed in lyrical and frequently obscure language. As a result, Blok himself discontinued work on this theme.

In the winter of 1909, Blok wrote two critical articles for *Rech* on the work of Merezhkovsky and Balmont, but contributed nothing more to *Zolotoe Runo* after his January 1909 "Rossiia i intelligentsiia." At the end of 1908 and in early 1909 a clear despondency and pessimism could be noted in Blok's poetry and correspondence; he felt lonely, dissatisfied, and prematurely old. On April 14, 1909, he and his wife left for Italy, to escape his friends, "art," and Russian political repression.

As one of his biographers has written, all he desired was "swimming in the sea, basking in the sun, plunging into Italian art."[46] More importantly, in Mochulsky's words, "the 'political' and 'social' period of the poet's life was finished. He was going to Italy to forget the past and to become a 'person.'"[47] Blok's journey to Italy was an event significant in his intellectual and personal life,[48] but in his journalistic life as well, because it marked the end of his work for *Zolotoe Runo.* His decision to stop actively collaborating on the magazine for which he had written some of his most interesting and thoughtful works must have been a major blow to *Zolotoe Runo,* its editors, and its circulation.

Summarizing Blok's work for *Zolotoe Runo* is not an easy task, and although more than a few scholars have attempted evaluations of his prose, all they have agreed on is its essential vagueness. Yet some kind of summary must be attempted, since Blok's essays constitute a major aspect of his creative work, and because Blok's articles were certainly the most remarkable series of works which appeared in *Zolotoe Runo*'s literary section. Much of what Blok wrote was incomprehensible because of its impressionistic style and because of the use of notoriously imprecise language, and many of his symbolist contemporaries felt he was over-reaching himself in even attempting to write critical and speculative essays. Blok was incapable of reducing complex questions to simpler terms, and could not develop a plan of action for the change he felt so necessary for Russian art and literature. Blok recognized this weakness in his essays, however, and directed their thrust elsewhere. V. A. Desnitsky's evaluation of Blok's critical essays is true of all his articles:

[Their] aim . . . is to stir the reader sympathetically, to inform him of the same mood which the author himself experienced in reading the evaluated books of poetry or stories.[49]

That Blok maintained a highly personal relationship between himself and the works he reviewed for *Zolotoe Runo* was clear from a letter he wrote Belyi in 1907:

As a man with the desire for health and simplicity, I write, or try to write. For example, "O lirike": I believe in the justice of the point of departure. I know that in "lirika" there is a danger of decay and I attack it. I beat *myself*, such in essence is the idea of my articles, independent of literary evaluations, with which it is possible to disagree as one pleases (even I myself admit the incorrectness of some of them). Beating myself for lyrical poisons, which also threaten me with decay, I try to warn others as well.[50]

This is Blok's fundamental statement on his work for *Zolotoe Runo*: all the essays represented aspects of Blok's personal reflections on the "diseases" he saw infecting both Russian symbolism and the Russian intelligentsia. It is for this reason that Blok's articles may be considered as a group alone, separate from the "mystical anarchism" espoused by Chulkov, Ivanov, and Gorodetsky. During these years Blok remained a profound individualist, never moving with or against symbolism as a school, or any subgroup within it, and (as we shall see in the next chapter) continually defending himself from any attempts to place him among one or another of the squabbling sects whose narrowmindedness he despised. Later, Blok restored his strained relations with the "esthetic" symbolists, in March 1910 defended symbolism in a speech in memory of Komissarzhevskaia,[51] and in the following summer even reached a firm reconciliation with Andrei Belyi. By that time, of course, *Zolotoe Runo* had ceased publication, as had *Vesy*, and symbolism appeared to be dying out. Yet Blok's two years of work for *Zolotoe Runo* remains an essential component in understanding his psychological and esthetic development, and the ideas he expressed in the magazine were to find reflection a decade later in the poetry and lectures he delivered during a greater, more far-reaching revolution.[52]

Without Blok's participation, it is unlikely *Zolotoe Runo* would have been able to continue publishing its literary section after the argument with the *Vesy* group. Despite his claim of independence, the opinions Blok expressed in his essays became intimately associated with *Zolotoe Runo* and the magazine played a primary role, even if from self-interest, in promoting Blok's critical activity, and in providing space for ideas which otherwise might have been unable to find a place in print. This service was mutually rewarding for Blok and for *Zolotoe Runo,* and it formed the basis for the relationship between the two.

VI

MYSTICAL ANARCHISM, REALISTIC SYMBOLISM, AND FURTHER PROBLEMS WITH *VESY*

Mystical anarchism...a very piquant, new, literary dish, a spicy sauce...with naive diligence, [Chulkov] cooks up mysticism and decadence, Vladimir Soloviev's cult of Sophia and Viacheslav Ivanov's orgiasm, and sprinkles it with the sugar of socialism, thinking it is anarchist salt.

>   Zinaida Gippius, "Vse protiv vsekh," *Literaturnyi dnevnik,* pp. 322-3.

>   Uvy! Bednye chitateli "Vesov"!
>   *Zolotoe Runo,* 1909, No. 2-3, 120.

It has been mentioned a number of times that one characteristic feature of *Zolotoe Runo* was its inconsistent editorial policy, a practice permitting the publication of conflicting opinions that seemed to deny the magazine any cohesive esthetic *Weltanschauung.* It should be repeated that this was a deliberate approach on the part of the editors and publisher during the first two years of the magazine's publication and that a substantial, but not complete, change in this policy was taken with the magazine's promise to examine realistic tendencies within Russian modernism. After the subsequent withdrawal of several significant symbolist contributors, *Zolotoe Runo* did adopt a more precise editorial and esthetic policy and did define its "face" somewhat more specifically, with Blok's sociological speculations and literary evaluations exemplifying the alteration. While representative of *Zolotoe Runo*'s new editorial position, however, Blok's articles were only secondarily related in the public's mind with what was widely considered to be the magazine's new "official" ideology—"mystical anarchism." It came to be associated with *Zolotoe Runo* when Georgy Chulkov decided to agree to become the magazine's literary editor. This personally devised esthetic and social program, described by Chulkov as the "path" of "mystical anarchism," was expounded and interpreted by Viacheslav Ivanov, Sergei Gorodetsky, and Genrikh Tasteven, whose articles, discussing and defending ideas introduced by Chulkov, appeared more and more frequently on the pages of *Zolotoe Runo.*

Opinions on the ramifications and meaning of mystical anarchism were varied and not uncommonly contradictory, but since they appeared so often on the pages of *Zolotoe Runo,* the magazine gained the reputation of being the "mouthpiece" of mystical anarchism. Much of this reputation was manufactured by *Zolotoe Runo*'s opponents, however, a further development of the 1907 break between *Vesy* and *Zolotoe Runo.* Neither Ivanov nor Gorodetsky (nor even Chulkov at times) admitted to being a mystical anarchist, but the philosophy was singled out by Belyi (*Vesy*'s official "ideologist") as the greatest contemporary threat to Russian symbolism. The resultant "symbolist debate"[1] became the most important and traumatic conflict within Russian modernism from 1907 until 1910. While it is by no means surprising that *Zolotoe Runo* would disagree with the positions of *Vesy*'s theoreticians, it was almost accidental that the argument was over mystical anarchism, an ambiguous, poorly-defined "path" *Zolotoe Runo* acquired with Georgy Chulkov.

Up until the beginning of 1908, Chulkov had contributed only two short poems to *Zolotoe Runo.*[2] He had been published elsewhere, however, and his ideas and works had been discussed in the magazine in some detail. Upon his return to European Russia from exile (for revolutionary activity), he became an active participant in a number of modernist and symbolist journals,[3] and published three issues of his own miscellany, *Fakely (Torches),* between 1906 and 1908. *Fakely*'s goal was not to print works of a single literary or artistic school, but to combine the works of adherents of various schools, in individual volumes, united on a single intellectual theme (an idea later partially adopted by *Zolotoe Runo*).[4] As a consequence, each issue included works of diverse literary and philosophical views: April 1906 included Blok's "Balaganchik" in its entirety, and other major contributions by Gorky and Andreev. Later issues included works by Viacheslav Ivanov, Blok, Sologub, Remizov, Zinovieva-Annibal (Briusov and Belyi had appeared in the first *Fakely*), as well as Andreev, Sergeev-Tsensky, Zaitsev, Bunin, and Shestov, and Chulkov continued requesting contributions from Gorky, Kropotkin, and Lev Tolstoy.

One significant feature of the *Fakely* miscellanies was their programmatic introduction of the basic tenets of what would soon thereafter become known as the theory of mystical anarchism. Because of his earlier political activity, Chulkov felt the 1905 revolution's failure acutely, and the direction this disillusionment was to take was indicated first, and best, in his notice to *Fakely*'s inaugural issue in 1906:

We think the meaning of the historical process is in the search for ultimate human freedom. We hail the socialist movement attempting to destroy the old economic order, but socialism is not for us the only goal and final form of society. Free thought and free creation by poets and artists, sages and prophets—this is the light on the path of humanity. We struggle for the emancipation of the individual personality from the flailing of moral, philosophical, and religious dogmatism and do not reconcile ourselves to a superficial world outlook which attempts to limit the sphere of spiritual experience. We raise our torch in the name of the assertion of individuality and in the name of the free union of people, founded on love for the future transformed world. In this sense we are anarchists....[5]

Chulkov had first used the term mystical anarchism in an article published in mid-1905,[6] and a later essay by his close associate Viacheslav Ivanov programmatically explored some of the ramifications of the theory.[7] The *Fakely* editorial was a development of these earlier formulations. All of them discussed the need to overcome "narrow individualism" and to turn toward a "sobornost," the need to find a new mystical experience in the midst of "miserable decadence," and of symbolism seen to have been decayed by bourgeois popularity.

The most concise expression of these ideas appeared in Chulkov's small 1906 book *O misticheskom anarkhizme (On Mystical Anarchism)*. It called for the assertion of individual personality in community, and for "mystical anarchists" to seek out a solution to the socio-political problems of the day, to surmount the difference between "freedom and necessity" through the irrational assertion of individuality, expressed not in "secluded individualism," but in a more perfect individualism seeking expression in society. One's individual personality could be unbound only within a society "based on a free anarchical union in love."[8] Finally, Chulkov posited mystical anarchism as an irreconcilable and rebellious attitude toward any authority, founded on a belief that the individual must destroy any regime restricting the activity of the human spirit.

Zolotoe Runo's initial reception of Chulkov's ideas was not the favorable one it would become in 1908 and 1909. Belyi's short notice on *O misticheskom anarkhizme* was anything but enthusiastic: "Mystical anarchism, as an independent principle in relation to life, has a place neither in religion nor in art."[9] Filosofov's longer and more analytical evaluation in the magazine's next issue[10] made it clear that *Zolotoe Runo* did not anticipate adopting the mystical anarchist philosophy, and was still even undecided on an editorial position on the question, the editors making no effort to disavow Filosofov's critical opinions. Filosofov described Chulkov's essays as being purely "psychological documents" with little value in themselves, and he criticized Chulkov's "disorganized, many-sided, and unrestrained" work, while nevertheless admitting that the book was an important indication of the real doubts and searching "which have taken possession of the modern soul."[11] Filosofov rejected Chulkov's political ideas and his program of social action,[12] and concluded that the reconciliation of the individual personality and society was only possible on a religious basis. Since the mystical anarchists were decadents, Filosofov wrote, they did not want to build on this foundation, and were therefore fated to failure.

Little else was written in *Zolotoe Runo* about either Chulkov or his esthetic and philosophical theories after Filosofov's broad examination, and it was only after the *Vesy* writers' exodus and the magazine's change of direction that Chulkov and mystical anarchism once again appeared on the pages of *Zolotoe Runo*. Much of the reason for Chulkov's acceptance of the magazine's literary editorship was his renewed friendship with Tasteven (the two had been close childhood friends) at the time of the break between *Zolotoe Runo* and the *Vesy* writers. Chulkov was especially interested in *Zolotoe Runo* because the literary editorship offer was made at a time when, in Chulkov's eyes, "the overcoming of individualism became a real solution"[13] to the problems plaguing Russian symbolism, and Tasteven and *Zolotoe Runo* were known to be the principal supporters of this "overcoming of individualism."

Chulkov was also attracted to *Zolotoe Runo* because of its openness to publishing views in opposition to those of *Vesy,* and its adopting of a tolerant editorial policy not unlike the one he had attempted with *Fakely.* While in practice this policy was often more accidental than deliberate, it did permit a new modernist examination of realist literature that was unthinkable in *Vesy,* and which appealed especially to Chulkov. While Blok's surveys were most prominent, other significant essays on contemporary realist writers had also appeared in *Zolotoe Runo.*[14] "Realistic symbolism," the product of such interests, became a basic feature of Chulkov's mystical anarchist philosophy: "In idealistic symbolism we have a world of ideal things, wishes, and possibilities, but abstract with regard to true existence; in realistic symbolism we have the symbolics of actual life."[15] As he wrote in *Zolotoe Runo,* for Chulkov, realistic symbolism was a way to recreate the individual and to change the world:

> In order to know the world not of imaginary, but of real values, we must recreate ourselves ... the evolution of symbolism from decadence to realistic symbolism is the direct path to the creation of the final value—Man.[16]

Chulkov had developed many of his ideas in conjunction with Viacheslav Ivanov, who had written the introduction to *O misticheskom anarkhizme.* Ivanov was a major contributor to *Zolotoe Runo* throughout its period of publication, but it should be noted that he had no close professional connections with the magazine's editorial board or affairs. In a series of long, philosophical, and generally obscure essays in *Zolotoe Runo*, Ivanov discussed the "modern crisis of individualism," realistic symbolism, and the problems of the symbolist poet's relationship with the masses.[17] The essays [combined with others to form his 1909 book *Po zvezdam (Among the Stars)*] discussed the evolution of the symbolist poet and of a symbolism which could not survive in Russia without a symbolist audience, an audience formed by raising the masses of people to a cultural level allowing them to appreciate symbolism. Eventually, Ivanov believed, every individual could become an artist in his own right: art would then become a broad communal experience instead of a narrow individual effort; the symbol would become a "myth," and art "myth-creation" ("mifotvorchestvo"); and symbolism would become democratized in the purest and best sense of the term.[18] Ivanov felt this was already occurring in the neo-populist poetry of Blok, Belyi (!), and even in Gorky's and Lunacharsky's "God-building." Ivanov's theories were clearly complementary to Chulkov's own positions, and the outspoken public support for Chulkov by Ivanov and by *Zolotoe Runo*'s editors helped initiate a new polemic between *Vesy* and what it called "the mouthpiece of mystical anarchism" over the nature and future of Russian symbolism.

Again, much of the controversy was personally motivated and directed, as had been *Vesy*'s criticisms of *Zolotoe Runo* throughout 1906 and 1907. At the same time, there was a feeling among all those involved, on whichever side, that symbolism was indeed undergoing a crisis that would alter it fundamentally. Both in this chapter and in the two previous ones, we have seen what *Zolotoe Runo*'s and the Chulkov group's position on the evolution of Russian symbolism was: an appreciation for realism and a need to find points of contact between new forms of symbolism and the masses of the Russian people, an attempt to find ways of making art relevant to a larger audience without degrading it, but on the contrary, revivifying it. *Vesy*'s basic criticism was that in going to a middle-class reading public to disseminate mystical anarchist and collective individualist ("sobornye") doctrines, *Zolotoe Runo* and Chulkov and Ivanov had, instead of democratizing symbolism, only vulgarized it. This position originated with Briusov, who believed that symbolism would have to evolve its esthetic canons further before popularizing its doctrines. In a review of *Fakely*, Briusov had dismissed the mystical anarchist program as being self-defeating: "The formula 'I reject the world' throws overboard all the material of artistic creativity—the whole world."[19] In Briusov's eyes, the entire movement would have to be exposed and stopped.

Belyi agreed with Briusov's interpretation, but understood the threat of mystical anarchism somewhat differently. Belyi felt that the new popularity symbolism enjoyed after the failure of the 1905 revolution was not the result of the mass of readers becoming symbolists or even of understanding symbolism, but that the ideological interpretation of symbolism had been twisted by Chulkov and Ivanov in a way to make it appeal to the mass public, the public finding its moods echoed in the slogans of mystical anarchism.[20] Finally, accompanying this new popularity and taking advantage of it was a "third generation" of symbolist writers, generally not as talented or dedicated as earlier symbolists. Belyi resented their early and enormous glory, and considered their growing influence one result of the spread of mystical anarchist theories.

While Gippius and Briusov published their own criticisms of the mystical anarchists in *Vesy* (Briusov called *O misticheskom anarkhizme* a "little anarchist bomblet"[21] and consistently satirized Chulkov's theoretical statements), it was Belyi who made the principal attacks on Chulkov, Ivanov, and Blok, whose essays were so readily published in the already reprehensible *Zolotoe Runo*. In a series of articles written in a highly rhetorical and at times frenzied tone,[22] Belyi criticized these primary contributors to *Zolotoe Runo,* their followers and merchant patrons who understood nothing of art,[23] and, for good measure, the "third generation" of symbolists, whom he described as "brats, tooting their whistles."[24]

It was Chulkov who received most of Belyi's venom. Belyi in no way considered Chulkov a true poet: as long as he occupied an editorial position within modernist periodicals, Belyi accepted him, but when Chulkov decided to organize and lead (from Belyi's point of view) a new artistic movement, Belyi directed a torrent of both critical and personal attacks toward him. He called Chulkov an "agent-provocateur" who would nevertheless fail to sway the dignity of Russian symbolism.[25] He compared Chulkov to a calf that had "sucked the milk of all the cows of Russian literature" and then "cursed the milk which it had poorly digested."[26] Finally, condescendingly, Belyi criticized Chulkov's purely artistic work: "One ought to feel ashamed to write reviews of [such] pitiful compilations of stolen phrases, which Mr. Chulkov calls a drama."[27] During 1908 and 1909, Belyi unleashed a flood of invective against Chulkov, his theories, and his works.[28] It was Andrei Belyi's attacks on Chulkov and mystical anarchism that provided the focus for Russian symbolism's self-reevaluation.

Much of Belyi's writing on the mystical anarchists was aimed at "exposing" various followers of Chulkov's philosophy who, in Belyi's eyes, refused to admit their adherence. It is interesting, and undoubtedly significant, that much of the "symbolist debate" itself consisted of accusations and denials of profession of mystical anarchism rather than of a discussion of the meaning and significance of the philosophy. Belyi and *Vesy* considered many writers "mystical anarchists" simply because they happened to contribute regularly to *Zolotoe Runo*. Blok was one of these. More emotionally than rationally, Belyi blamed mystical anarchism for turning Blok into a "painter of vacuity...whose 'Beautiful Lady' had disintegrated into a prostitute, into an imaginary quantity, something like the square root of minus one."[29] Blok himself was concerned at this time primarily with the problem of the intelligentsia and the people, and for Blok personally the 1907-1909 years were ones of unhappiness, melancholy, and drunkenness.[30] While he was never overly happy working for *Zolotoe Runo*, Blok remained close friends with Chulkov and was influenced by the theories of mystical anarchism, especially in the context of the revolutionary events of the time: his play "Korol na ploshchadi" ("The King in the Square," published first in *Zolotoe Runo* in 1907) shows obvious influences of mystical anarchist ideas, for example. Others disagreed about Blok's debt to mystical anarchism: although Kornei Chukovsky's *Zolotoe Runo* review of "Balaganchik" described the play as the single accomplishment of mystical anarchism,[31] Sergei Gorodetsky, who was close to both Blok and Chulkov, said on the contrary that the ideas of the two men were fundamentally opposed.[32]

In the face of these differences of critical opinion and of Belyi's growing virulent attacks, Blok felt compelled to renounce publicly any adherence to mystical anarchism. In late summer 1907 he wrote an open letter to *Vesy* denying he was a mystical anarchist, but maintained his independence by refusing to sever relations with *Zolotoe Runo*. Blok's continuing participation in *Zolotoe Runo* was an indication that while Belyi and his collaborators on *Vesy* considered *Zolotoe Runo* purely a mystical anarchist magazine, its contributors felt no compunction to accept any official philosophy in order to remain on *Zolotoe Runo*'s staff. Blok wrote to Chulkov, explaining his decision to publicly disavow mystical anarchism,[33] and Chulkov did not consider Blok's announcement a betrayal, since they both accepted the significant differences between their poetic and political views.[34] It did indicate the artificial nature of the categorizing Belyi had employed in his attacks on Chulkov and *Zolotoe Runo*, and points up the extent to which Belyi created a mystical anarchist philosophical movement for his own ends. This categorization of contributors to *Zolotoe Runo* as possessing by definition mystical anarchist sympathies reached a climax in conjunction with a July 1907 *Mercure de France* article describing Blok, Gorodetsky, Viacheslav Ivanov, and Chulkov as the leaders of a group aimed at creating a new mystical anarchist literary school.[35] Blok's letter was written in response to the article, and Chulkov himself heatedly denied in public that mystical anarchism was attempting to be a literary movement.[36] Clearly, mystical anarchism was not the cohesive threat to "pure symbolism" that *Vesy* and Belyi made it out to be. Nevertheless, the *Vesy* attacks had made mystical anarchism appear to be a philosophical and literary movement, and the *Mercure de France* article seemed to confirm the suspicion that some new destructive activity was at work within Russian symbolism. Even Viacheslav Ivanov (undoubtedly Chulkov's strongest supporter and closest collaborator at this time) felt compelled to disavow mystical anarchism in *Zolotoe Runo*'s summer 1907 issue, adding that his relationship to the magazine "continues to remain as before, [one] of simple literary collaborator."[37] Ivanov's statement indicates that most Russian symbolists probably felt that "collaboration" with *Zolotoe Runo* inevitably included acceptance of mystical anarchist principles. Otherwise, Ivanov would have seen no need to distance himself from the magazine's editorial board by so loosely defining his relationship to the magazine. Nonetheless, this mistaken belief was one exploited by *Vesy*. Finally, the whole tenor of this increasingly absurd discussion of who was or who was not to be classified as a mystical anarchist was set in an article by Filosofov in the newspaper *Tovarishch (Comrade)*, in which he wrote that no matter how much Blok, Ivanov, and even Chulkov denied being mystical anarchists, they were anyway and their denials were meaningless.[38]

Throughout all this confusion, Chulkov himself, while surprised at the enormous response to his theoretical works, preferred to publish subdued critical or analytical articles in *Zolotoe Runo*. In general, he felt that the attacks made on him by Belyi "seemed to have no relation whatever to literature"[39] and were purely personal, requiring no journalistic response. Chulkov's analytical essays did include some oblique discussions aimed at *Vesy*, however. In his "Razoblachennaia magiia" ("Exposed Magic") of 1908,[40] for example, Chulkov wrote that *Vesy* had died along with the decadence which had outlived itself and perished, that it recognized its ideological defeat, and was now imprisoned in the bonds of immobile dogmatism.[41]

While Chulkov remained relatively aloof in face of the *Vesy* attacks on his theories and interpretation of the ultimate fate of Russian symbolism, other writers on *Zolotoe Runo*'s staff did not, and published a number of critical evaluations of *Vesy*'s positions and counterattacks on Belyi, in particular. Most prolific was Sergei Gorodetsky (1884-1967),[42] whose venomous tone most closely equalled Belyi's own. He wrote the enraged reply to Gippius' description of mystical anarchism quoted at the beginning of this chapter,[43] and later expanded the attack to Briusov and *Vesy* in general.[44] He did write other more theoretical essays repeating general themes adopted by *Zolotoe Runo*'s official program, but sections of each of them continued his polemic with Belyi and *Vesy*. Gorodetsky's "Idolotvorchestvo" ("Idol-creation")[45] was an exposition on the contrasting values of realistic symbolism and idealistic symbolism, represented, he felt, by *Zolotoe Runo* and *Vesy*, respectively. Perhaps in emulation of the pseudo-scientific (and at times even pseudo-logical) techniques employed by Ivanov and Belyi in some of their theoretical speculative articles,

Gorodetsky even devised a chart summarizing his view of the differences between these two approaches to symbolism.[46] He concluded with a frantic attack on what he described as Belyi's "idolotvorchestvo" in contrast to the "mifotvorchestvo" expounded by Ivanov. On another occasion, he noted a new awakening of the "national idea" in Russian symbolist verse, and described "decadence" as a ten-year prologue to the real history of modern Russian poetry.[47] Gorodetsky was a major contributor to *Zolotoe Runo* during its final two years of publication, and one of the magazine's principal polemicists. His articles repeated and expanded on the themes of realistic symbolism and the national element in art introduced in *Zolotoe Runo*'s 1907 manifesto. Finally, late in 1909 it was Gorodetsky who would write the most scathing attacks on the journal *Apollon,* which he saw as a dangerous and "retrogressive" threat to the development of Russian modernist culture.

Other writers for *Zolotoe Runo* contributed more considered, but no less hostile, criticisms of *Vesy*'s presumption in envisioning itself the defender of "pure" symbolism in Russia. Tasteven, as a close friend and admirer of Chulkov, and as the man who was actually in charge of the production of *Zolotoe Runo*'s literary section, was the most important of these. Tasteven's significance in the entire controversy over mystical anarchism may be seen in his encouraging publication in *Zolotoe Runo* of articles by Chulkov and Ivanov that would never have been accepted by *Vesy,* still the only other major purely symbolist periodical in Russia.[48] Tasteven wrote two criticisms of *Vesy*'s "pure symbolism" in 1908, calling it "castrated symbolism" and a "recipe for the production of symbols" that was capable of producing only such "dry stylizations" as Briusov's *Ognennyi angel.*[49] As he had done during *Zolotoe Runo*'s earlier polemics with *Vesy,* Tasteven threw some of *Vesy*'s criticisms back in its face, describing Belyi, for example, as being incapable of explaining his own theoretical position, balancing somewhere between individualism and "sobornost," all the while maintaining a pose of almost scriptural sanctity. He satirized Belyi's nebulous statements, accepted as truth by his fellow collaborators on *Vesy*'s staff.[50] He was never quite as awed by the specter of Briusov, lurking behind Belyi's judgments, as were some of the other contributors to *Zolotoe Runo* (even Chulkov attempted to avoid personally antagonizing Briusov), and in his second article of 1908 dismissed Briusov's attempts in *Vesy* (under the pseudonym V. Bykov) to find Chulkov's and Tasteven's ideas in contradiction as being nothing more than amusing.[51]

Tasteven continued his campaign against *Vesy* in a number of 1909 articles enthusiastically reviewing new books by Chulkov and Ivanov. The first essay, dealing with Ivanov's *Po zvezdam,* discussed the transition of individualist art to its antithesis, the "vsenarodnoe iskusstvo" described in

Ivanov's book.[52] Tasteven summarized what he considered the significance and value of Ivanov's book: that modern decadence had disintegrated into the worship of subjective idealism, the idealistic principle that
would logically lead to nihilism, expressed in the social sphere in the
complete dissolution of the collective religious consciousness.[53] Tasteven
was writing little that was new here, and to a great extent stubbornly
repeating and refuting arguments *Vesy* had made against Ivanov, but his
firm positive stance on the book was in direct contrast to the reception
Ivanov's works received from *Vesy*.

Similar were Tasteven's two articles on Chulkov appearing in *Zolotoe
Runo*'s final issue of 1909.[54] He praised Chulkov's originality and wrote
that his "synthetic" style was restoring true style, sorely missing in modern
Russian literature. Tasteven stressed that the overcoming of subjective
impressionism in art derived from individual feelings synthesized together,
and expressed by a new religious experience, an experience Tasteven felt
was inherent in Chulkov's mystical anarchism. It was this "synthecism"
("sintetichnost") that was a fundamental goal of *Zolotoe Runo*'s official
artistic policy, something to be strived for, yet never really defined any
more precisely than Tasteven had done here. Tasteven saw in Chulkov's
work the evolution of impressionism to the point of realistic symbolism,
the aim toward which *Zolotoe Runo*'s change of direction had been made.
Tasteven wrote that this was a development noticeable in painting as well
as literature, and rather obtusely attempted to tie the two arts together. For
Tasteven and for *Zolotoe Runo,* the realistic symbolism present in
Chulkov's, Ivanov's, and Gorodetsky's works was the same as that in the
newest paintings of Sarian, Goncharova, and Larionov, a realistic
symbolism which could have an intuitive, if not mystical, understanding, a
philosophy with which the readers of *Zolotoe Runo* and the broad masses of
Russian people could come to agree.

While realistic symbolism, "synthecism" and attacks on *Vesy*'s
definitions of "pure" and "vulgarized" symbolism might find ready
support from almost all *Zolotoe Runo*'s contributors and collaborators,
the theories of mystical anarchism, remaining unclear and undefined on
the magazine's pages, did not. *Zolotoe Runo*'s tendentious tone became
increasingly extreme toward the end of its existence, and its writers
attacked even those whom it had formerly held in the highest esteem.
Tasteven criticized Andreev for abandoning realistic symbolism and for
setting out "on the path of a theomachy that is anti-religion."[55] Nor did
Gorodetsky's attacks on *Apollon* (discussed in Chapter 9) help elucidate
the topics under discussion within a symbolism so fragmented that any
objective analyses had become impossible. Within the context of such
personal and ideological conflict, the real significance of mystical anarchism both for *Zolotoe Runo* and for Russian symbolism was never

actually determined. Any clarification was complicated by the fact that while the magazine adopted the theories of realistic symbolism and "sintetichnost," it never officially adopted Chulkov's mystical anarchism, even though it did defend him and his theories.

Chulkov's role within the mystical anarchist/*Zolotoe Runo-Vesy* controversy is unclear even today. Belyi noted correctly that all along Chulkov as a personality, thinker, and poet lacked not only the talent but also the appeal necessary for a successful leader of a philosophical movement, and that those who followed mystical anarchist tenets were converted by the immensely stronger character of Viacheslav Ivanov. Chulkov never stopped trying to explain the controversies that arose in conjunction with mystical anarchism,[56] yet he never admitted that mystical anarchism was anything more than a "path." Perhaps the greatest difficulty in pinning down the theory and its significance for both Russian symbolism and *Zolotoe Runo* arises from its very definition. Chulkov's admitted "carelessness" left his explanations as obscure as his original statements. Contemporary critics and literary historians have been no more successful.[57] Theories of anarchism usually lack rigid formulation, of course, and in the case of Chulkov's theory, it was precisely this constant possibility of misinterpretation and misunderstanding that led to the whole debate over mystical anarchism.

For the "masses," even such "vulgarized" symbolism as mystical anarchism was incomprehensible, and for the symbolists themselves it allowed such latitude as to make it meaningless. Most of the mystical anarchist threat to "pure" symbolism was manufactured by Belyi and *Vesy,* as was the mystical anarchist "movement" itself and the definition of *Zolotoe Runo* as a "mystical anarchist mouthpiece." For *Vesy, Zolotoe Runo*'s opening its pages to the "heretical" writings of Chulkov and his supporters seemed an affront to the "true voice" of Russian symbolism, which had already rejected such philosophical positions as dangerous to the very essence of that symbolism. To a certain extent, *Zolotoe Runo* was forced to become associated with Chulkov's mystical anarchism when the *Vesy* writers refused to participate in the journal, and when no significant Russian symbolist would agree to accept the magazine's literary editorship, even only partially. That Chulkov accepted proved profoundly important for *Zolotoe Runo,* but the fact remains that none of the major works of mystical anarchism were published in the magazine, and the relationship between *Zolotoe Runo* and mystical anarchism remained one more of association than anything else.

While the controversy over mystical anarchism raged around *Zolotoe Runo,* the magazine on the whole devoted only a small percentage of each issue to the polemic. In the end, mystical anarchism emerged as a paper tiger, a speculative experimental balloon sent up by Chulkov that resulted in a far greater uproar than he anticipated. In the case of *Zolotoe Runo,* the pages dealing with the polemic amounted to a considerably greater number than did those devoted to the theory itself or to any of its applications in prose, poetry, or even original speculative thought.

While *Zolotoe Runo* did not become the "mystical anarchist mouth-piece" Belyi and *Vesy* made it out to be, there were certain points of agreement between the two which helped define post-1905 Russian symbolism. With the growth of widespread popular recognition, the general level of symbolist literature and art had deteriorated because of the large number of people trying to produce symbolist works without the necessary talent. Belyi had warned that a spread in symbolism's popularity, and the debasing of symbolism from being the work of a few very talented individuals to something anyone could reproduce, would vulgarize it, and such a threat was conceivable within Chulkov's theory. Belyi felt *Zolotoe Runo* was encouraging the new untalented "third generation" of symbolist writers. The magazine was doing this to a certain extent, of course: its program repeatedly stated that it encouraged "new young talent" to submit works for publication, although this was due partially to the need for obtaining contributions after the *Vesy* group's exodus. On the other hand, *Zolotoe Runo's* editors were not dependent on this "third generation," and did maintain certain critical standards. While symbolism may have been "vulgarized" at this time, it was not because of *Zolotoe Runo's* publication of the essays of Chulkov, Ivanov, Blok, and Gorodetsky, all of whom wished to find points of contact between the mass of people and the symbolists, but none of whom ever succeeded in reaching those masses.

To discover such points of contact, and to revive what it considered a symbolism increasingly irrelevant to Russian reality, *Zolotoe Runo* had adopted realistic symbolism. No single programmatic article was ever published explaining exactly what was meant by this term, despite the examinations of the question by Gorodetsky and Ivanov, and it remained as imprecise as did mystical anarchism. Yet everyone within Russian symbolism, and with whatever particular prejudice, felt he knew what the term meant, and what its ramifications were. *Zolotoe Runo* accepted mystical anarchism as an aspect of this new realistic symbolism, and combined it with an interest in redefining the "national element" in Russian symbolist poetry and art. This was a significant step both for Russian modernism and for *Zolotoe Runo,* and in painting more so perhaps than in literature. By 1907, the symbolists associated with *Zolotoe Runo*—Blok, Chulkov, Ivanov, Gorodetsky—shared a strong disappointment in the failure of the 1905 revolution. While much of Russian society retreated into a new "decadence," the modernists about *Zolotoe Runo* became obsessed with the reevaluation of national Russian traditions, with finding connections with the people before the symbolist intellectuals were destroyed in the new upheaval felt to be inevitable. One reason for *Zolotoe Runo*'s enthusiastic reception of Gorodetsky was the natively Russian influences in his poetry. Chulkov wrote that Gorodetsky was a good symbolist poet, but with a realistic Russian nature, and that the real strength of his poetry came from his purely Russian character.[58] As we shall see in the following chapter, Gorodetsky's work was paralleled in *Zolotoe Runo*'s artistic section by the neo-primitivism of Larionov and Goncharova, based on indigenous traditions. As Blok, Chulkov, and Ivanov attempted to turn away from their earlier "purely" symbolist stage, so too did Kuznetsov and Sarian move from their *Golubaia roza* symbolism to native, national neo-primitivism. To the dismay of all those writers and poets, "the people" never felt any more affinity with such consciously national attempts than they had with *Mir Iskusstva* or *Vesy*. Still, in a somewhat perverse way, *Zolotoe Runo*'s mystical anarchism-realistic symbolism episode helped pave the way for the further development of Russian modernism. The contributors to *Zolotoe Runo* made much of the statement that "decadence" was dead, that it had been outgrown and a new movement made necessary. Although they speculated vaguely on what would succeed it, the contributors to *Zolotoe Runo* would have been surprised to learn that it would become a "classical" Acmeism (Chulkov, and even *Apollon*'s archenemy Gorodetsky, moved in this direction) or a more radical Futurism (Tasteven became a major propagandist for the new movement). In the early years of the twentieth century's first decade, symbolism, and Russian modernism as a whole, had been fairly united as a movement. Its popular success after 1905 divided it into a number of competing groups, and after 1910 it became splintered. *Zolotoe Runo*'s experiments and support for generally unpopular positions within symbolism encouraged this splintering, and prodded on the constantly accelerating development of Russian cultural modernism.

VII

NON-JOURNALISTIC ACTIVITIES: COMPETITIONS, EXHIBITIONS, AND THE BIRTH OF RUSSIAN NEO-PRIMITIVISM

> Kuznetsov was lively and clever ... Drittenpreis was cheerful and kind, young-looking and tall ... he looked like a romantic from Göttingen. And everywhere flashed ... the somewhat ridiculous, sunburnt artist Arapov; like the moon, a melancholic throughout, a little dreamily, bent as if broken, Sapunov palely became silent ... And the pale, black-bearded Greeks came up—the Miliotis: the talented brother, Nikolai, with the untalented, evil intriguer, Vasilii, our enemy ... I remember Sarian, who, his black moustache hanging down, gloomily and absentmindedly walked around, dryly sticking out his hand, not noticing to whom he offered it.
>
> Andrei Belyi, *Mezhdu dvukh revoliutsii*, p. 236.

> A plenitude of sophistication narrowing into decadence—this means that primitivism will soon follow.
>
> Irving Howe, "The Idea of the Modern," p. 32.

During 1906 and 1907, the editors and publisher of *Zolotoe Runo* were concerned primarily with the magazine's production alone, but some related projects were undertaken as well, the most minor being the "Zolotoe Runo Publishing House." By the end of 1906, it had issued four books of disparate character which were nevertheless consistent with the interests of the magazine and, it was hoped, of prospective purchasers. The first work published was Balmont's collection of folkloristic poems, *Zlye chary (Evil Spells),* which never reached bookstore shelves, however, because it was seized by order of the successor to the former government censorship. Appearing at the same time was Riabushinsky's novella *Ispoved (The Confession,* written under his pseudonym, N. Shinsky), his only prose work printed outside his magazine. One book, already published in part in *Zolotoe Runo,* was Alexei Remizov's collection of stories, *Posolon.*[1] Finally, a considerably more expensive scholarly work (costing ten rubles, in contrast to the one or one-and-a-half ruble price for the other books) by the art historian and frequent *Zolotoe Runo* contributor Alexander Uspensky, was published by the magazine. His *Ocherki po istorii russkogo iskusstva (Essays on the History of Russian*

Art) was produced with a luxury typical of *Zolotoe Runo* (where parts of the book had been originally published) and included a large number of illustrations.

In its attempts at book publishing, *Zolotoe Runo* hoped to establish for itself a position similar to that of other Russian modernist periodicals. *Vesy,* for example, was printed by Poliakov's "Skorpion" (Scorpio) publishing house, and the two were so closely related that Belyi called them "twins."[2] "Skorpion" also published the miscellany *Severnye Tsvety (Northern Flowers)* and similar connections existed between *Pereval* and Sokolov's publishing house, "Grif" (Gryphon). While "Grif" and "Skorpion" were located in Moscow, there were two important modernist publishers in St. Petersburg as well. "Ory" and "Shipovnik" (Sweetbrier), with no journals of their own, did publish miscellanies. "Ory" was associated with several Petersburg symbolists belonging to Viacheslav Ivanov's circle, and also issued Chulkov's heterodox series of miscellanies, *Fakely.* "Shipovnik" was rather less modernist on the whole, and occupied a middle position similar to that of *Fakely.* It published not only works by Blok, Belyi, Briusov, Remizov, and Sologub, but also those of Plekhanov, Chernyshevsky, Marx, and Lunacharsky, almost the whole range of Russian writers from the symbolists to Gorky's *Znanie* school.

Unlike these Petersburg publishing houses, *Zolotoe Runo* did not consider it necessary to print collections of works outside the magazine since it allotted a great deal more space to *belles-lettres* from the beginning than did its major competitor *Vesy,* for example. On the contrary, it directed its attention toward publishing individual works which had usually already appeared in the magazine. By the end of 1909, *Zolotoe Runo* had issued a total of only nine books. Besides the four already mentioned, there was Nikolai Roerich's *Stati i snimki (Articles and Impressions);* Sologub's collection of poems *Plamennyi krug (The Flaming Circle,* with a cover designed by Riabushinsky and a portrait of the author which had appeared in *Zolotoe Runo);* Blok's collection of poems, *Zemlia v snegu (The Earth in Snow);* Chulkov's critical articles *Pokryvalo Izidy (The Veil of Isis);* and Stanislaw Przybyszewski's novel *Den sudnyi (Day of Judgment).* As was the case with most modernist works at the time, these books were published in relatively small editions: two thousand copies was probably average for symbolist works between 1905 and 1910, and Blok's *Zemlia v snegu* was published in an edition of two thousand, while Chulkov's collection of essays had a printing of only twelve hundred copies. At the same time, these books were not bought up rapidly, and new editions rarely appeared. As Soviet scholars frequently point out, this was at a time when *Znanie* publications were selling out editions of many tens of thousands.[3]

Zolotoe Runo's attempts at book publication remained limited because of competition with other, more experienced modernist publishing houses, but also for more unforeseeable reasons: Przybyszewski's novel, for example, was published simultaneously by three different Russian companies, even though the author had given *Zolotoe Runo* sole rights of publication in Russia. Despite such problems, the number and variety of books published by *Zolotoe Runo* remain an interesting and not entirely unsuccessful aspect of the magazine's activities and aspirations.

Book publication remained a peripheral concern to *Zolotoe Runo*'s editors, but a decision to devote individual issues of the magazine to specific themes, in conjunction with an open competition, was not. In May 1906, *Zolotoe Runo* announced that it would mount a series of exhibitions connected with certain future issues of the magazine being devoted to specific themes of current interest. January 1907 would deal with "the Devil" ("artistic, poetic, and religious-philosophical conceptions"), while the May 1907 issue would be dedicated to the theme of the "life and art of the future." A competition would also be held, and eleven prizes (ranging from 125 down to 50 rubles) in the literary and artistic sections given for the best drawings, vignettes and headpieces, poetry, fiction, and articles. Finally, it was announced that the recipients of the prizes would be determined by the editors, with the help of "artistic and literary individuals"[4] whose names were given in the October 1906 issue: the literary section was composed of Briusov, Blok, Viacheslav Ivanov, Kursinsky, and Riabushinsky, and the artistic section of Dobuzhinsky, Kuznetsov, Vasily Milioti, Riabushinsky, and Serov.[5]

Apparently there was little publicity for this first competition except for the notices appearing in the magazine itself, and beyond those individuals immediately involved, not much excitement or undue interest seems to have been aroused. Nonetheless, the "Devil" issue appeared in January 1907 as had been promised. There were several drawings on the artistic section's first few pages, including Kuznetsov's "Awakening of the Devil," Dobuzhinsky's nightmarish political conception of the Devil (a reflection of his continuing revolutionary sympathy), and other rather evocative drawings by Vasily Milioti, Arapov, and Feofilaktov. Concluding the artistic section, and not entered in the competition, was the single most impressive contribution to the issue, Uspensky's article "Bes" ("Demon"), which followed a series of reproductions of depictions of the Devil in ancient Russian painting. Uspensky's study was excerpted from a larger work, and dealt in detail with the esthetics of the depiction of the Devil in pre-Petrine Russian art.

The issue's poetry section consisted of a number of second-rate works by poets who generally remained as unknown after the competition as they had been before it. There were only two works of fiction, Kuzmin's disappointing epistolary story "Iz pisem devitsy Klary Valmon k Rozalii

Tiutelmaier" ("From the Letters of the Maiden Clara Valmon to Rosalie Tütelmaier"), and Remizov's fascinating long story "Chertik" ("The Little Devil").[6] Finally, there were two articles on the Devil theme: Sologub's discursive "Chelovek cheloveku—diavol" ("Man is Devil to Man"), in which he proposed that there was a devil in modern society existing in each of us, and that we were devils to each other; and "Satana v muzyke (Istoricheskaia zametka)" ["Satan in Music (An Historical Note)"] by I. A. S. (Ilia Sats), a discussion of the evolution of the feeling of Satan in music as being analogous to the development of the comprehension of the beginning of good and evil in religion. The remainder of the January 1907 issue (the predominant part) was composed of the magazine's regular features, and was unrelated to the "Devil" theme.

The report of the juries and a recapitulation of the competition was placed at the beginning of the issue's chronicle. It noted that the judges for the literary section had met in December 1906 to examine 61 works, with the result being that "the jury did not find a single item deserving first prize,"[7] either in poetry or prose. The situation was even worse among the artistic entries: the jury had decided that none of them were worthy either of a prize or of reproduction in *Zolotoe Runo*'s competition issue, and they agreed to dissolve the competition and to discontinue any plans for a related exhibition.

This was certainly a remarkable outcome for the magazine's attempt to stimulate interest in itself and in the concept of theme competitions. It was to the juries' and the editors' credit, of course, that they made such an embarrassing decision. The editors, with the agreement of both juries, did decide to give some prizes, however: a second prize of 50 rubles was given to Kondratiev for his poem; two first prizes were given to Remizov and Kuzmin for their stories; and *Zolotoe Runo* published the other poems in the issue with the usual remuneration to the authors. Curiously enough, the best works in the "Devil" issue were not entered in the competition itself, but apparently had been commissioned in advance. This was the case with the Kuzmin and Remizov stories, the Uspensky article, and the drawings. Why the competition was such a failure is unclear. It may have been considered rather ridiculous by those talented enough to expect to win the prizes (not negligible amounts of money for modernist writers). The failure may also have been due to a continually increasing antipathy among symbolist writers to any of Riabushinsky's projects. For whatever reason, the outcome of the "Devil" competition forced the editors to discontinue the whole concept. They must have felt that the very idea of a competition associated with a theme issue was a mistaken one since the motif of demonism was omnipresent at the time in Russian modernist art and literature.[8] Instead of making an attempt at combining exhibitions, competitions, and theme issues, *Zolotoe Runo* decided to return to the example of *Mir Iskusstva,* and sponsor exhibitions of art alone.

The magazine's first effort at organizing an art exhibition took place later in 1907 in association with the artists of the *Golubaia roza* group. *Zolotoe Runo* had included designs by these artists in every one of its issues, and as *Iskusstvo* had been, it too became a platform for the artistic and doctrinal views of the group. Their ties were so close, in fact, that Riabushinsky and Vasily Milioti, the magazine's art editor, were even considered members of *Golubaia roza.* The magazine gave its full financial and publicistic support to the exhibition and devoted a great deal of its May 1907 issue to it, including four photographs of the exhibition hall itself. The issue's pictorial section consisted entirely of reproductions of the exhibited works of Vasily Milioti, his brother Nikolai (1874-1962), Pavel Kuznetsov (1878-1968), Nikolai Sapunov (1880-1912), the sculptors Pavel Bromirsky (1884-1919) and Alexander Matveev (1878-1960), Sergei Sudeikin (1882-1946), Nikolai Feofilaktov (1878-1949), Martiros Sarian (1880-1972), Riabunshinsky, Ivan Knabe (1878-1910), V. Drittenpreis (?-?), Nikolai Krymov (1884-1958), and Artur Fonvizin (1882-1973). Certainly one of the most interesting features of the issue was Sergei Makovsky's laudatory review of the show.[9] Makovsky began by describing the exhibition as a "chapel" within the cathedral of art, an experience directed not toward the masses, but intended for the few elect individuals who could understand the works of art: "It is light. Quiet. And the pictures are like prayers,"[10] an expression of collective searching. He characterized the artists as being in love with the music of color and line, and while inspired by Borisov-Musatov and Maurice Denis, to Makovsky these new works were deeper, more intimate, soulful, and Russian than anything done before. Makovsky praised Kuznetsov's decorative panels for emerging from the regions of decorative art into the area of myth-creation (Viacheslav Ivanov's "mifotvorchestvo"), for showing to their viewers the "life of the soul."[11] He concluded that the artists of *Golubaia roza* were using a new primitivism as a means for seeking their artistic ancestors, and that this primitivism was a formless fog out of which would grow bright clear stars.[12] Makovsky's enthusiasm for the vagueness of these artists' works is surprising coming from the man who was to be the founder of the neo-classicist *Apollon* three years later, but the article was consistent with the atmosphere of the exhibition and the works included.

Both because of its organization and the subject matter of the paintings themselves, the *Golubaia roza* exhibition created a sensation in Moscow. Held in the Kuznetsov building in the center of the city, it ran from March 18 until April 29, 1907 and attracted five thousand visitors. Organized by Pavel Kuznetsov, the leader of the group, it was completely financed by Riabushinsky through *Zolotoe Runo.* The goals of the exhibition's physical organization had been stated some months earlier in

a *Zolotoe Runo* article by Alexander Rostislavov. In his discussion of the
current exhibition of the Union of Russian Artists, Rostislavov considered
the esthetics of artistic exhibition. Calling the Union's show a haphazard
grouping of paintings, he wrote that

> that time has long since passed when exhibitions [could be] simple collections of
> paintings, confusedly organized, in coarse frames. Not only are artistic works
> necessary, but artistic organization as well. The exhibitions themselves must be
> complete works of art, clear, beautiful, a complete picture of modern art.[13]

Kuznetsov and Riabushinsky did everything possible to fulfill this
Gesamtkunstwerk ideal for the *Golubaia roza* exhibition. With his usual
exhuberance, Riabushinsky gave a banquet in the Metropol Hotel to
celebrate the exhibition's opening: " ... the tables are covered with forget-
me-nots, a bear carved out of a block of ice holds a bowl of oysters, there
are 40 participants, the cost is 32,000 rubles."[14] The walls of the exhibition
hall were covered with dark-gray material and the floor carpeted; the
scents of hyacinths, lilies, and daffodils filled the air, and a string quartet
played. A series of literary-musical afternoons and evenings were held in
conjunction with the exhibition: Belyi, Briusov, and Remizov read their
newest works; musical works by Russian composers were played by the
pianists Igumnov, Beklemishev, and Buden; and a "Ms. K-ia" performed
Greek dances. The presence of the exhibiting artists at these performances
also helped ensure their success, and at each occasion the hall was reported
to be "overfull."[15]

Despite such supplementary activities, the exhibition's principal
concern was to provide exposure for the artists and their works. The
Golubaia roza artists had previously had only one small exhibition, under
the name *Alaia roza (Crimson Rose)*, in Saratov in 1904. Several had
contributed designs for *Vesy* and *Zolotoe Runo,* and beginning in 1906,
Sapunov and Sudeikin were commissioned to design sets for the Komissarzhevskaia Theater in Petersburg. A few had also exhibited with the *Mir
Iskusstva* artists and with Diaghilev's Russian section of the 1906 Salon
d'Automne in Paris.

The public knew them best for their dream-like, ethereal works that
seemed typically decadent, if not symbolist. This was how Tarovaty had
characterized their contributions to the *Mir Iskusstva* exhibition for
Zolotoe Runo in early 1906:

> An intoxicating dream invites one into a world of airiness and transparent outlines.
> Dreams in azure of pale blue and dull, quiet tones, trembling, unearthly silhouettes,
> transparent stems of mystical flowers, covered [with the light of] dawn, and on
> everything the mist of an ineffable, only vaguely comprehensible presentiment.[16]

Tarovaty's description of the works of the future *Golubaia roza* artists was still applicable to the paintings shown at the 1907 exhibition. Most of the works included in the later exhibition had been completed in 1905 and 1906, and the exhibition itself took place at a time when the artists were moving toward a neo-primitivist technique and beginning to abandon their former themes. Still, this retrospective collection was to be the only complete showing of works from their purely symbolist period. Paintings emphasizing themes of death, dreams, and visions of hazy reality were typical[17] and were the kinds of works the public came to see, if not to buy. They also provided a convenient point of departure for the caustic reviews written by most of the Moscow art critics.

This "exhibition of pictures of the newest direction,"[18] was received condescendingly by the *Moskovskii Ezhednevnik:*

> —Que ce que c'est la rose bleue?
> —C'est la rose, qui ne rougit jamais.
> The blue rose has been found and the secret of beauty has been fathomed. If you want to convince yourself of this, then go to Miasnitskaia Street, to the Kuznetsov building to the exhibition by the *Zolotoe Runo* circle.[19]

The tone of this criticism of artistic pretentiousness was not unlike that Gippius had used in her article on *Zolotoe Runo*'s appearance in 1906, and in fact, *Vesy*'s review of the exhibition, written by Igor Grabar (1871-1960), was surprisingly acidic toward the artists and fairly typical of the press's reception in general. Grabar credited the organizers with attaining an intimacy lacking in earlier Moscow exhibitions, and admitted that there were a number of talented and cultured individuals among the *Golubaia roza* artists. He did pick out some for serious criticism, however:

> Sudeikin has an excellent inventiveness and perfectly charming ideas, but he should do miniatures, or should be dragged to the Sistine ceiling. His "taste" would be very proper in crumbling bagatelles, in headpieces (with which he is successful), generally in things that are more graphic than painterly, and finally, perhaps in articles of jewelry. But in large things he is intolerable unless they are such frankly ornamental panels as "Birds" or the excellent "Basket of Flowers." I would sooner be satisfied to live in a room painted with the moustachioed women of Knabe—*ganz verrükter Knabe*—than to know that the rosy-fragrant "Venice" and "Defiles" and other sweetnesses would be looking at me for years from my walls. One could eat black bread every day...but my God! To be nourished on "Turkish Delights" one after another for two years would be impossible. Even Riabushinsky's "Gateway" painting and the absurd nonsense of Fonvizin is preferable to such walls.[20]

Grabar concluded his review with a suggestion that these artists should abandon their morbid and perverse themes and come outside into the sun:

Return the "devils" to Merezhkovsky, the "angels" to Rozanov and the symbolism to Maeterlinck, and don't believe in the "setting sun." Right now it's looking at me straight in the eye and laughing at you.[21]

Years later, Makovsky explained such vehement antagonism toward the *Golubaia roza* works by the fact that Russian society was not as yet accustomed to the rapid and encompassing changes in direction that were seen in this exhibition:

Even in the progressive camps of Petersburg and Moscow it was not possible to excuse the decadents of *Zolotoe Runo* the immature pretension of imitation of Maurice Denis and other post-Impressionists, about whom Russia was just hearing.[22]

Makovsky at the same time clarified his own earlier enthusiasm for the works by remarking that he had seen in them an important new direction in which Russian art should be encouraged to develop: not toward ever more subtle symbolist blues and grays, but toward a primitivism that demanded bolder and more vivid colors.

This *Golubaia roza* exhibition was the first and last show of the united Moscow symbolist artists. Financially it was not a success, but this was of little importance either to the artists or their sponsor. The aim of the exhibition, and of the publicity given it in *Zolotoe Runo,* had been to make the artists widely known, and by mid-1907 this had been accomplished. Artistic developments were moving so rapidly in Russia at this time, however, that by the end of that year these formerly *avant-garde* artists were to be eclipsed by the more forcefully expressed neo-primitivism of Goncharova, Larionov, and the Burliuks in their *Venok-Stephanos* (Wreath-Stephanos) exhibition, also organized under the general auspices of *Zolotoe Runo.*

Both the *Golubaia roza* and *Venok-Stephanos* exhibitions had been put together on a scale and with an attentiveness to esthetic detail never before seen in Moscow, and the public was justifiably impressed by the quality of the mounting of the exhibitions, if not by the exhibited works themselves. These experiences were to assure the artistic success of the succeeding exhibitions *Zolotoe Runo* was to sponsor under its own name in 1908 and 1909.

The first "Salon Zolotoe Runo" had its opening delayed because of organizational difficulties. Intended as a large exhibition representative of the full range of contemporary Russian and French art, the organizers wrote all the major Russian artists asking for their support. From their letter to Serov inviting him to take part in the "Salon," it seemed clear that the organizing committee (Utkin, Vasily Milioti, Larionov, Riabushinsky, Kuznetsov, and Iakulov) expected a wide range of participation in the exhibition.[23] Accompanying Serov's invitation was a note from Milioti saying that not only had almost all the *Golubaia roza* artists agreed to participate, but that the committee had also received the consent of Somov, Dobuzhinsky, Lanseray, Bilibin, Roerich, Golovin, Maliavin, and Korovin among others, and was expecting the participation of Benois and Bakst as well.[24] Apparently some kind of unofficial boycott developed among these predominantly Petersburg artists, however, although it is unclear whether it was the result of distaste for Riabushinsky, the *Golubaia roza* artists, or the invited French artists. In any case, and despite a misconceived if not deliberately misleading summary of the actual situation in Milioti's letter to Serov, the exhibition's Russian section came to consist almost entirely of the latest works of the former *Golubaia roza* artists, with the addition of Larionov and Goncharova, who had only recently begun showing their paintings.

The difficulties the committee experienced with regard to the exhibition's Russian section were equalled by those involved in collecting and organizing the French works. Riabushinsky had originally intended to show both French and Russian works at the exhibition, and with his contacts with French art dealers and his frequent visits to Paris, he became the principal organizer for the French section.[25] As a result, many of the Fauve paintings seen for the first time at the 1905 Salon d'Automne in Paris reappeared at this initial "Salon Zolotoe Runo" and the Moscow exhibition was the first important showing of Matisse's works outside France. Riabushinsky had hoped that along with his own recent French acquisitions, he would be able to exhibit works borrowed from the extensive modern collections of Ivan Morozov and Sergei Shchukin,[26] but they proved as hostile to his plans as had the Petersburg artists. Both declined to participate, replying that they were organizing their own exhibition and could therefore not be expected to lend anything to the "Salon" (no such exhibition ever took place, by the way). Riabushinsky was probably not unduly surprised at Morozov's decision, since he generally kept his collection to himself and rarely opened it even to artists, the public at large knowing the works comprising it only from hearsay or from occasional references in journals.[27] Shchukin's case was entirely different, however, and his collection and its accessibility had become famous throughout Europe as well as Russia.[28] It was clear to Riabushinsky that Shchukin's excuse for not participating was a fabricated one and a veiled insult. In the face of such a negative attitude, the importance of the "Salon" seemed even greater to Riabushinsky and *Zolotoe Runo*. The Morozov-Shchukin collections were the only comprehensive presentations of contemporary Western art in Russia, and until 1908 very few reproductions of modern French art had appeared in any Russian periodicals; Sarian wrote in his memoirs that he did not see an Impressionist picture until 1906. *Zolotoe Runo* recognized that only if the "Salon" were successful would there be a public Russian showing of Impressionist and post-Impressionist works. Riabushinsky was forced to import a considerably larger number of paintings from the West than originally intended, as well as to contribute most of his own modern collection in the interests of the exhibition. A number of these works had to be sold off the walls of the exhibition itself to help finance the show.[29]

Surmounting these frustrating financial and contributional problems, the "Salon Zolotoe Runo" finally opened at the Khludov building in Moscow at the beginning of April, and continued until June. Once again, attention was given to the physical setting's every detail, and six thousand spectators came to view the total of 282 canvases and 3 sculptures. The "Salon's" French section was an unqualified success: it included two sculptures by Maillol, one by Rodin, and paintings by almost all the Nabis—Bonnard, Vuillard, Sérusier, Valloton, and Maurice Denis; the Fauves were represented by Derain, Marquet, and Van Dongen, and headed by Matisse with four works; the older Impressionist school was seen for the first time in Russia with the works of Pissarro, Sisley, Renoir, and Toulouse-Lautrec; finally, the post-Impressionists were represented by Gauguin, Van Gogh (one of whose five exhibited works, "Le Café de Nuit," was sold to Ivan Morozov during the run of the exhibition), and Cézanne. In conjunction with the exhibition, during the summer of 1908 a special number of *Zolotoe Runo* was devoted to the French works.[30] The issue's entire illustrated section consisted of reproductions of paintings from the exhibition, including Van Gogh's "Le Café de Nuit" as a full page in color. In addition, a number of articles on modern French art followed the illustrations: Tasteven translated an article by Charles Morice on new tendencies in French art, Voloshin wrote about recent French artistic trends, and Tasteven about Impressionism.[31]

The exhibition's Russian section did not enjoy the critical success the French one did. The Russian works, hung separately from those of the French artists, were unable to compete on the whole with the originality and richness of the French paintings. In one contemporary critic's opinion:

> It's like a mass suicide. On the one hand French originals, on the other Russian imitations... You get the impression of a zealous bear trying to dance a minuet with a pomaded marquise.[32]

Mikhail Larionov (1881-1964), who had the largest number of works in the exhibition's Russian section, had worked primarily in a semi-Impressionist style that did owe an obvious debt to his French predecessors. Similarly, the French influence on the former *Golubaia roza* artists was equally clear: Kuznetsov's works, for example, were never more reminiscent of those of Maurice Denis than they were at this time. This Russian emulation of French models was the product of a new intensive interchange between Moscow and Paris, however: Kuznetsov had developed an interest in Gauguin's works after his own regular exhibitions at the Paris Salons, and the artistic horizons and development of Larionov and Natalia Goncharova (1881-1962) had been broadened and accelerated with their participation in Diaghilev's 1906 Paris exhibition of Russian art. More significantly, this emulation of French models was an important stage for young Russian artists in their development of a primitivist style based on native Russian or Central Asian themes and traditions. And it was the Russian artists exhibiting in the "Salon Zolotoe Runo" who would pioneer this development.

As it had for the French artists, *Zolotoe Runo* devoted a special issue to the Salon's Russian section.[33] Numerous reproductions (principally of works by Kuznetsov, Sarian, Vasily Milioti, Goncharova, and Larionov) were included, with Sarian's "Poet" being the only one in color. Many of these paintings burned in the fire which destroyed Riabushinsky's villa a few years later, and this issue of *Zolotoe Runo* remains the only source for a pictorial appraisal of them. As a whole, the issue was unimpressive in comparison with the French number, as were the Russian works themselves, and was no doubt reflective of the disappointments encountered in putting together the Russian section.

Successful despite numerous difficulties, the first "Salon Zolotoe Runo" brought to a focus the problems confronting Riabushinsky and his magazine in sponsoring such exhibitions in the face of strong criticism and lack of support. When Igor Grabar's review of the exhibition appeared in *Vesy* in June, criticizing "noticeable haste" in the exhibition's organizing, and calling its general arrangement one of "dilettante *poshlost,*"[34] Riabushinsky felt it necessary to reply not only to Grabar, but to all those who refused cooperation in the exhibition and who were generally negative toward anything undertaken by *Zolotoe Runo*. His angry "Iskusstvo, ego druzia i vragi" ("Art, Its Friends and Enemies") appeared soon after Grabar's review, and was an expression not only of Riabushinsky's general state of mind, but of that of all the major collaborators of *Zolotoe Runo* as well. Writing in a satiric tone, Riabushinsky began by discussing Russian art criticism, and particularly the recent reviews of the "Salon Zolotoe Runo":

> The critic from *Novoe Vremia,* having written the day before on the high prices of meat in Moscow, also gave his opinion. Petersburg and the provinces, reading this newspaper, would have to have taken a negative impression on the exhibition, because the critic, abusing and spitting, pushing the artists and their pictures to the sidelines, even began to counsel shooting a canvas in which he noticed a bird, apparently still under the impression this was the article about the high price of meat.[35]

After mentioning innumerable such "oddities" by "journalistic and artistic ignoramuses," Riabushinsky moved on to explain his, and *Zolotoe Runo*'s, conception of art and the artist. Art was not some kind of commercial activity that could be dictated by economically powerful, but artistically uninformed individuals (a clear reference to many of the Russian Maecenases). True art was advanced by those who suffered for it, who were dissatisfied, and who would continually strive for beauty:

> Intoxicated by an inner inclination, these people were unable to renounce their religion. Persecuted, they did not renege on their convictions; despised, without income, they starved and endured poverty, but in that deprivation, they loved their art even more, and with an even greater energy preached that with which their restless, misunderstood soul lived and breathed.[36]

With this idealized conception of art, Riabushinsky was referring precisely to *Zolotoe Runo* (and to the artists and writers associated with it), which despite enemies' attacks, would never renounce its allegiance to true art.

Next, Riabushinsky discussed those who were the major critics of this "true art" that could be seen in the "Salon Zolotoe Runo." First, the Russian "philistines":

> Standing before a picture, the philistine demands clarity from it, so that he will not have to work to understand it, and mainly so that it will not contradict those traditions upon which he has built all his inner well-being. A canvas not satisfying such demands is suddenly deprived in his eyes of everything valuable and profound in it. The philistine rushes about the exhibition, behaves noisily, is indignant, infects the other people who are still hesitating in their opinions, and in such a way magnifies the families of ignoramuses who do not take the trouble to understand even a little of what is going on, what the indignation is all about; he brands the pictures, brands the entire exhibition with the general term "decadent."[37]

Surprisingly, Riabushinsky remarked, this closed-mindedness about art was as present in those Russians who had read about and who had even made collections of art, as it was in those who attended exhibitions "not to buy paintings, but only to judge them." Riabushinsky described the tyranny of art "critics" and "experts" over Russian art collectors who knew very little about art themselves, and who were interested more in the artist's reputation than in his work:

> One of them bought a work which he liked a lot, thinking it a bronze by Maillol. Examining the catalogue, the exhibition secretary noticed that there had been a mistake and informed the collector that the bronze should not have been attributed to Maillol, on the threshhold of celebrity, but to the talented, but less well-known Getscher. The collector rejected it, saying: "In that case, I don't want it."[38]

Riabushinsky faulted such people for buying pieces of art for investment without having any feeling for the works themselves or for the artist's vision.

While private collectors bought works purely for economic considerations, Riabushinsky continued, the government-sponsored public museums refused to collect any modern works of art at all because of outmoded esthetic standards. When they finally did "come to their senses" they found that all the best Russian modernist works had already been purchased, and that they would have to be content with the leftovers. As a result, Riabushinsky wrote, the public had no way to follow the gradual development of Russian modernist, and particularly symbolist, art. The poorly-organized exhibitions of symbolist art appearing recently had only, in Riabushinsky's eyes, made conditions worse in that they were made up of imitative and talentless works recognizable as such even by the "philistine" public. Such exhibitions, and the artists whose works filled them, were only doing a disservice to Russian modernist art.

To counter this dismal state of affairs, Riabushinsky explained, *Zolotoe Runo* decided to mount an exhibition of all contemporary Russian artistic currents, with the addition of modern French works which "would clarify the influences and origins of the new movements in Russian art."[39] He then mentioned some of the difficulties any such undertaking would involve, while noting that *Zolotoe Runo* naturally hoped for the sympathy and support of Russian "lovers of art." Instead, obstacles were deliberately placed in the magazine's path. When the Petersburg artists declined to cooperate, it was left to those of *Golubaia roza* to represent modern Russian art, but even there the "transience of blue roses" took its toll, and several refused to participate. Finally, and with regard to the exhibition's French section, Riabushinsky noted *Zolotoe Runo*'s request for assistance to Morozov and Shchukin. Through barely veiled anger, Riabushinsky mentioned their "curt reply" and pointed out the baselessness of the reasons the two had given for denying any aid. But despite such difficulties and general lack of support, Riabushinsky concluded, "the Salon Zolotoe Runo opened on the fifth of April."[40]

To a large extent, Riabushinsky's article repeated charges of spiteful opposition that *Zolotoe Runo* had been making throughout its existence, although this time, with the mention by name of Morozov and Shchukin, it was on a more personal level. Above all, it had become clear both to Riabushinsky and the magazine's other editors that they could hope for little support or encouragement either from many of the Russian artists themselves, from a press (both modernist and non-modernist) that seemed intent on continually ridiculing anything *Zolotoe Runo* attempted, or from many of the major Russian collectors and promoters of modern art. As bitter as this sense of isolation must have seemed to *Zolotoe Runo*'s editors, it did reinforce their own publicly-expressed views of themselves as fighters and possible martyrs for the development of truly progressive art in Russia. Surprisingly enough, the editors were able to maintain their position in the face of the ridicule and opposition they encountered, and went on to sponsor two more exhibitions in 1909.

The second "Salon Zolotoe Runo" ran from January 11 until February 15, 1909, and exhibited French Fauve and pre-Cubist works alongside the (still) symbolist works of Kuznetsov and the early neo-primitivism of Larionov and Goncharova. Although more Russian works were included on this occasion, once again no Petersburg artists were represented. Many of them undoubtedly had been insulted by some of Riabushinsky's public comments, and in any case most were currently participating in Makovsky's Petersburg "Salon," intended to represent all the modern movements in Russian art. *Zolotoe Runo* claimed credit for Makovsky's conception ("[it] apparently arose from ideas stated already in *Zolotoe Runo*,"[41] the magazine noted), and because of his success in gaining the participation of such diverse groups as the *peredvizhniki,* the *miriskusniki,* members of the Union of Russian Artists, and even some members of *Golubaia roza,* the magazine felt compelled to attack the exhibition. "S. Iu." (probably Siunnerberg) wrote that Makovsky did not have a good selection of the latest Russian artists;[42] Larionov commented that the great mass of artistic material had been poorly arranged and exhibited with no apparent plan,[43] and Larionov and Goncharova boycotted the exhibition entirely. Much of *Zolotoe Runo's* reaction resulted from envy, but interestingly, Makovsky's "Salon" proved to be almost entirely retrospective and in general was rather staid (perhaps the product of bringing so many different artistic schools together) in comparison with the *Zolotoe Runo* exhibitions. It is likely that it was this enforced but not entirely uncultivated isolation of the artists associated with *Zolotoe Runo* that helped encourage artistic developments whose beginnings had been suggested at the magazine's first "Salon."

Indeed, the second "Salon Zolotoe Runo" was conceived in part as means in a conscious search for a new artistic method to replace symbolism. The exhibition catalogue's introduction expressed this desire:

> A distinctive feature of what Russian art is undergoing at the present time is the decomposition and necrosis of previous groups... Distinguished by the *Golubaia roza* exhibition organized by *Zolotoe Runo* and appearing now for the second year this group of artists has broken with the group of esthetes and symbolists in its searches. Its essential feature is its aspiration to overcome formulae which have already become stagnant: of estheticism which has broken the link between the colorful joys of the eye and those, more profound, which excite the spirit; and of historicism which has narrowed the area of personal experiences... (the French are more sensual, the Russian artists have more spirituality)... Here we see the overcoming of estheticism and

historicism, there is a reaction against neo-academism into which Impressionism degenerated. If the forefathers of this movement in France were Cézanne, Gauguin, and Van Gogh, the first stimulus in Russia was provided by Vrubel and Borisov-Musatov.[44]

This new attitude toward the development of Russian art was paralleled by the similar change in *Zolotoe Runo*'s general esthetic position, with its new emphasis on the appreciation of "realism" and primitivism.

Addressing more directly the problem of the relationship between new artistic endeavors and "realistic symbolism" than had the catalog introduction, was Tasteven's "Neskolko slov o vystavke *Zolotogo Runa*" ("A Few Words about the *Zolotoe Runo* Exhibition"),[45] which appeared in early 1909. Tasteven wrote that Kuznetsov, Vasily Milioti, and Utkin had overcome the "decadent estheticism which had confined the field of painting" by aspiring toward the new realistic symbolism espoused by Gorodetsky, Chulkov, Ivanov, and (even) Remizov on the pages of *Zolotoe Runo*. Tasteven felt that "the most important fact of modern artistic life is the liquidation of decadence, the striving for a new, sunny, and joyful art, free from the fatigue and reticence of decadent experience," that "the search for a new realistic symbolism, indissolubly connected with the search for a new *non-decadent, non-individualist,* but *religious connection* to life is occurring both in painting and literature."[46] He concluded with a summary of the Russian works in the exhibition:

> The basic tendencies are these:
> In the philosophical sphere—the overcoming of subjectivism through realistic symbolism.
> In the sphere of *painting*—a synthetic method, a combination of Impressionism with decorativeness; the liberation of painting from graphicness.[47]

While Tasteven's characterization of the exhibition sounds at times like so much nonsense, it does express the attitude of those associated with *Zolotoe Runo* in so far as this striving for a new kind of art is concerned. Certainly Russian art during the next few years did not overcome subjectivism in form, although it did liberate painting from "graphicness." Tasteven's, and *Zolotoe Runo*'s, expectations did not find quite the precise realization in Russian art that they expected. It must be repeated, however, that *Zolotoe Runo* was the only established active supporter of this search for new means of artistic expression, and it was only *Zolotoe Runo*'s exhibitions that gave these experiments wide public exposure during 1908, 1909, and 1910.

Again, few criticized the physical arrangement of the second "Salon Zolotoe Runo," and it attracted eight thousand spectators. Larionov had helped in the exhibition's organization, while Riabushinsky supported it financially, again relying on purchases of the paintings for reimbursement.[48] The exhibition differed from its predecessor in that it was not intended as an introduction of French art to the Russian public, and only incidentally of new Russian painting, per se. As Camilla Gray has pointed out, "It was instead an exhibition of works by artists of similar ideas, regardless of nationality,"[49] and as if to prove this, the French and Russian works were hung side by side. While significant pre-Cubist works by Braque were shown, the exhibition was limited primarily to the Fauves Matisse, Vlaminck, and Marquet, Van Gogh and Rouault (of whom Riabushinsky was the first major collector in Europe). There were noticeable changes in the works of the Russian artists. Kuznetsov's and Sarian's paintings were no longer derivative copies of their former French *maîtres*, for example; their tentative primitivism had already taken on an eastern quality, and Kuznetsov's cold symbolist themes were replaced by more ordinary scenes painted in warmer colors. New works were shown by Kuzma Petrov-Vodkin (1878-1939) and Robert Falk (1886-1958),[50] both of whom would later make significant contributions to Russian and Soviet art. The exhibition was a coming-of-age for the young artists and an indication of the new independence of Russian art in general.

Zolotoe Runo devoted special issues to the exhibition in early 1909.[51] One work by Van Dongen was reproduced in color, but it was Kuznetsov who received the magazine's greatest attention, certainly an indication that the earlier disagreements between Kuznetsov and *Zolotoe Runo* had been resolved. For financial reasons, however, and representative of the smaller number of paintings exhibited in the second "Salon," there were far fewer reproductions in these issues than had been the case with the earlier exhibitions sponsored by *Zolotoe Runo*.

The magazine's first two issues of 1909 announced that yet another "Salon Zolotoe Runo" would be held at the end of the year, and it was to be the last.[52] As usual, the accommodation of the exhibition was luxurious, with vases of flowers, a string orchestra, soft carpets, and a buffet. One important difference was the absence of any foreign artists in the exhibition, Riabushinsky's rapidly deteriorating financial condition and the continuing hostility of Morozov and Shchukin no longer permitting the appearance of their works. Instead of providing comparisons between French and Russian art, the exhibition helped point out the differences between those few artists still clinging in part to *Golubaia roza* symbolism and those rapidly adopting a national neo-primitivism. The exhibition was quite successful (there were five thousand visitors), and marked the full appearance of a number of important new artists with some of their best and most distinctive works, including Peter Konchalovsky (1876-1956) and Ilia Mashkov (1881-1944), who made impressive contributions to the "Salon." Older, better-known artists received wider appreciation than they had enjoyed previously: Sarian's striking self-portrait was included in the exhibition (and reproduced in color in *Zolotoe Runo*'s June 1909 issue), and so impressed Shchukin that he commissioned the artist on the spot to paint his son's portrait in a similar style.[53] The two artists contributing the most interesting works, however, were Larionov and Goncharova, who firmly launched their primitivist style at this exhibition. Goncharova had spent the summer of 1908 in the Kaluga countryside where she had been especially struck by peasant toys, pastries, embroideries, and the simplicity of peasant life in general. This experience, combined with her acquaintance with the work of Gauguin and Cézanne in particular, allowed her to produce her own peculiarly personal interpretations of peasant life. Larionov's works were equally notable in their innovations, and although his colors were less vivid than Goncharova's, his formal compositions foreshadowed an incipient Russian abstractionism.

In the very last issue of *Zolotoe Runo,* A. Toporkov attempted to analyze the significance of this final exhibition.[54] Toporkov felt the neo-primitivists who had been given full exposure in the third "Salon" were making an essential united attack on the no longer relevant principles of *Golubaia roza,* and were striving against the artistic fragmentation so prevalent in 1908 and 1909. Attempting to explain why the transition to neo-primitivism was necessary, he wrote that the *Golubaia roza* artists' paintings appeared to have no substance, no "density," and that such works were no longer acceptable; their subjectivity must be overcome, a feeling for actuality must appear; people now wanted to touch reality. To these young artists and their supporters, subjectivity was being attacked in the increasingly abstract works of such artists as Goncharova and Sarian, and an attempt to reach true, if hidden, reality was being made. Toporkov tried to clarify this apparent contradiction by explaining what he saw as the goals of the artists taking part in the most recent *Zolotoe Runo* exhibition:

> We believe that the young artists grouped around *Zolotoe Runo* in their search for new synthetic methods will be able to unite organically both forms of estheticism, to find that magic point where the art of the "creator" becomes the art of the "spectator."[55]

Toporkov expressed remarkable insight about the initial steps of truly twentieth-century art forms. Brecht's "epic theater," Picasso's "Guernica," and Eisenstein's theories of montage all shared the ideal Toporkov described, and it is not surprising that Toporkov himself attempted to find this "magic point" in the industrial art of the 1920's.[56] Toporkov succinctly described what the neo-primitivist artists felt, and what Tasteven and Riabushinsky had unsuccessfully tried to explain themselves.

In his book on Russian Futurism, Vladimir Markov has emphasized the importance of this final exhibition's neo-primitivist stress as being essential to the development of Futurism in Russia:

> Russian primitivism was broad in its extent and complex in its sources. It included
> not only painting and poetry, but music as well (the best example is Stravinsky's "Rite
> of Spring"). Its beginnings were, in one sense, connected with the symbolists' wide
> interest in Slavic mythology, as well as with the theme of the human beast in the Russian
> prose of the period (Leonid Andreev, Artsybashev). In a more specific sense, however,
> Russian primitivism began in December, 1909, with the third exhibition of the *Golden
> Fleece,* which boasted not only examples of the Fauvist line and the abstract use of
> color, but also specimens of folk art, such as lace, popular lithographs *(lubok),* icons,
> and even ornamented cookies. Soon after that, Kulbin wrote about "the art of children
> and prehistoric men" in the same context with manifestations of beauty in nature
> (flowers, crystals). Even the conservative *Apollon* showed interest in children's
> drawings (the article by Bakst in no. 3, 1909).[57]

Despite his recognition of *Zolotoe Runo*'s role in the promotion of
Russian primitivism, Markov failed to note that an interest in children's
art and psychology had been maintained in *Zolotoe Runo* throughout its
entire period of publication.[58] While Kulbin and *Apollon* recognized a
trend, therefore, they were certainly not the first in Russia to discuss the
importance of children's art and *Weltanschauung* in conjunction with
Russian modernism.

Siunnerberg was especially interested in the study of children's art and
in their conception of the world: he wrote enthusiastic reviews of talented
Russian artists' attempts at producing children's books,[59] praised the value
of the artist's seeing the world through children's eyes,[60] and even
personally organized and sponsored an exhibition of children's art in
Petersburg. Maximilian Voloshin wrote a long and interesting article on
the psychological and artistic value of children's games, illustrated by
Dobuzhinsky's drawing of a complicated traditional wooden child's toy.[61]
Zolotoe Runo also gave particular attention in its chronicle to any
developments in adult appreciation of children's art, stressing the importance of such an interest not only for the previously ignored children,
but for the adult himself (especially for the artist), who from such
appreciation would be able to look at a world that was "fantastical and
mysterious...[and] endlessly interesting."[62] Finally, Remizov's *Zolotoe
Runo* stories, particularly those in *Posolon,* often deal with children and
their games, and use children's language.[63]

Jacob Bronowski has suggested that an appreciation of childhood,
accepting it on its own terms, rather than forcing it to conform to adult
conceptions, is an important indication of a truly civilized society.[64] If we
accept Bronowski's idea, and to it add a willingness to see, and indeed a
cultivation of seeing the world through children's eyes as a sign of a society
sophisticated enough to attempt to deal with its deepest emotional and

psychological problems (if not to solve them), we discover that such conditions existed among most of the artistic and literary intelligentsia of Russia by 1910. Within Russian modernist art and literature, no one supported this attempt at viewing the world through the unsophisticated, yet prescient, eyes of children more than did *Zolotoe Runo,* and particularly by means of its exhibitions.

Originally intended to show new Western art to the Russian educated public, the *Zolotoe Runo* exhibitions provided Russian artists with models for a primitivism that could be based on their own experiences and backgrounds, and helped promote the stylistic developments of a number of important and influential Russian artists. Above all, by breaking down previous artistic barriers (as it had done with its support for the *Golubaia roza* artists, who produced the quintessentially symbolist Russian art), *Zolotoe Runo* helped pave the way toward an abstractionism that would predominate in Russian and European art for years to come. *Zolotoe Runo's* 1907 manifesto announcing its change in direction (encouraged by its disillusionment with its "devil" competition) had promised a re-examination of the national question in art and literature. Those who had ridiculed the magazine's decision must have been surprised when it became clear that it was from this very decision that would come the primitivism which was the next major step in the development of modern art as a whole. Despite the abuse and ridicule heaped on it by the press and by individuals who felt themselves considerably more sophisticated and knowledgeable in questions of esthetics than was *Zolotoe Runo,* the magazine and its editors were responsible in their non-purely journalistic activities for a similar achievement whose significance few recognized at the time.

N. Gay, *Sud* (*Le jugement*), *ZR.*, No. 4, 1909

VIII

CONCENTRATION OF FOREIGN INFLUENCES, INTERESTS, AND CONTRIBUTIONS

... the issue of *La Toison d'Or*, 1909 #6 ... devoted its entire art section to Matisse, reproducing thirteen paintings and three drawings, most of them radical, recent works, right up through the big study for the *Dance* ... which must have been finished only a few weeks before ... This was the most complete single publication on Matisse in any language before 1920.

Alfred Barr, Jr., *Matisse*, p. 110.

I

Zolotoe Runo's Foreign Concerns

There is a general misconception that throughout its publication, *Zolotoe Runo* maintained little contact with, and interest in developments in Western European art and literature, especially in comparison with such Russian magazines as *Vesy, Mir Iskusstva,* or *Apollon.* There is some evidence that tends to lend credence to such a view. When *Zolotoe Runo* decided to discontinue its French text, it appeared the magazine had sharply circumscribed its original goal of becoming an important means for acquainting the West with the latest Russian cultural developments. A second apparent indication of *Zolotoe Runo's* orientation toward purely Russian concerns was its change of program in 1907 and the resultant discussion of the "national question" in Russian art and literature, an interest for which the magazine became best known during its last two and a half years of publication.

Although such a characterization of *Zolotoe Runo* as being primarily interested in Russian modernist culture is true on the whole, there are a number of exceptions to this generalization. In fact, the magazine's interest in foreign developments led in *Zolotoe Runo's* artistic section to a serious examination and promotion of modern French art, to an extent equalled by no other contemporary Russian periodical, and paralleling the exhibitions sponsored by the magazine.

The magazine's literary and theoretical sections were not on the whole particularly concerned with foreign literature or esthetics, nor did the editors print many Russian translations of works by foreign writers as *Vesy* often did, for example.[1] *Zolotoe Runo* was particularly impressed by the Polish writers Wyspiański and Przybyszewski, however, and published works by and about them. Stanislaw Wyspiański (1869-1907) was given serious attention in *Zolotoe Runo* only after his death, when the importance of his verse plays in the evolution of the new Polish theater was becoming clear. His "posthumous tragedy" "Sudi" ("Sedzia") was printed in the magazine in 1908,[2] and later that year E. Zagorsky wrote an article describing Wyspianski as the "Prometheus of Young Poland,"[3] and decrying his death as a serious blow to Polish cultural life. *Zolotoe Runo*'s new interest in Wyspianski in 1908 was understandable in that the Polish writer had begun to suggest the rejection of the worship of Art as an absolute, feeling it was time to adopt a new variety of commitment—a problem discussed in almost every issue of *Zolotoe Runo* after mid-1907, of course.

In contrast to Wyspianski, Stanislaw Przybyszewski (1868-1927) was almost a regular contributor to *Zolotoe Runo,* publishing two long poems in 1907,[4] an article on sexual ethics,[5] and a serialized novel that was one of *Zolotoe Runo*'s major publishing ventures during 1909.[6] With the abolition of censorship restrictions, almost all Przybyszewski's works appeared in Russian translations, and during the next few years he himself enjoyed his greatest popularity and renown in Russia.[7] Przybyszewski's ethical and philosophical positions, his typically "decadent" interest in such abnormal psychic states as hysteria, hallucination, and satanic possession, his belief that sexual desire was the demon at the core of man,[8] at times must have been difficult for *Zolotoe Runo*'s editors to endorse in light of their own new program, even though the magazine's initial manifesto had expressed ideas similar to those in Przybyszewski's earlier writings.[9] His popularity among Russian readers was undoubted, however, and *Zolotoe Runo* desperately needed works that would attract a diminishing audience. The magazine's esteem for Przybyszewski was certainly less than that for Wyspianski, but it was based on hard economic fact and the desire by the editors to print whatever the educated Russian public found interesting, or in this case, stimulating.

Other than the attention given these two Polish writers, *Zolotoe Runo*'s literary-philosophical sections published few works by, or dealing with, non-Russian literary figures. A. Malakhieva-Mirovich's essay on Maeterlinck[10] and Balmont's on Wilde[11] were notable in their singularity, and Chulkov's "Pokryvalo Izidy,"[12] ostensibly dealing with Mallarmé, was more concerned with the current "mystical anarchism" debate. Finally, it should be repeated that during its first year of publication, when *Zolotoe*

Runo's critical section published individual reviews of new books, few foreign works were included, and the only other subsequent such review was a long analysis by A. Toporkov in 1909 of a new book by Henri Bergson.[13] Except for some short references to non-Russian literary events in the chronicle, there was little concern in *Zolotoe Runo* for literary developments outside the country unless they were directly related to events within Russia.

In contrast to the almost entirely Russian orientation of its literary department, *Zolotoe Runo's* artistic section expressed a steadily increasing interest in French artistic developments, to a great extent reflective of the magazine's exhibition activities. From the beginning, *Zolotoe Runo* had officially maintained correspondents in Paris who sent sporadic reports on artistic events in the French capital. This rather incidental concern for French art changed considerably in mid-1908, however, when the editors decided to include a number of articles in the magazine aimed at familiarizing its Russian readers with the different currents in contemporary French painting, thereby increasing their appreciation of the French works being exhibited at the *Zolotoe Runo* "Salons." The July-August-September number was the first of a series whose artistic sections were devoted in large part to French art. More than half the issue was given over to an examination of modern French artistic developments, and was published in part as a companion to the first "Salon Zolotoe Runo," with 94 reproductions of works from the exhibition. For those Russians interested in modern French art who had been unable to see the exhibition itself, the issue was invaluable, and it proved to be the best pictorial survey of contemporary French painting printed in Russia until that time. Accompanying the reproductions were explicatory articles by Charles Morice[14] and Maximilian Voloshin,[15] and an essay by Tasteven discussing Impressionism in light of more recent artistic developments.[16]

Significantly, not only was *Zolotoe Runo* beginning to publish articles by Russians on French art, but it also was accepting original and critical essays by French writers and artists. Charles Morice (1861-1919) was an important figure in French artistic life at this time, for example. Morice had been a close friend of Gauguin, had helped him write and publish *Noa-Noa*, Gauguin's account of his experiences in Tahiti, and was later to publish an entire book on the artist. Undoubtedly, it was with some assistance from Morice that *Zolotoe Runo* was able to devote a special issue to Gauguin in January 1909 which included 15 reproductions of his wood sculptures (of particular interest to Russian neo-primitivists because of their similarity to Russian peasant wood-carving), a translation of a *La Plume* article about the artist, and the first installment of a Russian translation of selections from *Noa-Noa*.[17] Later that year an article by Morice himself on Gauguin as a sculptor appeared in *Zolotoe Runo*.[18]

Considering interest in the work of such modern European artists to be widespread in Russia, *Zolotoe Runo* also arranged for the translation of some of Van Gogh's letters.[19] Realizing that Van Gogh's and Gauguin's works were still relatively unknown or misunderstood in Russia, the editors asked the well-known French artist and theoretician Maurice Denis (1870-1943) to write an essay on the two artists. Denis' "Ot Gogena i Van-Goga k klassisizmu" ("From Gauguin and Van Gogh to Classicism"),[20] a description of an incipient neo-classicism based on principles found in the work of Gauguin, Van Gogh, and the Pont Aven School, certainly must have met with some criticism from the Moscow neo-primitivists supported by *Zolotoe Runo*. Denis' relations with the magazine remained cordial, however, and when he visited Moscow in 1909, he stopped by *Zolotoe Runo*'s editorial office and met with Riabushinsky a number of times.[21] Although most of the new artists associated with *Zolotoe Runo* would have agreed more with Gauguin's statement that "to me barbarism is a rejuvenation,"[22] than Denis' that Gauguin was a stage in a movement toward classicism, they could nevertheless welcome Denis and his opinions because of his own intimacy with a French art they appreciated, but felt they were transcending.[23]

While Gauguin and Van Gogh did receive special attention in *Zolotoe Runo*, and other post-Impressionist and Fauve painters were reproduced on the pages of the magazine as well, Henri Matisse was given unusually extensive treatment. As a result of the magazine's June 1909 issue, and because of the prominent exposure Matisse was given in the *Zolotoe Runo* exhibition, Belyi wrote that he "was considered a 'Muscovite' artist"[24] when he visited Russia a few years later. In 1909, Matisse's works were generally still considered shocking, and such Parisian graffiti as "Matisse will drive you crazy! Matisse is worse than absinthe!"[25] could as easily have appeared on walls in Moscow. Matisse's most recent works were being collected avidly by Sergei Shchukin, and exhibited and reproduced by *Zolotoe Runo*, and both created continual uproar and general disapproval from the Moscow public and from the artistic establishment. *Zolotoe Runo* was well known for supporting unpopular artists (as the *Golubaia roza* exhibition had shown) and was expected to do the same for such "wild beasts" as Matisse by the public of what Alfred Barr called "one of the most conservative cities in Europe."[26] Nevertheless, while the Moscow "philistines" might shake their heads at what they considered Shchukin's immodesty in hanging Matisse's explicit nudes in his house, they actively protested *Zolotoe Runo*'s public diffusion of Matisse's work. Even Benois considered Matisse's work "incomprehensible." Taking this into consideration, the magazine's stubborn devotion to the French artist and his admirers is all the more extraordinary.

The Matisse issue included an article by Mercereau (still *Zolotoe*

Runo's official artist-correspondent) on Matisse and contemporary art.[27] More important, however, was the translation of Matisse's own "Notes d'un peintre," the most complete statement about art Matisse ever wrote, and in which he expressed the theory of Fauvism.[28] In a calm, reasoned tone, directly contrasting his bold painting, Matisse discussed color and composition, the heritage of Gauguin, and defined a work of art as a symbol whose principal reference was to the feeling of the artist. He described his hope for art:

> What I dream of is an art of balance, of purity and serenity devoid of troubling or depressing subject matter, an art which might be for every mental worker, be he businessman or writer, like an appeasing influence, like a mental soother, something like a good armchair in which to rest from physical fatigue.[29]

At first reading, there would seem little in such remarks that would appeal to Matisse's Moscow admirers, whereas their *miriskusniki* competitors might accept his statements wholeheartedly, even if they felt it did not apply to Matisse's works or to those of his followers. When these comments are placed together with his concluding lines, however, the esthetic ties between Matisse and those artists exhibiting in the final "Salon Zolotoe Runo" become clearer:

> Rules have no existence outside of individuals: otherwise Racine would be no greater genius than a good professor. Any of us can repeat a fine sentence but few can also penetrate the meaning. I have no doubt that from a study of the works of Raphael or Titian a more complete set of rules can be drawn than from the works of Monet and Renoir but the rules followed by Monet and Renoir were suited to their artistic temperaments and I happen to prefer the smallest of their paintings to all the work of those who have merely imitated the "Venus of Urbino" or the "Madonna of the Goldfinch." Such painters are of no value to anyone because, whether we want to or not, we belong to our time and we share in its opinion, preferences and delusions. All artists bear the imprint of their time but the great artists are those in which this stamp is most deeply impressed. Our epoch for instance is better represented by Courbet than by Flandrin, by Rodin than by Frémiet. Whether we want to or not between our period and ourselves an indissoluble bond is established.... [30]

None of the artists grouped around *Zolotoe Runo* would have disagreed with Matisse's conclusion: to them the situation in Russia seemed exactly as he had described. It was at this time, for example, that Benois was painting his series dealing with Versailles as it looked during the last years of Louis XIV's reign, Bakst was recreating personal visions of archaic Greece, and *Apollon* was preparing to begin publication with what the Moscow artists considered a "retrospective" and "retrogressive" program. There was little doubt in the eyes of *Zolotoe Runo*'s contributors that these artists did not bear the stamp of their time, while the Moscow neo-primitivists did.

More importantly, Matisse's stress on the "indissoluble bond" between an artist and his time, the recognition of which ideally would create
an art of "equilibrium, purity, and tranquillity," had been a central interest
of *Zolotoe Runo* from the time it promised to explore realistic symbolism
and the national question in Russian art and literature. *Golubaia roza* had
reflected pictorially the essence of Russian symbolism, and neo-
primitivism, based on Russian national styles and traditions, was
indicative of the modernist intelligentsia's post-1905 interest in
reestablishing relations with the peasants and with nature. However
spurious these connections between Matisse's theory and *Zolotoe Runo*'s
conception of it with regard to Russian reality may seem, it was certainly
for this reason that the French modernist painters received *Zolotoe Runo*'s
attention. The *Zolotoe Runo* artists valued Matisse for stating a position
with which they agreed, and for creating a new, highly personal art of his
own from which they could learn. In printing the articles by Matisse, Denis,
and Morice, as well as reproductions of the works of Gauguin and Van
Gogh, *Zolotoe Runo* publicly declared that it was maintaining as its goal
the promotion of the newest tendencies in Russian and European art.
Initially, *Zolotoe Runo* had hoped to acquaint Western Europeans with
Russian art. When this proved unfeasible because of economic,
contributional, and technical problems, the magazine altered its program
to some extent, and attempted to familiarize Russians with Western artistic
developments, especially those in France, which had by this time taken a
predominant place in European modernist art. In making this decision,
Zolotoe Runo laid foundations for a wider experience among young
Russian artists and helped move forward Russian art as an independent
entity.

Throughout this final year and a half discussed here, *Zolotoe Runo*'s
interest in foreign artistic developments helped reestablish its public
position as a continually provocative and progressive magazine that
promoted native and foreign artists and movements that few others in
Russia would. The success of what at the time was a controversial
undertaking may be seen in Matisse's later reception in Moscow "as a
'Muscovite' artist"—more than anything else, it was *Zolotoe Runo* which
could be credited with guiding the Russian public to such a general
European level of sophistication and familiarity with the latest currents of
modern art.

The interest in foreign developments so prevalent in *Zolotoe Runo*'s
artistic section found some expression in its musical department as well,
now composed almost entirely of articles by Emily Medtner (who
continued using the pseudonym "Volfing" exclusively). Certainly the most
important work Medtner contributed during this second period of
publication was a series of articles dealing with the 1907 Munich festival of

Wagner's operas. The articles, each characteristically subtitled "notes of a non-Wagnerian," began with a description of Munich, the festival theater, the audiences, and the performers, and finally moved on to evaluate in turn each of the operas performed. He discussed "Tannhäuser" (writing that despite all his criticisms of the production, he had to admit that only a caricature of this opera had ever been given in Moscow), "Die Meistersinger" (described as one of the greatest, and perhaps only, German comedy), "Tristan und Isolde," and finally "Der Ring des Nibelungen."[31] Medtner's essays had formerly dealt with European musical developments in general, and he continued some of his earlier themes in his 1908 *Zolotoe Runo* articles. "Modernizm v muzyke" ("Modernism in Music") dealt with the problem of form in music, this time in conjunction with the ideas of Felix Weingartner, Mahler's replacement as conductor of the Vienna Philharmonic. Once again, Medtner concluded that the "decline of modern music" was due to such musicians and composers as Strauss and Reger.[32] Finally, "Estrada" ("The Stage") discussed stage performance as a whole, the art of the symphony orchestra conductor, and the current phenomenon of *Wunderkinder*.[33] Much of the article consisted of Medtner's own repeating (surprisingly for a "non-Wagnerian") of Wagner's racist ideas about Jews causing a decline of "Aryan" music in Europe: Reger and Strauss were "Jewish-influenced," and in their impact on modern music, the Jewish *Wunderkinder* were considered as pernicious as was Mahler. Except for these outspoken essays Medtner sent from Germany, *Zolotoe Runo*'s musical section at this time was taken up almost exclusively by straightforward reports of Russian musical events.

During this second period of publication, *Zolotoe Runo* did expand its coverage of foreign periodicals and of Russian artistic activities abroad. Summaries of recent issues of *La Chronique des Arts*, the *Bolletino d'Arte*, the *Gazette des Beaux Arts*, and the *Zeitschrift für Bildende Kunst* appeared regularly in the chronicle. Mercereau sent a report on the 1908 Salon d'Automne[34] and noted the French reception of such visiting Russians as Meyerhold and Princess Tenisheva. The editors also quoted compliments made by Western Europeans about the new Russian art, one of the most gratifying of which came from the Viennese critic Ludwig Hevesi:

It wasn't very long ago that people were saying *grattez le Russe*, and you will find a barbarian. Now we understand this more correctly, and in this barbarism we find a great artistic advantage. This fund of raw material, nourished by geographic and ethnographic peculiarities, is a national treasure from which the Russians will be able to draw for a long time to come. A few years ago Western art had to acknowledge the invasion of the Japanese. Last spring at our architectural exhibition the Russians participated and attracted universal attention to themselves. We had to envy them for those remains of barbarism which they have managed to preserve, at a time when in the

West everything has become some kind of common meeting ground. As in the last years of the Roman Empire, we have been invaded by different and strange peoples. And at a time when they wish to learn from us, it turns out that they are becoming our teachers. The barbarian embraces the most refined modernist, and each complements the other.[35]

In the end, this was the very goal *Zolotoe Runo* had hoped to accomplish by increasing its coverage of foreign artistic developments: to bring Russian culture, and especially Russian art, to a level equalling that of Western Europe, to make it a full contributing member of European culture. Despite the continual controversy surrounding the groups and ideas it sponsored, *Zolotoe Runo* did play a fundamental role in promoting the development of the kind of Russian art Hevesi had described.

II

Other Concerns of *Zolotoe Runo*'s Non-Theoretical Sections

Despite this predominance of foreign influences and interests, as well as the emphasis on continuing the discussion of "mystical anarchism" and realistic symbolism during its last two years of publication, *Zolotoe Runo* did continue to print a number of stories, poems, and critical articles similar to those which had appeared in the magazine in 1906 and 1907. The percentage of each issue devoted to fiction and poetry declined steadily after 1907, however, and by the last few issues, the fiction section consisted proportionally of a much smaller number of works. The most prominent contributors were Remizov, Balmont, Sologub, Gorodetsky, Chulkov, Kuzmin, and Riabushinsky, and only a few works by other writers appeared in the magazine. The only major pieces of fiction printed in *Zolotoe Runo* during this second period were Kuzmin's short novel "Nezhnyi Iosif" ("Gentle Joseph") and Przybyszewski's "Den sudnyi" ("Day of Judgment"), both of which appeared serially during 1909. Undoubtedly the decline in the number of contributors to the magazine's fiction and poetry sections was a result of the *Vesy* group's exodus in 1907 and the personal conflicts between the editors and contributors. By early 1909 even Blok had discontinued any participation in, and contribution to, *Zolotoe Runo*. Space previously devoted to *belles-lettres* was more and more given over to the arguments with *Vesy,* to philosophical-speculative essays, and to critical articles on literature which were to a great extent interrelated with the "symbolist debate."

Zolotoe Runo did not change its focus entirely, however, and maintained an interest in as wide a range of subjects as it had during 1906 and 1907. This was particularly true of the magazine's concern with exotica. The artistic section of one entire issue early in 1908 was devoted to Persian art, with 46 illustrations and an article by Tasteven praising the "pantheistic" nature of Persian art, and contrasting it to the differentiation from nature Tasteven saw as being so prevalent in Western art.[36] Similarly, the last issue of 1908 included reproductions of eighteenth-century Russian peasant bone carving accompanied by Uspensky's interpretive essay.[37] Both these topics had obvious relation to *Zolotoe Runo*'s new interest in primitivism, which was finding expression throughout the magazine, and could be seen as inspirational models for Russian artists. Somewhat different in focus were Balmont's interpretive travelogues from Brittany and the Balearic Islands,[38] Boris Zaitsev's sketches from Italy,[39] and Sergei Auslender's account of his visit to Capri.[40] These last three reports continued the descriptive tradition begun during *Zolotoe Runo*'s first two years and had little significance beyond their expression of a simple interest in foreign landscapes, peoples, and customs.

While *Zolotoe Runo*'s artistic section was concerned predominantly with new French art and progressive Russian developments, it did devote several issues to other subjects during 1908 and 1909. The practice of giving entire issues over to individual modern artists was continued, and the June 1908 issue dealt with Pavel Kuznetsov (who probably received more exposure in *Zolotoe Runo* during its four years of publication than did any other single contemporary Russian artist except Vrubel) and included a Kuznetsov self-portrait and an appreciative article by Vasily Milioti.[41] Lanseray was given similar attention later that year, with reproductions of his work, Somov's portrait of him, and Rostislavov's interpretive essay.[42] Other numbers were concerned with more retrospective or purely historical subjects: May 1908 dealt with the artist Iakov Kapkov; May 1909 with Vrubel's watercolors and drawings; April 1909 with Ge; October 1909 with Nikolai Lomtev ("an almost unknown artist"[43]); and the magazine's final issue with the French artist Monticelli. Finally, two issues were devoted to more purely historical topics, one on the collection of miniatures in the Hermitage, and another on Russian enamel ware. Although interest in these historically-oriented subjects appeared to predominate in *Zolotoe Runo*'s artistic section, the magazine's spirit clearly was directed toward the vanguard of contemporary art, and the value these artists from earlier periods and their works had for the further development of modern art was the primary reason they received *Zolotoe Runo*'s attention.

Two issues of *Zolotoe Runo* in particular emphasized that its fundamental allegiance was to modernist art. The first, appearing in January 1908, was a pictorial survey of current exhibitions and included reproductions of works from the Union of Russian Artists, *Venok-Stefanos,* and *peredvizhniki* exhibitions. Refusing to disguise *Zolotoe Runo*'s modernist prejudices, the issue praised the *Stephanos* artists

(especially Aristarkh Lentulov and David Burliuk), while remarking that
the exhibitions of the *peredvizhniki* "become worse and weaker year by
year."[44] Again, it should be repeated that such a pictorial survey of current
exhibitions was attempted by no other Russian periodical, and in this
respect, *Zolotoe Runo's* service to the Russian public interested in art was
unsurpassed. The second special issue appeared in mid-1909 and dealt with
decorative art in the theater. Despite the remarkable innovations of the
miriskusniki and subsequent artists in theatrical design, the general public
still considered the products of such activity second-rate in comparison
with "pure art," and no comprehensive examination of contemporary set
and costume designs for the theater had appeared in Russia until the
Zolotoe Runo issue. It included 68 reproductions, with designs by Korovin
(whose "Don Quixote" set was reproduced in color), Vrubel, Golovin,
Dobuzhinsky, Bakst, Lanseray, Stelletsky, Benois, Sapunov (including his
set and costumes for Meyerhold's still controversial production of Blok's
"Balaganchik"), Sudeikin, Roerich, and Bilibin. Rostislavov wrote an
essay to accompany the illustrations in which he noted the low level of
popular appreciation for set and costume designs, even though many of
them had appeared at various exhibitions over the previous few years. He
concluded with the hope that this situation would soon change and that
theatrical decorative art would receive the attention it deserved.[45] With this
issue *Zolotoe Runo* aided in establishing a public recognition of the value
of theatrical designs as works of art, and of the importance of their
preservation. Even today, the issue is considered a landmark in the
appreciation and preservation of theatrical design.

The remainder of each of *Zolotoe Runo's* issues during this second
two years of publication was taken up almost exclusively by notices and
critical reports typical of the magazine's chronicle of 1906 and 1907.
Developments in the theater were given special attention: Sologub wrote
an enthusiastic review of Isadora Duncan's Moscow performance, and
somewhat later Anastasia Chebotarevskaia wrote rapturously of Duncan's
"Zarathustran" dancing: "...in truth we may regard her as a great
intimation, a beautiful dawn, a joyful prelude to a great, beautiful,
inexpressibly joyful Symphony of the future."[46] Rather less emotional were
reports on Vsevolod Meyerhold's activities in the theater: B. Diks
commented on the director's dramatic accomplishments, Meyerhold
himself contributed selections from his "letters on the theater," and a
summary of a lecture by Meyerhold's associate Nikolai Evreinov was
printed in 1909.[47] More general in their discussion of the Petersburg theater
were Sergei Auslender's "Pisma iz Peterburga" ("Letters from Petersburg,"
to a certain extent a continuation of Dymov's articles of 1906), which did
give special attention to the achievements, failures, and controversies

within the Komissarzhevskaia Theater, however, and which appeared from the end of 1907 until early 1909.

Except for Medtner's articles on the Munich Wagner festival, *Zolotoe Runo*'s musical section consisted of reportage similar to Auslender's. With the magazine's reorientation in 1907, the editors had promised that original pieces of music would also appear on its pages, but the attempt proved abortive, and only one piece of music, Nikolai Medtner's score for a poem by Belyi, appeared in early 1908. Emily Medtner himself wrote a few other essays on such topics as Rakhmaninov as a performer, on the theory of musical criticism, and on the opening of a new musical publishing house in Moscow. The anonymous "Moskovskaia muzykalnaia khronika" ("Moscow Musical Chronicle") appeared in 1908 and 1909 and reported on such events as the Russian opera season in Paris, the musical promise of the young Stravinsky, and described Scriabin's "Poem of Ecstasy," for example, as "an event of outstanding importance, all the more so because in no other contemporary work of art do we find so clearly expressed the incarnation of the artistic strivings of our time."[48] The chronicle's severely modernist position was repeated in two essays contributed by Nikolai Zhiliaev (1888-1938) about Rimsky-Korsakov. Zhiliaev, a friend and associate of Scriabin, wrote a surprisingly critical obituary of Rimsky on his death in 1908, and repeated his remarks a few months later in reviewing a production of Rimsky's "Zolotoi petushok" ("Le Coq d'Or"), which he felt should never have been staged in the first place.[49] Although this type of negative attitude toward the now more "traditionalist" composers had not been true of *Zolotoe Runo* earlier, by the end of 1909 it was representative of the magazine's general tone of almost hysterical youthful rejection of anything not blatantly modernist, an attitude inflamed by the appearance of the "retrogressive" *Apollon*.

During *Zolotoe Runo*'s second two years of publication, the magazine did experience some deterioration both in technical and literary quality. The continual loss of contributors hurt the magazine seriously, and by 1909 the literary section had to rely on a small group of writers, who were with only a few exceptions closely connected with the esthetic theories of "mystical anarchism." Since most of them were necessarily preoccupied with battling the "esthetic" tendencies of the *Vesy* group, the quality and extent of their non-theoretical work for *Zolotoe Runo* suffered correspondingly. Undoubtedly, *Zolotoe Runo*'s editors hoped to compensate for the decline in the number of short fiction and poetry contributions by publishing the two novels by Kuzmin and Przybyszewski in rather more installments than might otherwise have been necessary. The chronicle suffered in much the same way: it was the individual correspondents who had provided a great deal of the section's personal insight and entertaining commentary during 1906-7, and their loss forced the editors to turn the chronicle into what was generally an anonymous recounting of Russian cultural developments and a summarizing of articles appearing in other publications, foreign as well as Russian. *Zolotoe Runo's* entire literary section, with few exceptions, suffered from the grim necessity of carrying on the debate with *Vesy* about the future of symbolism, to an extent that more time and effort were taken up debating where symbolism was going than in moving it anywhere.

Zolotoe Runo's artistic section, on the other hand, continued to be as brash and progressive as it had been before the magazine's reduction in format, and with the exception of fewer color reproductions and illustrations in the text, remained equally impressive. The useful retrospective articles on living and only recently dead artists, the issues devoted to formerly unknown painters, and the examination of exotic and ignored national primitivist traditions were equal in quality to anything the magazine had attempted in 1906 and 1907. But it was certainly *Zolotoe Runo's* concern for foreign artistic developments that remains most impressive. Modern French artists had received attention from Russian periodicals before, of course; one of the last issues of *Mir Iskusstva* had even devoted some space to Gauguin's works. But no one had given the exposure to the post-Impressionists and Fauves that *Zolotoe Runo* had, and no one was as active in propagating their work among the Russian public in the face of "philistine" opposition, to which *Zolotoe Runo* had become accustomed from the beginning of publication. In adopting such a position and maintaining it, *Zolotoe Runo* helped change the face of Russian art and bring it into European art as a full and contributing member which could even, as Hevesi remarked, provide an example from which the West could learn.

IX

DECLINE, "RETROGRESSION," FAREWELL

I

Zolotoe Runo's Decline and Its Attack on *Apollon*

The academy of formalism has united with the academy of historicism and created *Apollon.*

Sergei Gorodetsky, "Formotvorchestvo," *ZR,* 1909, No. 10, 57.

As has been noted, *Zolotoe Runo* had never been financially successful, either in its non-journalistic activities or in the publishing of the magazine itself, whose economic problems grew steadily more serious. Although it is unlikely that any magazine such as *Zolotoe Runo* could have been financially independent in Russia, one major reason for *Zolotoe Runo*'s increasing financial difficulties was the rise of a number of periodicals which shared some of *Zolotoe Runo*'s artistic concerns and which appealed to the same audience. While competition with *Vesy* in literary and philosophical matters had split *Zolotoe Runo*'s readers along primarily ideological lines, the magazine's artistic competitors usually dealt with non-controversial topics which did, however, appeal to specialized readers not always satisfied with the general, often all-inclusive concerns of *Zolotoe Runo.*

In its attempt to present both modern and forgotten aspects of Russian and Western art, *Zolotoe Runo* found itself from its inception dealing with some topics closely related to the major interests of the Petersburg journals *Khudozhestvennye Sokrovishcha Rossii (Artistic Treasures of Russia),* and *Starye Gody (Olden Times).* In these two periodicals *Zolotoe Runo* found continuing competition for readers interested in earlier periods of art. *Zolotoe Runo*'s decision to place as much emphasis on non-contemporary art as it did was certainly not a sound one economically, particularly during its final two years of publication. Yet it should be remembered that *Zolotoe Runo* conceived of itself as fostering, promoting, and representing the most progressive artistic interests of contemporary Russia. One notable feature of this

period was the rediscovery and appreciation (if not emulation, certainly) of
the art of the not-too-distant past, an interest first given expression only a
few years before in *Mir Iskusstva*. Becoming more widespread after 1905,
this enthusiasm for "antiques" was a means of escaping from the
disappointments of the present, whether political, ideological, or in some
cases, artistic. It began as an impulse toward rescuing art ignored and even
reviled during the ideological dominance of the utilitarianism of the 1860s-
1890s, but after 1905, such interest

> was considered a sign of good taste...collections of antiques were made. Apartments
> and villas were filled with period furniture, porcelain, bronzes, engravings. In
> Petersburg there appeared one after another societies, circles, commissions, having as
> their goal the study and preservation of the monuments of Russian art.[1]

Zolotoe Runo reported on these activities and supported them without
hesitation, and never gave anything but praise to its two main competitors
in Petersburg. *Zolotoe Runo* considered itself both complementary and
supplementary to the two magazines, never competitive. Unfortunately, to
the specialized audience counted on to support such publishing ventures,
Starye Gody and *Khudozhestvennye Sokrovishcha Rossii* were more
relevant than was the more expensive and only intermittently interesting
Zolotoe Runo. By adopting a broad artistic program, *Zolotoe Runo*'s art
editors found themselves attempting to appeal to an audience significantly
more sophisticated both in its means and in its tastes than had been the case
before 1905, when *Mir Iskusstva* was being published. While *Zolotoe Runo*
stood alone journalistically in its promotion of modern Russian and
French art, this was clearly not the case with pre-modernist art (although
such issues as the one on Persian miniatures were more closely related to
modernist artistic "searching" than to the retrospective appreciations
typical of *Starye Gody*). Because of the editors' unwillingness to circum-
scribe *Zolotoe Runo*'s artistic program, the consequent competition
Zolotoe Runo had to face with the two Petersburg magazines only
deepened its financial difficulties.

Similarly, Kiev's *V Mire Iskusstv (In the World of Art)* and *Iskusstvo i
Pechatnoe Delo (Art and Printing)* were warmly welcomed by *Zolotoe
Runo* and both led to serious competition for the Moscow magazine in the
Ukraine. A decidedly more significant rival was *Apollon,* whose first issue
appeared in Petersburg at the end of 1909. All this publishing activity
indicated the growing technical competence of a Russian periodical press
able to produce, and attract audiences for, a number of magazines and
newspapers dealing with modernist art and literature. Inversely, by further
splintering the modernist periodical reading audience, this development
only compounded *Zolotoe Runo*'s economic problems.

Zolotoe Runo's unviable financial condition had become well known to the public, and in 1907, for example, V. Burenin described the situation in *Novoe Vremia:*

> According to [the editor's] report, in the last year the journal's expenses were something like 80,000 [rubles], but the subscription was about 11,000 [rubles], which would mean that in the first year the editor spent 70,000 [rubles]. This whole business could continue on as it began, but it is impossible not to be surprised at the editor's decision to continue it. Apparently this editor is a hero of generosity. Apparently, he possessed not only the printed *Zolotoe Runo*, resulting in a 70,000 loss, but a real golden fleece as well, which provided greater riches.[2]

As Burenin's comments suggest, and as is to be expected, *Zolotoe Runo*'s success or failure was closely tied to Riabushinsky's own financial condition. Since the magazine was financed almost entirely by Riabushinsky's fortune, and since any possibility of its becoming self-supporting grew increasingly less likely with the passage of time, Riabushinsky's own financial fate determined that of his magazine.

Riabushinsky continued spending money lavishly. A great deal was required for the construction of his villa, and afterwards he made it a center for Moscow's "bohemia" with his spectacular (and costly) parties. He continued what he considered his necessary role as Maecenas and patron of the arts: his project for a "Palace of the Arts" was a notable failure, and on the tenth anniversary of the founding of the Moscow Art Theater he donated one thousand rubles to the theater, more than did any other contributor on the occasion. Eventually, Riabushinsky's financial prospects became so bleak that discontinuation of *Zolotoe Runo* became unavoidable. Not even Riabushinsky's family would help him in maintaining its publication.[3] His oldest brother Pavel was already supporting two newspapers, his own weekly *Utro Rossii (The Morning of Russia,* 1907, 1909-18),[4] and the political and literary weekly *Rannee Utro (Early Morning,* 1907-18), for which he provided financial aid. The other brothers considered *Zolotoe Runo* not only embarrassing, but as an economically unsuccessful venture, inexcusable. Riabushinsky's profligacy in general, which they considered deplorable enough, and the problems plaguing *Zolotoe Runo*'s publication from the beginning convinced them of the magazine's hopeless situation. Several issues appeared late, and were accompanied by a number of excuses: strikes among the print shop workers (1907, No. 3), technical difficulties (1907, No. 6), and failure to meet publishers' deadlines because of insufficient time for preparation (1908, No. 6). Attempts to solve these recurring problems were made by combining several issues, but even these appeared later than promised. Many of these difficulties are understandable in light of the serious upheavals continuing in Russian society during the magazine's first period of publication, and were compounded by the fact that the entire magazine was printed within Russia, rather than abroad (as *Mir Iskusstva* had been), so that as a consequence it felt the full brunt of the disruptive revolutionary activity.[5]

Zolotoe Runo had made a continuing effort to attract subscribers throughout its existence, but never with great success. Hoping to counteract the magazine's growing deficit, the editors announced at the end of 1908 that the subscription rate would be reduced from 15 to 12 rubles, and that a ten percent discount would be given to schools.[6] Attempts were made in conjunction with other Russian modernist publications to encourage subscriptions during the first years, allowing discounts to those already subscribing to *Vesy,* for example.[7] So many more issues of the magazine were printed each month than were sold, however, that from the last issue of 1906 until *Zolotoe Runo*'s ceasing publication, new subscribers were promised all the magazine's back issues.[8]

Other problems plagued the magazine. Advertising, which it had been hoped would yield some income (rates ran from 100 rubles for a full page to 25 rubles for a quarter-page), was discontinued after appearing in the first few issues. Difficulties with the reinstated censorship became more prevalent, and one issue was seized with no explanation.[9] Finally, on a number of occasions, *Zolotoe Runo* seems to have been the target of rumors, practical jokes, and even sabotage by some of its competitors and enemies.[10] Added to these technical difficulties in the magazine's production and distribution was the fall in circulation following the withdrawal of the writers later associated with *Vesy*. This was compounded in mid-1909 by the *miriskusniki*'s abandoning *Zolotoe Runo,* accusing Riabushinsky and his magazine of encouraging artistic licentiousness and individualistic arbitrariness.[11] To most of these artists, it seemed that Benois' warning of the danger of individualistic anarchism had found realization on the pages of *Zolotoe Runo.* When the new *Apollon* appeared in Petersburg in the autumn of 1909, the *miriskusniki,* as well as most of those literary figures who had left *Zolotoe Runo* to contribute primarily to *Vesy,* welcomed it wholeheartedly. By the end of 1909, *Zolotoe Runo*'s venomous debate with *Vesy* had ended, and in December *Vesy* discontinued publication. By that time, *Zolotoe Runo* had discovered what it considered dangerous "retrogressivism" in *Apollon,* however, and during the last few months of its existence, carried on a one-sided battle against the Petersburg magazine.

Apollon (Apollo, 1909-17) was founded, edited, and published by Sergei Makovsky, a former *Zolotoe Runo* contributor,[12] and its reception within the Russian press was considerably different from that given its modernist predecessors:

...the general attitude toward the symbolist press had undergone a certain change. The novelty of the modernist movement had worn off, the new critical values were appreciated and often accepted, the enrichment of the Russian poetic style was acknowledged, and such a serious *tolstyi zhurnal* as *Vestnik Evropy* did not hesitate to welcome the new arrival.[13]

In accordance with the mood of its reception, *Apollon* adopted no firm position, and had no interest in persuading or teaching the public, as most previous modernist periodicals had: its goals were described as "purely esthetic, independent of...[any] ideological shades (social, ethical, religious)"[14] and it conceived of itself as being a creative accommodation of divergent views. It hoped to give a "full picture of contemporary literature and art"[15] both in Russia and abroad:

> Giving an outlet to all new sprouts of artistic thought, *Apollon* would like to call its own only the strict search for beauty, only the free, harmonious, and clear, only strong and living art beyond the bounds of the sickly disintegration of the spirit and pseudo-innovation.[16]

Apollon considered itself more directly in the tradition of *Mir Iskusstva* than of its more immediate predecessors, *Vesy* and *Zolotoe Runo*. As Denis Mickiewicz has pointed out, *Apollon* felt a greater affinity with the "less dogmatic youth" of Petersburg, with the tastes and cosmopolitan élan of Diaghilev and Benois, an antidote to the daring of the Moscow avant-gardists: "Not as lavish as the *Golden Fleece*, *Apollon* was more reminiscent in its restrained *Schlichtheit* of the age of Pushkin."[17]

The new magazine avoided a stand on partisan modernist issues, and found it possible to attract both a large number and a variety of names to its list of contributors, excluding only the neo-primitivist artists and those writers still intimately connected with *Zolotoe Runo*'s editing and publishing. Viacheslav Ivanov was chairman of *Apollon*'s executive committee, and its editorial board included Annensky, Makovsky, Kuzmin, Blok, and Gumilev. *Apollon* was determined to "assert rather than destroy norms" and such a position attracted men like Benois, Bakst, Blok, and Voloshin, all of whom were by now sated by continual innovation and change, and were searching (often desperately) for substance and permanence.

It is not surprising that *Zolotoe Runo*, believing itself the vanguard of modernist art, did not give *Apollon* a friendly reception, and criticized what it called the new journal's "ideological timidity and banality." Tasteven reviewed *Apollon*'s first issues, questioning what he considered the new magazine's certainty that it was "the most progressive, last word in the area of art,"[18] and asking what connections *Apollon* truly had with modern artistic life:

The directors of the journal are convinced that they are fighting for the future, but in this they are cruelly mistaken: repeating the old thesis of the independence of art from "ethical and religious principles," the authors clearly show that they are alien to the whole movement of modern art, to all its urgent and innermost problems; they simply revive once again the old theory of art for art's sake ... the dogma of the "primacy of art." This isn't even the estheticism of *Vesy,* which, in all its reaction, at least had a moral-philosophical position; this is the old theory of "l'art pour l'art." We say that art will perish if it does not create a new synthetic form, if it does not overcome the tragedy of individualism. Instead of an answer, they demand from us that we sing hymns. "The time has come. It is time to learn to compose hymns, so that we can greet the promised sunrise in the appropriate manner. It is time to rush from the stuffy atmosphere"—this is what Benois, one of the main inspirers of the journal, dreams.[19]

Tasteven was referring to Benois' essay "V ozhidanii gimna Apollonu" ("Awaiting the Hymn to Apollo"), which had followed the editors' introduction to *Apollon*'s first issue.[20] Tasteven attacked Benois for not considering the philosophical and esthetic bases of his position:

One cannot decide the question of future forms of art without touching on one hand the internal changes in the religious-moral structure of the contemporary spirit, and on the other the external social forms, among which is possible the destruction of the discord between beauty and life, about which Benois dreams so poetically.[21]

Tasteven felt that "in general, *Apollon* carries us twenty years or so backwards, to the period of the first genesis of decadence,"[22] and he concluded that, judging from its first issue, "*Apollon* is completely foreign not only to the new strivings of Russian art, but in general to all its organic developments and urgent tasks."[23]

Tasteven's attitude was representative of that of *Zolotoe Runo* as a whole toward *Apollon* and above all, to the "retrogressivism" the new magazine was felt to represent. Even before the appearance of *Apollon,* perhaps as a result of the lack of support *Zolotoe Runo* had received for its exhibitions from any but fervently *avant-garde* artists, every department of *Zolotoe Runo* carried attacks on this growing "retrogressivism" which was subsequently found to be intensified in *Apollon.* In April 1909, Vasily Milioti described the *miriskusniki* as having inherited the position within Russian art that the *peredvizhniki* had occupied only a few years before.[24] The strongest criticism of "Apollonizm" was made by Gorodetsky and directed at Benois, who now symbolized the new magazine's esthetic position for *Zolotoe Runo.* Ostensibly reviewing Benois' series of newspaper articles, "Khudozhestvennye pisma" ("Art Letters"), Gorodetsky instead wrote a bitter, at times hysterical, personal attack on Benois for being intellectually dishonest in pretending to be knowledgeable about and enthusiastic for modern art when he in fact despised it.[25] He discussed Benois' negative attitude toward the Matisse school, and concluded that

Benois himself was as anachronistic as were his ideas and his friends. Gorodetsky expanded this theme in a later article, "Formotvorchestvo" ("Form-Creation"), an examination of backwardness in Russian art and literature in general, which he found centered among previous Russian modernists around the Petersburg *miriskusniki* and *Apollon*, frozen at a stage beyond which Russian art and literature had already passed.[26]

Behind these attacks on *Apollon* was *Zolotoe Runo*'s sincere belief that there was nothing in the new journal leading and contributing to future Russian art, and that the danger of such a situation becoming widespread was frightful. Not only did "Russia not need such a journal,"[27] but its existence could in fact be harmful, especially since it was becoming clear to *Zolotoe Runo* by the end of 1909 that it would be unable to continue its own publication much longer. Much of the tone of *Zolotoe Runo*'s attacks on *Apollon* may be explained by what had probably become an equivalency in the editors' minds between the new magazine's apparent "retrogressivism" and the "philistinism" which *Zolotoe Runo* felt was growing ever stronger in Russia.

We have seen this sense of isolation in the struggle with the "philistines" in Riabushinsky's article on the first "Salon Zolotoe Runo." It was later expressed even more forcefully in the magazine, and on one occasion even Briusov, certainly not greatly esteemed in the magazine's editorial offices, was defended from a "barbaric...provincial" crowd in Moscow.[28] The growing power of the censorship had intensified *Zolotoe Runo*'s sense of desperation, and the forbidding of productions of Rimsky-Korsakov's "Le Coq d'Or" and Wilde's "Salomé" prompted the editors' comment that "all this administrative zeal is causing serious fear for the fate of Russian art."[29]

Two other major confrontations with "retrogressive philistinism" took place at much the same time as *Apollon*'s appearance. The first was the police's seizure and confiscation of some privately exhibited paintings by Goncharova at the instigation of a Moscow newspaper's notice calling them "decadent and pornographic," which Larionov reported in detail in *Zolotoe Runo*.[30] Considerably more important for understanding the quality of *Zolotoe Runo*'s reaction to *Apollon* is the eulogy to Vera Komissarzhevskaia (1864-1910) published in the last issue. Komissarzhevskaia had been considered the "poetic image" of Russian modernist drama, and after its opening in Petersburg in 1904, her theater became the center of dramatic experiments by modernist writers, artists, and composers. With the church censorship's banning of her production of "Salomé" in the fall of 1908, her theater was forced to close, and soon thereafter, while on tour attempting to raise money to reopen the theater, she died of smallpox. Her relations with *Zolotoe Runo* had always been friendly and warm,[31] and it is not surprising that her death should have

been taken by *Zolotoe Runo* as another serious blow to Russian
modernism:

> You, you all-Russian giggling *poshlost,* having killed Her impetuous theater, have
> also killed Her. You do not understand this. The coffin was barely lowered into the
> grave when you prepared masks for yourself and tuned up violins for dancing, even
> before the first sun had set and the first night fallen—you were already dancing, a
> mummer, and grimacing to please your baseness.
>   How terrible, how awful it would be, if the earth were not lit up by such flames as
> Vera Fedorovna Komissarzhevskaia.[32]

The death of Komissarzhevskaia, and of Vrubel soon thereafter, seemed to
Zolotoe Runo unparalleled disasters for Russian culture. Though *Apollon*
also mourned Komissarzhevskaia's loss, *Zolotoe Runo* nevertheless
faulted it for betraying modernism to expedience, for retreating in the face
of ignorance.

While the extent and quality of *Zolotoe Runo*'s reaction to *Apollon*
may best be understood in light of its attitude toward Russian "philistinism" in general, one final development, the change of focus of Russian
culture from Petersburg to Moscow, should be considered. The energy,
brashness, and presumption associated with Moscow found its best
representative in *Zolotoe Runo*. Similarly, *Apollon* was equated with the
northern capital's refinement, sophistication, and respect for past traditions. That *Zolotoe Runo* possessed this "Moscow consciousness" is
clear from an article about Vrubel, "Moskva i demon" ("Moscow and the
Demon"), which Chulkov wrote after visiting Moscow (from Petersburg)
in April and May 1909.[33] He asked rhetorically what Vrubel's connection
with Moscow was, and answered that it was there Vrubel first exhibited his
"Demon," that it was Moscow's Tretiakov Gallery which first bought his
works for exhibition, and that the artist had been given little attention by
Petersburg's *Mir Iskusstva,* to whom his "spirit" always seemed strange.[34]
Identifying Vrubel with Moscow, and by implication, *Zolotoe Runo,*
Chulkov summarized the significance of his visit from the capital:

> The cold and mocking Petersburg is unable to reconcile itself to the provincialism
> of Moscow, but in provincialism there is sincerity, and this sincerity, unbearable in
> everyday life, unexpectedly becomes beneficial soil for an exceptional [person], for a
> genius.
>   In Vrubel there is no longer any irony, no dandyism, no metropolitan foppishness:
> this is a provincialism which with one gesture wipes the smile from the face of the most
> refined mocker and skeptical epicure.
>   The cold smile is proper in Petersburg, but in the [country] you don't smile in such
> a way. Moscow is still a [country] town; it grew firmly into the earth and Vrubel's genius
> is from the earth; his soul is not woven from fog.[35]

Zolotoe Runo had firm ideological reasons for opposing the existence and publication of Apollon, yet as we have seen, much of this opposition arose from circumstantial emotional and geographical considerations. Even though many of those who wrote for Zolotoe Runo during its last few years of publication were from Petersburg (Chulkov, Ivanov, Blok), it is clear that even they saw in Moscow a strength lacking in the over-sophistication of the capital. Apollon could have existed only in Peters-burg, and did continue publication there until the 1917 revolutions, maintaining in its own fashion the traditions of modernist Russian periodicals. Nevertheless, it was in Moscow that Russian art and literature continued to develop most freely and spontaneously, unhindered by the "forms" demanded by Petersburg "Apollonizm." The vanguard of Russian modernism, of which Zolotoe Runo was an essential part, continued its existence in Moscow rather than Petersburg. Although Zolotoe Runo would be outlived by Apollon, it was from the Moscow magazine that the Russian modernist art and literature of the 1920s would draw their tradition.

II

Farewell and Post-Mortems

> Zolotoe Runo, that journal no one needs.
> Andrei Belyi, Vospominaniia o Bloke, p. 556.

In its title itself the journal projected its goal—the stubborn search for that same Golden Fleece which is hidden not in some mysterious Colchis, but here in the depths of the Russian national soul.
> "Ot redaktsii," ZR, 1909, No. 12, 105.

Zolotoe Runo's decision to cease publication came abruptly, and with no warning. Throughout 1909 a number of prospective contributions were listed in each monthly issue. As late as the July-August-September number, the editors were promising articles "by a series of French theoreticians and artists," including Denis, Morice, and Rodin;[36] stories and articles by Remizov, Balmont, Sologub, and Auslender were men-tioned by title as future contributions, and the same was done for poems by Ivanov, Blok, Kuzmin, Gorodetsky, and Chulkov; finally, a portrait of Kuzmin by Somov was promised for sometime in the indefinite future. Almost none of these appeared in Zolotoe Runo, and Kuzmin's portrait was eventually reproduced in Apollon in 1910. The editors obviously hoped to continue Zolotoe Runo's publication as long as possible, and the high quality of the magazine's last few issues gave no indication of imminent demise: the June issue on Matisse and the July-August-September issue on decorative art in the theater were two of the best-produced and most successful numbers of the magazine. By late autumn it became clear that serious problems were not being solved by *Zolotoe Runo*'s editors, however: the October issue was not published until after the end of January 1910, and did not ask, as had earlier ones, for future subscriptions. The final double issue appeared only after the deaths of Komissarzhevskaia and Vrubel some weeks later in April, and included an appended notice from the editors announcing their decision to discontinue the magazine's publication.

Certainly pressure from Riabushinsky's brothers played an important role in convincing him to close the magazine, as did his own financial situation, which forced him within a year to auction off a number of works from his personal art collection. Undoubtedly of contributing importance was *Vesy*'s demise in December 1909. In spite of its own apparent vitality, *Vesy* had undergone a serious deterioration during the previous year. Briusov had withdrawn as an active editor in February 1909, and had disclaimed responsibility for any articles in *Vesy* except for those appearing over his own signature.[37] He had in fact been losing interest in the journal for a number of years, had begun publishing in such "thick" journals as *Mir Bozhii* and *Obrazovanie,* and upon leaving *Vesy,* he joined the staff of Peter Struve's *Russkaia mysl.*[38] Balmont announced in June that he would no longer continue to contribute to *Vesy,* "considering its role as a journal completely played out."[39] With the unsatisfactory conclusion of the *Vesy-Zolotoe Runo* debate, and with the loss of interest in the magazine on the part of Briusov and several other writers, the publisher Poliakov decided that *Vesy* had outlived its usefulness. *Vesy*'s farewell must have been read with more than a little interest by *Zolotoe Runo*'s editors, particularly since the final notice from *Vesy* attempted to explain the reasons for the decision:

> These two missions of *Vesy* (the promotion of new ideas, the cultivation of young talent) as a result created "the symbolist movement" in Russia, organized it, transformed symbolism from being a subject of rejection and repudiation into an all-penetrating cultural development, rejected on principle by no one any longer ...
>
> While the problem posed by *Vesy* remained unsolved, *Vesy* did not fear to go forward. Its external enemies did not increase, but decreased with time. Its path led from complete rejection to an almost complete recognition, to the triumph of ideas dear to it. We think and announce that in this triumph of ideas is included the basic reason for the present discontinuation of *Vesy.*
>
> *Vesy* was a sluice which was necessary up until the time when there merged the two intellectual standards of the age, and it became useless when this was finally achieved by its own activity. At the same time as the victory of the idea of symbolism in the very form in which it was professed and had to be professed by *Vesy,* the journal itself became unnecessary. The goal was attained and *eo ipso* the means are unnecessary! .. [40]

Zolotoe Runo might have questioned *Vesy*'s goals as well as the extent of its success in achieving them, but *Vesy*'s statement that it had become "unnecessary" must have struck a note of sympathy within its competitor. *Zolotoe Runo* stumbled along for a few months longer than did *Vesy*, but it was clear that it suffered a similar malaise. Interestingly enough, although *Zolotoe Runo* did not comment on *Vesy*'s demise, it did have the last word in their polemic in Chulkov's notice on *Vesy*, which appeared in *Apollon* in July 1910. In it, Chulkov wrote that after 1906 (when *Vesy* began its sharpest criticism of *Zolotoe Runo*), "the journal stopped being interesting and significant: it was no longer a living personality, nor an ideological whole...."[41] With its competitor gone, and with *Apollon* apparently promoting positions inimical to both Moscow modernist journals, *Zolotoe Runo* must have considered its continued existence essential for the future development of Russian modernist culture. Unfortunately, this proved impossible.

Zolotoe Runo's final issue embodied all the contradictions present in the magazine from its inception. Its art section was devoted to Adolph-Joseph-Thomas Monticelli (1824-1886), a French Second Empire painter who had little to do with modern Russian artistic movements. The issue's literary and critical essays were decorated with designs by Roerich, the former *miriskusnik*, and Utkin, whose work had remained stylistically much the same as when he exhibited with *Golubaia roza*. This montage of styles contrasted directly with the distaste shown in the issue's chronicle for the "philistines," Benois, and *Apollon*. One peculiar coincidence of this last issue was that it appeared soon after Vrubel's death, another serious psychological blow to the editors' morale. *Zolotoe Runo* had dedicated its first issue to Vrubel, and strangely enough found itself closing with his death. To *Zolotoe Runo* Vrubel had continued to be the true genius of modern Russian art and as late as May 1909 the magazine's artistic section dealt exclusively with his drawings and watercolors. *Zolotoe Runo* had come to identify Vrubel's battle for the acceptance of his art with itself and its own struggle against philistinism and backwardness. The concluding lines of Gorodetsky's eulogy for Vrubel were intended as much for *Zolotoe Runo*'s loss as for Vrubel's: "Woe to you, Russia and the entire world, if you lower into the ground your creators after bringing them to such a state."[42]

It is surprising that in light of the continuing conflicts and disappointments *Zolotoe Runo* had experienced throughout its publication, its farewell notice was no more bitter than it was, that it was not filled with the kind of invective the magazine had directed at *Vesy* and *Apollon*. Instead, it was a subdued and rather self-satisfied summary of what the magazine's editors felt they had accomplished during the previous four years of publication, and included little of the braggadocio for which *Zolotoe*

Runo's opponents had so often criticized it. Following *Vesy*'s example, the
editors explained that they would attempt to clarify how well the goals
Zolotoe Runo had set for itself had been achieved. Recounting the period
of sharp social and political crisis during which the magazine had
appeared, and with the advantage of hindsight, the editors wrote that "in
no way ignoring the connection of art with society," the magazine "set its
mind on being the representative of all branches of pure art in Russia . . ."[43]
They noted that artists associated with Petersburg as well as Moscow had
been participants in the magazine, and described with special pride the
"gallery of portraits" *Zolotoe Runo* had commissioned.[44]

The editors next attempted to summarize *Zolotoe Runo*'s relationship with the other artistic groups in Russia. While not denying its
connections with the accomplishments of *Mir Iskusstva*, the editors
reiterated their opinion that

> the formula of "estheticism" and "historicism" prevailing then in literature and painting
> must inevitably lead Russian art to a blind alley, enclose it in an ivory tower and deprive
> it of its connections with the great masters of the West.[45]

It was for this reason, the editors explained, that *Zolotoe Runo*
undertook the task of providing public exposure for the new currents
within Russian painting ("to throw new light on the legacies of Vrubel and
Musatov"[46]) and to acquaint Russian society with modern Western art, a
program occurring in two stages, represented by the *Golubaia roza* show
on one hand, and the "Salon Zolotoe Runo" on the other. Conscious of its
duty to the requirements of the new Russian art, the editors continued,
Zolotoe Runo felt it had to become the champion of young Russian
painters, "standing in opposition to Petersburg estheticism,"[47] and of
necessity reexamining the theoretical bases and foundations of the
prevalent world-view of Russian art.

The editors noted that a similar task had been undertaken in the
magazine's literary section, and they prided themselves on understanding
and clarifying the close connections between religious experience, realistic
symbolism, and synthetic art: "[*Zolotoe Runo*] recognized that for the
revival of art it is necessary to pass from purely negative subjective
individualism to a new religious life-confirmation."[48] Although disappointed that the subsequent discussion of this problem had degenerated
into a polemic, the editors felt it was to their credit to have initiated the
examination of the ideas of realistic symbolism.

Recounting the names of the writers who had appeared on *Zolotoe
Runo*'s pages, and mentioning the titles of some of their best-known
works, the essay concluded optimistically. Refusing to make any interpretive evaluation of *Zolotoe Runo*'s activity because of a lack of proper

perspectives, the editors recapitulated their experiences and their hope for the future:

> Parting with our readers, we in no way feel ourselves to be tired. Neither constant battle, which we have carried on for more than three years for the future art so dear to us, nor the enormous technical difficulties of publishing the artistic section; neither the systematic confiscation of our issues and publications by the censorship, nor the indifference and campaign of the newspaper critics hindered our energy. But now we feel clearly that the currents we defended in the area of literature as well as in the area of painting have already grown sufficiently strong that they will be able to express themelves independently in the future, and that *Zolotoe Runo* has fulfilled its mission in this respect. Ending up our four-year labor, we leave with a calm certainty that nothing will be able to suppress and destroy those artistic principles for which *Zolotoe Runo* struggled.[49]

Considering the hysterical tone of much printed in *Zolotoe Runo*'s last few issues, this farewell is unusually subdued, conciliatory, and modest. It might have been expected to be a great deal more self-congratulatory in its summary of what it considered *Zolotoe Runo*'s very considerable achievements, especially in light of the "presumptuous" editorial notices made at the magazine's inception and at the time of its change of direction. Its modesty was particularly notable in comparison with the more ostentatious self-praise of *Vesy*'s final editorial. *Zolotoe Runo*'s farewell attacked no one, and made a point of offending no one; as a result, most of the magazine's readers and even its frequent critics had little negative to say about this straightforward summary of what *Zolotoe Runo* had hoped, and felt it had, accomplished.

Both *Vesy* and *Zolotoe Runo* mentioned no real immediate reasons for their ceasing publication. As a general explanation for the decisions, both gave the accomplishment of their initial goals, but neither found itself able to admit that time had passed them by and that they were no longer relevant to the condition of Russian cultural life in 1910. The arguments carried on between the "esthetic" and "realist" tendencies within symbolism had lost their intensity, and when it appeared that *Zolotoe Runo* was attempting to begin a polemic with *Apollon* at the end of 1909 (perhaps with the expectation of revitalizing the magazine's readership), the Petersburg journal offered no response. The Russian educated public was more sophisticated and knowledgeable than it had been only five years before, and had adopted a general commitment to the modernism *Vesy* and *Zolotoe Runo* had promoted. While *Zolotoe Runo* remained in the "vanguard" of art in 1909, and continued to sponsor artistic groups whom the general educated public would appreciate only much later, it was impossible for *Zolotoe Runo* to maintain its momentum. Above all, *Zolotoe Runo*'s attempt to represent all the newest and best developments in Russian culture had become an unrealistic goal for a single magazine within the pluralistic artistic and literary life of the Russia of 1910. The immediate reason for *Zolotoe Runo*'s ending publication was Riabu-shinsky's insurmountable financial difficulties, but even had the magazine been able to attract other financial support, its position remained an unviable one. The break-up into warring factions that had plagued Russian modernism after 1905 continued for the next decade or more, and until after the October Revolution, none of the feuding groups which came to constitute the Russian modernist *avant-garde* felt they should be associated with any other group, or should contribute to "bourgeois, philistine" journals. Neither *Zolotoe Runo* nor, in fact, any other single magazine could maintain contacts with all these progressive groups, while at the same time attracting the less radical modernists as well.

While *Zolotoe Runo*'s passing did not go unnoted in the Russian press, the only lengthy evaluation of it appeared in *Apollon* late in 1910, and was written by Alexander Rostislavov, a previous collaborator on the now-defunct magazine.[50] Neither praising nor maligning, Rostislavov gave a balanced summary of the history of *Zolotoe Runo*'s publication. He recounted the difficulties the magazine had faced at its outset: he felt it was fated to failure because its essays and articles were always above the educational level of the general public, and never being able to bring its own standards together with theirs, it suffered from the opposition of the press and of the "crowd," both of whom ridiculed the magazine. Rostislavov believed that the magazine, having begun publication at a time when society had more immediate concerns than problems of art, had adopted a program that was too wide and general, "a banner rich in gold, but insufficiently defined."[51] He faulted *Zolotoe Runo* for maintaining a "combative" character thereafter, without ever determining a clear, defined, and consistent position of its own, and in conjunction apologized for *Zolotoe Runo*'s partisan attacks on such highly respected individuals as Benois. Rostislavov explained the magazine's final hysteria as resulting from the loss of perspective accompanying the rapid changes in art and literature which took place during the four years of *Zolotoe Runo*'s publication. Finally, Rostislavov described some of the magazine's accomplishments: he wrote that no one could disagree on its purely artistic achievements, and gave *Zolotoe Runo* the credit for recognizing the importance of Vrubel and Borisov-Musatov as founders of the new tendencies in Russian art, as well as for supporting and emphasizing the new French art which had since become so influential in Russia. Rostislavov concluded that whether or not *Zolotoe Runo* had fulfilled its mission would be a problem for the future to decide.

As did *Zolotoe Runo*'s self-evaluation, Rostislavov's summary elicited little response. Rostislavov's attitude most likely was shared by the magazine's other contributors, who felt that since *Zolotoe Runo* no longer existed, recrimination or boasting was pointless. Undoubtedly believing Rostislavov's evaluation to have been a fair one, no one else felt it necessary to publish any direct comments on *Zolotoe Runo*. *Apollon*, for example, considered Rostislavov's article as sufficient comment on a magazine that it did not see as its own direct predecessor, which it felt had lived out its usefulness, and whose attempts to begin a strident debate with *Apollon* itself seemed only embarrassing. On the other hand, those artists closely connected to the magazine had now been taken up by the rush of Russian artistic life, and had little time for retrospection. Such artists as Kuznetsov, Sarian, Larionov, and Goncharova had now, as *Zolotoe Runo* congratulated itself, proved themselves capable of continuing the development of their art by their own efforts. The magazine's editors themselves had their own immediate concerns. Riabushinsky, of course, was forced to concentrate primarily on his worsening financial situation. In addition, the general antagonism toward him on the part of Russian literary and artistic figures precluded any attempts he might have made to say anything more about what at best had been a difficult enterprise for him. Riabushinsky had been interested mainly in the magazine's artistic section, preferred the purely symbolist art of the *Golubaia roza* artists, and had some difficulty accepting the neo-primitivism replacing it, although in the interests of the "unceasing development of Art," he used his magazine to help promote the new tendencies. Considering that Riabushinsky undoubtedly felt overtaken by artistic changes of which he could not keep abreast, he must have been relieved to put the magazine behind him. While Vasily Milioti certainly shared Riabushinsky's feelings, Tasteven on the other hand experienced no such emotional break with his work for *Zolotoe Runo*: in his attachment to Russian Futurism, he felt he was refining ideas and theories first expressed in conjunction with Riabushinsky's magazine. For all these people, *Zolotoe Runo* had served its purpose, and soon became part of the past; none of them saw any point in dwelling on it when other more important immediate tasks remained to be accomplished.

As *Mir Iskusstva* had done to a certain extent, *Zolotoe Runo* provided economic and spiritual support for what would later become disparate groups, maintaining them at their most vulnerable moments. By 1910, the artistic and literary tendencies aided by *Zolotoe Runo* no longer needed its help. Had *Zolotoe Runo* not existed, it is doubtful that Russian modernist culture would have developed as rapidly as it did, and, if at times confusingly and incomprehensibly, continued to move forward at the pace it did. Considering *Zolotoe Runo* from this point of view, as a cultural catalyst, its success was implicitly tied to its very failure.

Part Four

Conclusion

X

ZOLOTOE RUNO, FIN DE SIECLE RUSSIA, AND RUSSIAN MODERNISM

Thought and culture in the reign of Nicholas II were by no means of uniform quality. Their achievements were great, their failures far from negligible. But even fifty years after the end of the Civil War, they cast their shadow, both in Russia and the West.
Donald Treadgold, *The West in Russia and China*, v. 1, p. 242.

The twentieth century was born in Russia. This is an unknown fact.
Mihajlo Mihajlov, "Russian Modernism," in his *Russian Themes*, p. 264.

The single most important historical development occurring during the period of *Zolotoe Runo*'s publication was the 1905 revolution. While *Zolotoe Runo*'s active participation in the revolutionary events themselves was negligible, the magazine could not help being influenced by the revolution's initial success, and ultimate failure. Russian social, economic, and political life were all seriously affected by the revolution, as were even the modernist artists, writers, poets, and philosophers. Blok's carrying a red banner at the head of a demonstration and Chulkov's imprisonment did represent a certain degree of spontaneous participation in the revolution by modernist figures, but in general, concerted revolutionary action did not appeal to the individuals surrounding *Zolotoe Runo*. They were excited at the idea of the revolution, but after early, highly emotional outbursts, preferred to settle down to a more individual exploration of the possibilities offered by the revolution's apparent success. During 1906, much of Russian society viewed the future optimistically, believing that the revolution had indeed made considerable changes in the autocratic, repressive Russia Nicholas II had inherited from his father. At the same time, however, for many this optimism had begun to fade in the face of the government's continual reassertion of powers believed destroyed. By the end of 1906, a mood of pessimism was growing prevalent. With the reestablishment of government control, a sense of disillusionment, disappointment, and hopelessness became increasingly widespread in the country. Seeking escape from an ever more disgusting reality, the Russian public at large discovered the Russian turn-of-the-century *poètes-maudits* and adopted their manner of looking at the world. While the decadents and symbolists of the previous decade had shared an attitude of *fin de siècle* gloom and license, with the failure of the revolution, their mood consciously became that of the Russian educated public in general.

The populist, realist movement that had paralleled what Mirsky called the "esthetic revival" of the 1890s lost its force when confronted with this new, disappointing reality. A schoolboy of the times remembered:

> Now it was no longer Marx and Engels, but Nietzsche and Baudelaire and Wagner and Leonardo da Vinci whom we passionately discussed; we did not sing revolutionary songs but recited to one another poems of contemporary symbolist poets and our own imitations of them. A new period had begun.[1]

Ilya Ehrenburg has described the period, and his youth, in considerably more detail:

> ...enlightened humanity was advancing to the foxtrot. Students argued over whether Artsybashev's Sanin was the ideal modern man: here there was both Nietzscheanism for the unexacting, an eroticism closer to the stable than to Wilde, and the outspokenness of the new age. A story by Anatoly Kamensky appeared, recounting in detail how a certain officer succeeded in seducing four women in one day. In the Art Theater they put on Leonid Andreev's "Zhizn cheloveka," a naive attempt to generalize a life, interpreted in the corner of the stage by "someone in gray." The polka from this play was sung or whistled by the Moscow intelligentsia. In the same theater Maeterlinck's "The Blind" was staged and from its symbolistic howling sensitive ladies fell ill with neurasthenia. None of them foresaw that after ten years there would be millet kasha and questionaires; life seemed too peaceful; people sought unhappiness in art like "defisitnyi" cheese. There began the epoch of God-seeking, of Scandinavian almanacs...
>   ...art penetrated even into my underground work. At night I read Hamsun—*Pan, Victoria, Mysteries,* abused myself for my weakness, but fell into admiration: I felt that there was another world—nature, images, sounds, colors. Chekhov shook me even then by a truth incomprehensible to me at the time, but indisputable; I whispered "Misyus, where are you?" I was in love with the "lady with the dog." I saw Isadora Duncan; she was in an ancient tunic, and danced completely unlike Geltzer.[2]

Ehrenburg felt compelled to remark, however, that despite all the excitement and brilliance of this period, "behind it all one felt weariness, disillusionment, emptiness."[3]

Such a sense of disappointment and hopelessness is essential to a *fin de siècle* age. The decade preceding 1905 had been one hopeful of regeneration and improvement, both among the Russian modernists and within Russian society as a whole. With the revolution's failure, all this changed. Briusov described the situation to his father in 1907:

> In the capitals there is great despondency. The government has closed almost all the progressive unions... the Cadets are dejected and Prince Trubetskoi is calling for an

agreement with the Octobrists...the socialist *Utro Stolichnoe* is hitting out against cheap novels.... The impression is that these are not revolutionary days, but the most severe times of the reign of Alexander III.[4]

Briusov's contrast of what had seemed "revolutionary days" with the repressive reign of Nicholas II's father must have been a thought omnipresent in the minds of most educated Russians. Politically, the revolution and its achievements were being undone by the government, yet the collapse of censorship still permitted broad discretion on the part of publishers. In this new context, for most of the educated classes of society, esthetic and physical pleasure were preferred to public service or political activity. The spirit of the age had caught up with the modernists, who for years had been attempting to free art and literature from any requirement of social utility, and to explore the deepest reaches of the individual mind and personality. It was ironic that at the very moment when the modernists were embraced by the Russian educated public, however, they themselves were preparing for a reexamination of "extreme individualism" and beginning to call for the establishment of connections between the intelligentsia and the people.

The slow reassertion of governmental censorship permitted an outburst of pornography and eroticism previously unexperienced in Russia. Such illustrated magazines as *Décolleté* ("a journal for adults, singular in its originality"), *Naturshchitsa (The Model, "sent in a sealed envelope")*, and *Noch Liubvi (Night of Love)* appeared on the market.[5] Books which would have been considered of questionable morality before the revolution could now be published: such was the case with Kuzmin's *Krylia (Wings)*, Zinovieva-Annibal's *33 uroda (33 Monsters)*, and Artsybashev's *Sanin*. The kinds of works published by Artsybashev are particularly indicative of the change in public reading tastes: in 1905-6 his stories dealt with the development of the revolution, while 1907's *Sanin* was concerned with sexual license, personal gratification, and freedom from any restrictive morality. Similarly, European works considering questions of sex were avidly translated, and Strindberg, Wedekind, and Weininger appeared to a large and appreciative Russian audience at this time, for example.

Such reactions to the disappointing outcome of the revolution were continually mirrored in *Zolotoe Runo,* and because of its tolerant editorial policy, it was the single magazine in Russia, either modernist or non-modernist, which kaleidoscopically expressed almost all aspects of the post-1905 *fin de siècle*. Escape was the fundamental desire of most Russians during this period of increasing repression. They began to appreciate the works of artists who had foreshadowed their own feelings but who had received little public encouragement before 1905. Vrubel's

"Bogatyr" of 1898 and "Pan" of 1899 represented a turning to the mythical past in response to what the artist considered the social and moral fragmentation of his own time. The "dreaminess" of Borisov-Musatov's works indicated a similar goal, and little could be more escapist than the early works of Musatov's students, the *Golubaia roza* artists. *Zolotoe Runo* maintained an interest in exotica throughout its period of publication: Balmont's travelogues, his translation of the Mayan *Popul Vuh*, Rozanov's descriptions of Egypt, and the special 1908 issue on Persian art were all examples of an interest in non-Russian actuality shared by *Zolotoe Runo*'s editors and the Russian periodical reading audience.

Closely related to this geographic or chronological escapism was the general public interest in fantasy, emotionalism, and mysticism. An editorial enthusiasm for the resurrection of myth and legend was present from the beginning of *Zolotoe Runo*'s publication until its end, as we can see from Ivanov's "Mifotvorchestvo," Gorodetsky's early "pre-Christian" poetry, and Sologub's "Prizyvaiushchii zveria."[6] Sologub's work in particular suggests irrationalism as well, the irrationalism of sex (present in Briusov's previously unpublishable "Voskresshie pesni" of 1906[7]) that Przybyszewski described as the "demon" at the core of man. Demonic irrationalism exerted a tremendous pull on post-1905 Russians, probably to an extent greater than at any other time in Russian history. Sologub's *Melkii bes*, Merezhkovsky's *Leonardo da Vinci*, Briusov's *Ognennyi angel* were all expressions of an almost compulsive interest in demonism and of the age's concomitant fascination with death and morbidity, for many a transparent, metaphoric vision of their own lives and their society.

Zolotoe Runo's "Devil" competition brought the problem of demonism to a focus. The special issue's articles on satanism in music, art, and society summarized aspects of the basic theme of demonism that had appeared in *Zolotoe Runo* until that time and which were to continue until the magazine's closing. *Zolotoe Runo* had reproduced evidence of Vrubel's fascination with the devil, while Kuznetsov's painting, "Probuzhdenie diavola" ("The Awakening of the Devil"), provided a definition and explanation of much of his symbolist art. Responding to public interest, the editors used Przybyszewski's concern with demonic possession and hysteria (an abnormal, semi-"possessed" state) to increase the magazine's circulation. Even political interpretations of demonism and death found their way into the magazine. Andreev's "Eleazar" dealt with the infection of life with death, and similarly, Blok felt that the Russian intelligentsia had been infected with a will to die by the triumphant demonism symbolized by Dobuzhinsky's highly politicized drawing of the devil. Such victorious political "demonism" encouraged a more introspective examination of the psychological composition of demonism. That much of it was superficial is readily seen by the failure of *Zolotoe Runo*'s abortive competition—while the problem was debated actively and was widely discussed, no specific explanation or general interpretation emerged and it remained more an indication than a primary component of the malaise of the time.

Most positively, *Zolotoe Runo*'s escapism was directed toward uncovering internal freedom, and its early discussion on the problem of individualism was related to this. After 1905, the Russian intelligentsia had become absorbed in its own narrow personal interests, in an amoral individualism prevalent among the modernists of the "decadent" 1890s. *Zolotoe Runo*'s predecessor *Iskusstvo* had emphasized "the science of the individual, the subjective 'I' "[8] and in light of the highly politicized nature of the early months of 1906, when *Zolotoe Runo* first appeared, such statements as Siunnerberg's that "beauty has nothing to do with morality or usefulness," Blok's call for a return to nature and the necessity to "feel" above all, and the *Golubaia roza* rejection of visible reality seemed anti-political in the extreme. Yet there was considerable confusion in this "apoliticism" and "individuality" of *Zolotoe Runo*'s. The members of the *Golubaia roza* group hoped to discover a collective, systematic imagery that would enable them to transcend individualistic, physical reality and reach an absolute level meaningful to everyone. Yet the artists and their experiments were understood in fact by almost no one (as was the case with Viacheslav Ivanov's "collective individualism"), and they remained inescapably isolated. The artists may have believed in their "searchings," yet as Makovsky pointed out in his review of their first exhibition, their experimentation was directed toward the individual and not toward the masses. And as Shervashidze, Rostislavov, and Voloshin wrote in the magazine's debate on artistic individualism, what was important was that art should be permitted to develop freely, that it "should go where it can and will," that too much talk of canons and formulas would only hinder its development. Such support for a rejection of intellectual or physical restraint, but on a broader, philosophical plane, corresponded precisely with the spirit of a post-1905, disillusioned Russian art. What appeared to be a call for "extreme individualism" was precisely what *Zolotoe Runo*'s wider audience wished to hear, and was the same feeling that ensured the success of books like *Sanin*.

Significantly, however, even within this debate over individualism, talk of "overcoming" it was also present. "Extreme individualism" had been a rallying cry for the decadents of the 1890s. By 1906, although it was being widely adopted as an ideal by much of educated Russian society, the modernists themselves had begun to question its value, and to yearn for something different. Tasteven's "Nitsshe i sovremennyi krizis" ("Nietzsche and the Contemporary Crisis")[9] introduced the "crisis of individualism" as an important issue for the first time in *Zolotoe Runo*, and was related to

Golubaia roza's artistic experiments, to Ivanov's "collective individual-ism," and to Chulkov's mystical anarchism. "Nitsshe i sovremennyi krizis" proved a bellwether of future developments within the magazine itself, but at the time it was printed, it was only one of a wide range of positions within Russian modernism which were reflected in the magazine. In giving space to whatever topical writings its contributors found interesting, *Zolotoe Runo* was able to provide a forum for opinions as diverse as those of Medtner and Karatygin, Blok and Briusov, Tasteven and Belyi—all of whom were representatives of extreme positions within Russian modern-ism in the post-1905 years, and whose latest works were attacked or defended avidly by the new devotees of Russian modernism. But when *Zolotoe Runo* began to talk more seriously, and at greater length, of "overcoming individualism" and of the need for more positive exami-nations of the realist writers, it foreshadowed the subsequent development of Russian modernism, and indicated the ultimate demise of the Russian *fin de siècle.*

The first stage in the magazine's reevaluation of previously rejected traditions was an attempt at finding some sort of connection with "the people," expressed in a typically modernist, although not necessarily *fin de siècle,* interest in primitivism. It was predictable that the period's preoc-cupation with the exotic would eventually result in an appreciation of earlier or simpler times, much as *Mir Iskusstva* had developed a concern for eighteenth-century and even medieval Russian traditions. Blok's "Kraski i slova," in *Zolotoe Runo*'s first issue, had called for simplicity in art and life, the simplicity of children, whose artistic vision of the world was just then first being appreciated in Russia. Blok was influenced by Kliuev's poetry, which had as its inspiration Russian peasant Christianity, with its traces of pagan rites and beliefs. Similarly, the stylized folk tales of Remizov's "Posolon" would evolve into Gorodetsky's conscious neo-paganism, and the simple, primitive *lubok* would be profoundly influential on Goncharova's art. All these were typical "searchings," and the second "Salon Zolotoe Runo" was touted as a conscious attempt at discovering a new artistic style to replace symbolism. As Gauguin had done, Kuznetsov and Sarian went to the "wilderness" in protest against the bourgeois world and capitalist civilization (although they owed their very professional existence to that civilization and to Riabushinsky, whom they both nonetheless resented), hoping to find there a world of natural man, of eternal values, "the essential underneath the superficial."[10] Not unlike Gauguin's discovery of Brittany, and Yeats' fascination with the Celts, Gorodetsky found his inspirations in the early Russian tribes (both Slavic and non-Slavic), Goncharova hers in Russian folk art, and Kuznetsov his in "Russian" Central Asia.[11] Once again, this indicates an important feature of Russian modernism, symbolism, and the Russian *fin de siècle* in general: its origins within Russian, rather than foreign, traditions. Blok continually stressed the native sources of Russian symbolism, and the *Golubaia roza* artists felt a sharp contrast between *Mir Iskusstva*'s "cosmopolitanism" and their own Russian roots in the works of Vrubel and Borisov-Musatov. While they emulated foreign models in much of their earliest work, the *Golubaia roza* artists later moved toward indigenous sources of inspiration, a change in direction Russian modernism would continue to follow for a number of years.

It was this appreciation for the native sources of Russian modernism that led to *Zolotoe Runo*'s desire to find new relationships with "the people," the peasants whose lives of "ideal simplicity" had supplied this new artistic inspiration. Viacheslav Ivanov's essays spoke of the need to find a force binding each individual to a common, absolute world order, a longing for a universal means of communication among men, and a desire for a common bond between the artist and "the people."[12] Chulkov's call for the assertion of personality in community was closely related to Ivanov's ideal "collectivity," but Chulkov added theoretical anarchism, to at least one European cultural historian, the major component of *fin de siècle* European culture.[13]

Both Chulkov and Ivanov hoped to overcome the "narrow individualism" employed by the decadents of the 1890s as a means to liberate Russian art and literature from the restrictions of realism. Gorodetsky and Tasteven believed that symbolism was one means to "overcome individualism" and to encourage the birth of a "new, organic age." "Narrow individualism" was identified with the Western *fin de siècle,* and seen as having been necessary at one time. Now, however, by relying on Russian traditions, it could be transcended. Commenting on Frank Wedekind's play "Frühlings Erwachen," Blok protested some of the negative influences of Western "decadence" on Russian literature and art:

> This question has never arisen in such a way among us in Russia, and if it occurs so now, it is only in closed circles, doomed to slow decaying, in classes from which emerge a corpse-like odor... We still have people not manufactured by machines—with wills, with hopes, with "dreams," with "ideals"—to use even vulgar words. Our life is higher and greater than this petty life.[14]

Blok's emphasis on indigenous traditions encouraged an examination of the ultimate sources of these traditions, the Russian people themselves, and an attempt to discover what it was that distinguished Russian symbolism and modernism from its Western counterpart. Blok wrote in 1907 that the distinction was to be found in Russian symbolism's "tendency to realism."[15]

As we have seen, Blok's interest in contemporary Russian realist literature produced one of the principal polemics involving *Zolotoe Runo,* but one debated on two different levels. While *Vesy* attacked the realists for using a shoddy literary technique and an outmoded style, *Zolotoe Runo* appreciated realism for its emotional and moral qualities rather than for its method. To Blok, the principal defender of the realists within *Zolotoe Runo,* realism was a path to the discovery of such values as truth and justice. With *Zolotoe Runo's* promise to uncover values wherever they lay, it was felt that modernist symbolism could only be enriched by an appropriation of such realist values. The most important of these was "simplicity," which many modernists felt they had lost and needed to recover. Nothing so infuriated *Vesy's* critics of *Zolotoe Runo* as did Blok's favorable comments about Gorky. His appreciation of the emotional, intuitive, and moral values of Gorky's works resulted in his consideration of the problem of the "intelligentsia and the people," and led him to warn his class of almost inescapable, ultimate disaster.[16] A sense of inevitable and imminent apocalypse was a major psychological component of the European *fin de siècle,* and among Russians it proved epidemic in the years following 1905. Yet it is a paradox of cultural history that while the predominant tenor of a time may be pessimistic and negative, an anticipation of disaster, the first traces of rebirth and renascence are present as well. This was certainly the case within the broader European *fin de siècle,* and even more so within Russia. To a great extent, Diaghilev's Tauride Palace speech of 1905 had been the real climax of the feeling of doom and hopelessness prevalent among the Russian intelligentsia's *avant-garde.* While Diaghilev's mood spread to large numbers of Russians after that time, a hesitant beginning at regeneration was also taking place. It was *Zolotoe Runo* which proved to be the most willing sponsor of this "revival."

One of the ironies associated with *Zolotoe Runo* was that it was charged by its enemies with the "vulgarization" of symbolism at a time when it was reaching an almost miniscule audience, a fact particularly surprising in light of the popularity of symbolism during the post-1905 years, a time when, in Pertsov's words, symbolism was crowned "with almost academic laurels."[17] The decadent *avant-garde* coterie of the 1890's found themselves welcomed wholeheartedly by the previously-despised "philistines," and a "third generation" of symbolist writers, poets, and artists had appeared. *Vesy's* criticisms notwithstanding, *Zolotoe Runo* did not rely on, nor give its support to this generally untalented new group of writers: the magazine's refusal to award any prizes to the inferior contributions to the "Devil" competition indicated that it did maintain high standards of quality. Similarly, *Vesy's* charges that *Zolotoe Runo* was endangering symbolism's "purity" by spreading symbolist ideas to people unable to understand them have little foundation in fact: Blok, Ivanov, and Chulkov may have talked of reaching the "masses" with their messages of transformation, but all their articles were directed toward other members of the predominantly modernist intelligentsia, who almost invariably rejected them. The public loved the superficial excitement, shock, and scandal associated with symbolism, but cared little for its essence: crowds of people flocked to the *Golubaia roza* exhibition, but few liked or purchased the paintings. *Zolotoe Runo* certainly did not "vulgarize" symbolism, nor did it even reap any benefits from a "populist" interpretation of symbolism. On the contrary, it found itself ever more isolated within Russian modernism as well as within the Russian periodical reading audience—an indication of the price of symbolism's public success.

Not surprisingly, such popularity encouraged symbolism's disintegration into warring groups and factions, and by 1909, in Joan Grossman's words, symbolism had "reached that fatal point where it was defining itself in retrospect."[18] A psychological change was taking place throughout Russian life: the educated classes were recovering emotionally and intellectually from the revolutionary years, and economic stability had given the middle classes a sense of security—industrial production was rising, the urban population was growing, and it appeared Russia was beginning to catch up with the West technologically. By 1910, the new material welfare of the middle classes (who had constituted most of the modernists' new audience) led them to the adoption of a new realistic attitude. This mood had been foreshadowed by *Zolotoe Runo*'s support of "simplicity" and "realistic symbolism," and soon found further expression in *Apollon* and Acmeism, antidotes to the excess of the previous few years.

The "symbolism" adopted by a mass audience after 1905 was in fact the old pre-revolutionary decadence; symbolism itself was now becoming something considerably different. This mass audience now wanted tangible contacts with reality, not hidden meanings, concreteness rather than abstraction, clear-cut descriptions rather than allusions. *Zolotoe Runo*'s publication of excerpts from Maurice Denis' *Théories* was an indication of this changing public and symbolist attitude: Denis recommended a return to tradition in art, and hoped for the day when the young symbolists would eventually "arrive at nature." Even the Fauve Matisse had called on the pages of *Zolotoe Runo* for an art of "equilibrium, purity, and tranquility."[19]

Symbolist self-evaluation paralleled the public reevaluation of taste, and not surprisingly, the symbolists again found themselves disagreeing with each other. Viacheslav Ivanov wrote that "symbolism did not want to be and could not be merely art,"[20] while Briusov countered that "symbolism wanted to be and was only art,"[21] but both agreed that symbolism had passed its apogee, and Briusov gave his support to the "clarists" of

Apollon.[22] Blok himself defended symbolism after earlier having been one
of its principal critics (an indication that he too recognized symbolism's
imminent demise and wanted to clarify his involvement in it).[23]

Calls for the establishment of new literary and artistic styles were
being made, not for a return to earlier symbolist "purity": Kuzmin's
"beautiful clarity"[24] of 1910 prefigured Gumilev's 1913 Acmeist manifesto,[25] and both were published in the "classicist" *Apollon.* Gorodetsky,
by that time supporting those he had earlier vilified, summarized the
difference between symbolism and the new Acmeism in his 1913 article
"Nekotorye techeniia v sovremennoi russkoi literature" ("Some Currents
in Contemporary Russian Literature"):

> The struggle between Acmeism and symbolism . . . is above all a struggle for this world,
> resounding, colorful, having form, weight, and time, for our planet the earth. In the
> end, symbolism, having filled the world with "correspondences," has turned it into a
> phantom. . . . For the Acmeists, the rose has again become good in and for itself, for its
> petals, its scent and color, and not for its conceivable similarities with mystical love or
> some other such thing.[26]

Gorodetsky defined the new movement as being against obscurity, against
"private" meanings, against the cult-significance of the poet and poetry. It
was in favor of ordinary speech, clear conventional form, and a down-to-
earth craftsmanlike attitude—if not a call for a new realism, at least a call
for an appreciation of some of the values and techniques of realism.
Finally, and unlike Russian symbolism, which did have some foreign
inspirations, this new Acmeism was based on native Russian modernism,
and, as did Russian Futurism, developed toward a national form of
literature and art. One of *Zolotoe Runo*'s major positive legacies was that
it had attempted to discover a vital and creative esthetic to replace a
decaying symbolism, and despite its attacks on *Apollon,* it was *Zolotoe
Runo* which had provided a forum for the discussion of ideas such as
Gorodetsky's which would eventually supercede symbolism.

In her book on *Die Jugend,* Linda Koreska-Hartmann wrote that
" . . . every epoch has the periodicals that it deserves, which correspond to
its view of the world, its spiritual needs and strivings as well as its general
level."[27] *Zolotoe Runo* certainly "corresponded" to its time, more so than
did any other modernist, or non-modernist periodical. It provided a
"synthesized" picture of the seething cultural spirit of the years between
1905 and 1910, and aspired toward "sintetichnost" as an esthetic ideal. As
an ideal, "synthèthisme" arose first among Western European *fin de siècle*
symbolists, as Lucie-Smith has noted:

> Synthesis is a particularly important symbolist concept: it involves an effort to combine
> elements found in the real world, or even borrowed from other works of art, to produce
> a separate, different, and certainly self-sufficient reality.[28]

Lucie-Smith's definition of "synthesis" was generally applicable to those who believed in symbolism's "theurgic" force, but by its nature as a magazine, *Zolotoe Runo* brought this theoretical synthesis down to a more everyday level. "Synthesism" had been an ideal espoused by *Mir Iskusstva,* but *Zolotoe Runo* had developed it further, particularly in that it had a native Russian source for doing so in the person of one of the magazine's "patron saints," Borisov-Musatov. In a letter to Benois, Musatov gave a concrete explanation of his view of "synthesism":

> The endless melody which Wagner found in music also exists in painting. This melody is in the melancholy northern landscapes of Grieg, in the songs of medieval troubadors and in the romanticism of our Russian Turgenevs. In frescoes, this leitmotif is an endless, monotonous, impassive line without angles.[29]

Musatov's model found expression in all of *Zolotoe Runo*'s activities, particularly in its exhibitions, where an attempt was made to unite art and life into a new reality. In its initial manifesto, *Zolotoe Runo* exhibited deep sympathy for "those working for the renewal of life" and Tasteven, Blok, Gorodetsky, and Chulkov all wrote of transforming the world, changing it toward a modernist ideal, an idealistic aspiration providing a clear contrast to the prevalent pessimism of the time. Predictably, the magazine's calls for "renewal" were not noticeably successful in rallying large numbers of educated Russians. Yet despite this failure, *Zolotoe Runo* did contribute to Russian cultural life important new ideas, concepts, and artistic forms whose significance would be appreciated only later. Although it was outspokenly on the side of revitalization, the task of completely redirecting Russian cultural life proved too great for the magazine: its own curious mixture of pessimism and optimism was a direct reflection of that general failure.

As most of *Zolotoe Runo*'s critics pointed out, the magazine never really determined an official consistent esthetic position for itself, and contradictory opinions frequently appeared on its pages. While the political confusion of the times explains many of the technical problems involved in the magazine's publication, it also provides some indication for why Gorky was severely criticized in some issues, yet praised in others, why Dobuzhinsky's highly political interpretation of the "Devil" appeared in what Gorodetsky later called "the citadel of merchant estheticism."[30] *Zolotoe Runo*'s lackadaisical and unpredictable editorial policy and practice was only reinforced by such contributions as Blok's "lyrical" articles, which contradicted each other and often only confused their readers. Such modernist rivals as *Vesy* or *Pereval* were ideologically too firm to allow the editorial inconsistency *Zolotoe Runo* did, and other more "popular" magazines never reached *Zolotoe Runo*'s artistic or literary level. For most of its existence, the magazine had no real competition, but in attempting to appeal to a broad audience, it ended up appealing to no single particular faction within a fragmented Russian modernism, and economic failure, if not esthetic or historical failure, resulted.

Zolotoe Runo's combination of populism, modernism, and "art for art's sake" was possible since the battle against the realists in art had been won by *Mir Iskusstva* at about the time *Zolotoe Runo* began its publication, and a similar struggle was being won by the first-generation symbolists against civic, utilitarian literature. *Zolotoe Runo* believed it could continue to move Russian art forward, freeing it even more from the fetters of the past, and ironically, found itself doing so by turning toward timeless, native traditions. The single major problem for *Zolotoe Runo* was the old one of Moscow or Petersburg, Russia or the West. *Mir Iskusstva*, with its conscious sophistication, Western orientation, and remarkable success, had made the question a real issue among the Russian modernists. One of *Mir Iskusstva*'s goals had been the introduction of modern Western art to the (relatively) artistically ignorant Russian educated public. After 1905, and certainly by 1910, such cultural education was no longer necessary, and such men as Shchukin, Morozov, and Riabushinsky knew more about artistic developments in the West than did most Westerners, for example. In fact, the cultural flow had reversed itself: Diaghilev's exhibitions, ballets, and operas were presenting a fully-developed Russian modernist culture to an amazed West, a culture which increasingly drew its inspirations from national Russian traditions, interpreted in a modernist Western way, and a culture fostered and promoted by *Zolotoe Runo*.

Mirsky's comment a number of years ago that the broad development of Russian symbolism was from foreign examples back to national traditions[31] may be expanded to include the entirety of Russian modernism. *Mir Iskusstva* had provided such examples, but its rediscovery of a previously forgotten or ignored Russian cultural past was undertaken from a Western standpoint, and symbolized by the *miriskusnik* "cult of Petersburg." *Zolotoe Runo* added native Russian primitivism. *Zolotoe Runo*'s concern with foreign developments in themselves was never as great as *Mir Iskusstva*'s or even *Vesy*'s. The most interesting Western artists to *Zolotoe Runo* were Gauguin and Matisse, and it was directly from Gauguin that the esthetic inspiration of the Russian neo-primitivists initially derived, in particular his pictures of life in Brittany and Tahiti.[32] Psychologically, the Russians were prepared to adopt this primitivism: the "consciousness of the primitive" had preceded the first models of primitivist inspiration.[33] Through special issues and through its exhibitions, *Zolotoe Runo* provided those models, ones influencing not only such artists as Sarian and Goncharova, but poets such as Gorodetsky and

Blok, and theoreticians such as Ivanov and Tasteven. Although it never proved capable of systematizing it, *Zolotoe Runo* was developing a broad primitivist esthetic (Volfing's musical tastes notwithstanding), and the implications of primitivism, including the desire for simplicity of form seen later in Malevich and the Constructivists, would lead to the culmination of Russian modernism. In only four years, because of the acceleration of Russian cultural life in general, *Zolotoe Runo* and Russia had experienced a true *fin de siècle* and the first stirrings of an esthetic world-view that would soon transform Russian and Western artistic consciousness.

Diplomatic and political historians usually see World War I as ending the nineteenth century in Europe, while those interested in cultural developments consider the twentieth century as having begun in the 1890s. *Zolotoe Runo* was published during what was a transitional period culturally, and toward the end of its existence, indications of later, post-World War I developments appeared in it: Toporkov's call for a union of the art of the creator and the spectator, Tasteven's early, initially hesitant support for Futurism, Larionov's "luchizm" ("rayonism"), all reached their full culmination in the 1920s, which was, in fact, the final flowering of the Russian Silver Age. For Russians, the twentieth century did begin in the 1890s—culturally and psychologically, a new age was being born. Life changed politically as well; 1905 seemed cataclysmic to many Russians, and 1917 was to be both an anticipated and feared apocalypse from which few expected to emerge. The years following the turn of the century witnessed a distinct reorientation in Russian and Western consciousness. Virginia Woolf wrote that "on or about December 1910 human nature changed,"[34] and while the precise dating would be different in the case of each European country, her expression of a sense of discontinuity between the traditional past and the uncertainties of the present and future was one felt throughout Europe. Subconsciously, Europeans were preparing themselves psychologically for a great disjunction in their lives. It was the Russians, now more than ever before active participants in European civilization, who felt most acutely the hope and fear inherent in this discontinuity. Within Russia, and to an extent equalled by no other competing periodical, *Zolotoe Runo* had continually, and almost unconsciously, expressed this change of mentality, and taken its place firmly on the side of the future.

NOTES

NOTES TO CHAPTER I

1. Gleb Struve prefers this term to the more commonly used "Silver Age." See his "The Cultural Renaissance" in Theofanis George Stavros, ed., *Russia Under the Last Tsar* (Minneapolis, 1969), 179-201.

2. "Modernism" is one of those terms that means everything and nothing. Its most concise definition is found in Irving Howe's "The Idea of the Modern" in his *Literary Modernism* (New York, 1967), and it is Howe's interpretation of this term that is used in this work.

3. Camilla Gray, *The Russian Experiment in Art: 1863-1922* (New York, 1970), 111.

4. Wladimir Weidlé, *Russia: Absent and Present,* translated by A. Gordon Smith (London, 1952), 92.

5. Jean Cassou, "The Climate of Thought" in Jean Cassou, Emil Langui, and Nikolaus Pevsner, editors, *Gateway to the Twentieth Century* (New York, 1962), 56.

6. See Oleg Maslenikov, *The Frenzied Poets* (Berkeley and Los Angeles, 1952), 9 ff.

7. The best source for background on *Mir Iskusstva* is Aleksandr Benois, *Vozniknovenie "Mir Iskusstva"* (Leningrad, 1928).

8. For Benois, see his *Memoirs* in two volumes, translated by Moura Budberg (London, 1964). This English version of his *Zhizn' khudozhnika* (New York, 1955) includes material not in the Russian edition. See also Mark Etkind, *Aleksandr N. Benua* (Moscow-Leningrad, 1965). For rather dated, but none the less useful background on Diaghilev, see Arnold Haskell with Walter Nuvel, *Diaghileff* (New York, 1935) and Serge Lifar, *Serge Diaghilev: His Life, His Work, His Legend* (London, 1940).

9. Benois, *Memoirs,* II, 157.

10. Sergei Diaghilev, "Slozhnye voprosy" *Mir Iskusstva,* 1899, No. 1, 1-2.

11. This is not entirely true, because *Mir Iskusstva* did sponsor the "Evenings of Contemporary Music" society, aimed at familiarizing the general public with the work of such young or unknown Russian and foreign composers as Ravel and Debussy, Reger and Schoenberg, and later, Stravinsky and Prokofiev.

12. Benois, *Memoirs,* II, 157.

13. See G. Iu. Sternin, *Ocherki russkoi satiricheskoi grafiki* (Moscow, 1964), 226 ff.

14. Benois, *Memoirs,* II, 217.

15. Alla Gusarova, *Mir Iskusstva* (Leningrad, 1972), 94. For a different view of *Mir Iskusstva* see John Bowlt, "The World of Art," in *Russian Literature Triquarterly,* No. 4 (Fall, 1972), 183-212.

16. Petr Pertsov, *Literaturnye vospominaniia 1890-1902* (Moscow-Leningrad, 1933), 273.

17. See Bowlt, "The World of Art," 214-15.

18. Mikhail Kuzmin, "Vospominaniia o N. N. Sapunove," in N. Sapunov. *Stikhi. Vospominaniia. Kharakteristiki* (Moscow, 1916), 46-7.

19. Valentine Marcadé, *Le Renouveau de l'Art Pictural Russe 1863-1914* (Lausanne, 1971), 61.

20. See N. P. Pakhomov, *Abramtsevo* (Moscow, 1969).

21. Valentine Bill, *The Forgotten Class* (New York, 1959).

22. See Michael Ginsburg, "Art Collectors of Old Russia: The Morozovs and the Shchukins," *Apollo* (December 1973), 470-85; and Pavel Buryshkin, *Moskva kupecheskaia* (New York, 1954).

23. A. M. Pankratova, editor, *Istoriia Moskvy*, vol. 5 (Moscow, 1955), 55 ff.

24. See P.A. Berlin, *Russkaia burzhuaziia v staroe i novoe vremia* (Moscow, 1922), 292 ff.

25. Alexander Solzhenitsyn mentions in his *Gulag Archipelago* I-II, translated by Thomas Whitney (New York, 1974), that a number of people were arrested in the USSR in the early 1920s, accused of being counter-revolutionary agents of Pavel Riabushinsky and his associates (p. 47).

26. Buryshkin, *Moskva*, 192.

27. Andrei Belyi, *Mezhdu dvukh revoliutsii* (Moscow, 1934), 72-3.

28. Sergei Shcherbatov, *Khudozhnik v ushedshei Rossii* (New York, 1955), 41.

29. John Bowlt, "The 'Blue Rose' Movement and Russian Symbolist Painting," doctoral dissertation, University of St. Andrews, 1972, 178.

30. Viktor Lobanov, *Kanuny* (Moscow, 1968), 179.

31. Bowlt, "Blue Rose," 180.

32. Shcherbatov, *Khudozhnik*, 41.

33. The neo-classicism of Riabushinsky's villa seems in direct contrast to his life-style in general, yet as Carl Schorske has pointed out with regard to Adolf Loos' central European houses, a geometrical, rationally ordered house could be a surrogate for a rational world gone awry outside. While Schiele's and Kokoschka's works hung best in Loos' houses, so too did Kuznetsov's and Arapov's in Riabushinsky's villa. See Carl Schorske, "Cultural Hothouse," *New York Review of Books*, v. 22, No. 20 (11 December 1975), 39-44.

34. Shcherbatov, *Khudozhnik*, 41.

35. Letter to John Bowlt from Mikhail Bakhrushin, quoted in John Bowlt, "Nikolai Riabushinsky: Playboy of the Eastern World," *Apollo* (December 1973), 488.

36. A notice about the projected "Palace of Arts" appeared in *Zolotoe Runo*, 1909, No. 1, 110-11.

37. Stepan Riabushinsky, quoted in John Bowlt, "Nikolai Riabushinsky," 487.

38. See, for example, Sidney Harcave, *The Russian Revolution of 1905* (New York, 1964); Lev Trotsky, *1905* (New York, 1971); David Walder, *The Short Victorious War: The Russo-Japanese Conflict, 1904-1905* (London, 1973).

39. These questions are discussed in more detail in the following works: V. Lobanov, *1905g. i zhivopis'* (Moscow, 1922); V. A. Desnitsky and K. D. Muratova, editors, *Revoliutsiia 1905 goda i russkaia literatura* (Moscow, 1956); E. P. Gomberg-Verzhbinskaia, *Russkoe iskusstvo i revoliutsiia 1905 goda* (Leningrad, 1960).

40. Benois, *Memoirs*, II, 214-15.

41. Alexandre Benois, *Reminiscences of the Russian Ballet* (London, 1941), 238.

42. Ibid., 226. A broader reaction to the war and revolution may be seen in the play "Makov tsvet" (1906), co-authored by Merezhkovsky, Gippius, and Filosofov. For more on Merezhkovsky and the 1905 revolution, see Bernice Glatzer Rosenthal, *Dmitrii Sergeevich Merezhkovsky and the Silver Age* (The Hague, 1975), especially Chapter 7.

43. Haskell, *Diaghileff*, 123.

44. M. A. Beketova, *Aleksandr Blok: Biograficheskii ocherk* (Petersburg, 1922), 97.

45. S. Diaghilev, "V chas itogov," speech reprinted in *Vesy*, 1905, No. 4, 45-6.

46. *Zolotoe Runo*, 1906, No. 1, 4.

47. Albert Guérard, *Art For Art's Sake* (New York, 1936), 72.

48. Hilton Kramer, "The World of Art in Exile," *The New York Times*, 3 May 1970, 23.

49. Holbrook Jackson, *The Eighteen Nineties* (New York, 1927), 18.

50. Ibid., 22-3.

51. No consistent definitions of the terms "decadence" and "symbolism," "first-genera-tion" and "second-generation" symbolists have yet emerged. See, for example, the discussion of this problem in Renato Poggioli, *Poets of Russia* (Cambridge, Mass., 1960); James West, *Russian Symbolism* (London, 1970); and Viktor Erlich, "Russian Symbolism and Polish Neo-Romanticism: Notes on Comparative Nomenclature of Slavic Modernism" in *American Contributions to the 7th International Congress of Slavists*, II (The Hague, 1973), 181-97. In general, in this work "decadents" and "first-generation symbolists" are considered roughly to refer to the same group, succeeded after 1905 by the "second-generation symbolists," who are this work's principal concern. Finally, these are primarily literary distinctions and do not mean quite the same thing when referring to artistic developments.

NOTES TO CHAPTER II

(In notes to this, and the following chapters, *Zolotoe Runo* will be indicated by *ZR*)

1. M. A. Mamontov, quoted in V. M. Lobanov, *Kanuny* (Moscow, 1968), 179.

2. *ZR*, 1906, No. 1, note inserted before p. 7.

3. On this group, see Andrei Belyi, *Nachalo veka* (Moscow, 1933), Chapter 1.

4. Ilya Ehrenburg, *Liudi, gody, zhizn'* (Moscow, 1966), 107.

5. Johannes von Guenther, *Ein Leben im Ostwind* (Munich, 1969), 134.

6. On February 1, 1906, Vrubel received the following telegram in the hospital: "Celebrating the appearance of the first issue of *Zolotoe Runo*, we drink to your health. Riabushinsky, Briusov, Belyi, Grabar, Milioti, Vinogradov, Kuznetsov, Feofilaktov, Vorot-nikov, Petrovskaia, Tarovaty." Quoted in Mikhail Vrubel', *Perepiska* (Leningrad, 1963), 135.

7. See P. Muratov, "Novye priobreteniia Tretiakovskoi Gallerei," *ZR*, 1908, No. 2, 72-4.

8. For a discussion of "Starinnye oktavy," see Bernice Glatzer Rosenthal, *Dmitrii Sergeevich Merezhkovsky and the Silver Age* (The Hague, 1975), 25-8.

9. For example, see Lev Trotsky, *1905*, translated by Anya Bostock (New York, 1971), "Censorship Battles."

10. See V. Kranikhfeld's review on pages 53-4.

11. D. S. Merezhkovskii, "Vse protiv vsekh," *ZR*, 1906, No. 1, 92.

12. For more on this, see Chapter 3.

13. K. Siunnerberg, "Sukhie listia," *ZR*, 1906, No. 1, 126.

14. Lobanov, *Kanuny*, 179.

15. M. A. Mamontov, quoted in Lobanov, *Kanuny*, 181.

16. Lobanov, *Kanuny*, 173.

17. Viktor Hoffmann, quoted in John Bowlt, "The 'Blue Rose' Movement and Russian Symbolist Painting," unpubished doctoral dissertation, University of St. Andrews (1972), 178. Viktor Lobanov has recalled Tarovaty's interest in decorative art in his *Kanuny*, 157-8.

18. "N. Ia. Tarovaty," *ZR*, 1906, No. 10, 74.

19. Andrei Belyi, *Mezhdu dvukh revoliutsii* (Moscow, 1934), 245.

20. Valerii Briusov, *Dnevniki 1891-1910* (Moscow, 1927), 137.

21. There are few primary sources on Tasteven. For example, Chulkov mentions in his memoirs a collection of 70 letters from Tasteven in his possession which apparently no longer exist in the USSR [Georgii Chulkov, *Gody stranstvii* (Moscow, 1930), 183]. V. N. Orlov also

notes in his introduction to *Aleksandr Blok. Andrei Belyi. Perepiska* (Moscow, 1940) that Tasteven's letters to Blok do not exist. There are no listings for Tasteven in the published guides for the Soviet archives beyond a few letters peripheral to his major activities.

22. Grabar letter to Benois, July 18, 1906, quoted in O. I. Podobedova, *Igor Emmanuilovich Grabar* (Moscow, n.d.) 137.

23. Chulkov, *Gody,* 183.

24. G. E. Tasteven, *Futurizm: na puti k novomu simvolizmu* (Moscow, 1914).

25. Lobanov, *Kanuny,* 99.

26. Ibid., 174.

27. "Vulgarno-zateilivoe izdanie," *Sovremennaia zhizn'* review (1906, No. 1, 155-7), quoted in B. A. Bialik, editor, *Russkaia literatura kontsa XIX-nachala XX veka,* volume 2 (Moscow, 1971), 490.

28. Vl. Kranikhfel'd, "Zolotoe Runo," *Mir Bozhii,* 1906, No. 4, 58.

29. Ibid.

30. V. Briusov letter to P. P. Pertsov, February 17, 1906, quoted in N. Ashukin, *Valerii Briusov* (Moscow, 1929), 217.

31. Belyi, *Mezhdu,* 73.

32. S. I. Mamontov, quoted in Lobanov, *Kanuny,* 99.

33. Vrubel', *Perepiska,* 119.

34. This is Lobanov's contention, and Bowlt repeats it in his "Nikolai Riabushinsky, Playboy of the Eastern World," *Apollo* (December, 1973), 491.

35. Valentine Marcadé, *Le Renouveau de l'art pictural russe 1863-1914* (Lausanne, 1971), 491.

36. Lobanov, *Kanuny,* 179.

37. V. Briusov, "Kliuchi Tain," *Vesy,* 1906, No. 1, 3-21.

38. G. Chulkov, "Vesy," *Apollon,* 1910, No. 6, 17.

39. Tovarishch German, "Zolotoe Runo," *Vesy,* 1906, No. 2, 82.

40. Ibid.

41. Ibid., 83.

42. Ibid.

43. Belyi, *Mezhdu,* 245.

NOTES TO CHAPTER III

1. *ZR,* 1906, No. 2, 136-7.

2. *ZR,* 1906, No. 4, 90-1.

3. Ibid., 91.

4. M. A. Vrubel, *Perepiska* (Leningrad, 1963), 134.

5. Ibid., 119.

6. Valerii Briusov, "Posledniaia rabota Vrubelia," in Vrubel, *Perepiska,* 264.

7. The work eventually found itself in the collection of Riabushinsky's brother Mikhail, and for this reason was not destroyed by the fire in the "Black Swan" [see S. P. Iaremich, *Mikhail Aleksandrovich Vrubel* (Moscow, 1911), 168a].

8. Briusov, "Posledniaia," 269.

9. Oleg Maslenikov, *The Frenzied Poets* (Berkeley and Los Angeles, 1952), 99.

10. For more on Musatov, see Alla Rusakova, *Borisov-Musatov* (Leningrad, 1975).

11. *ZR,* 1906, No. 3, 63-5.

12. *ZR,* 1906, No. 3, 67-71.

13. A. Shervashidze, "Aleksandr Benua," *ZR,* 1906, No. 2, 3-7.

14. V. Rozanov, "M. V. Nesterov," *ZR,* 1907, No. 4, 3-7.

15. A. Sredin, "Biograficheskii ocherk," *ZR,* 1907, No. 2, 7-8.

16. S. Makovskii, "N. Rerikh," *ZR,* 1907, No. 4, 3-7.

17. A. Rostislavov, "Individualizm Rerikha," *ZR,* 1907, No. 4, 8-10.

18. "Drevne-russkaia zhivopis' (XV-XVIII vv.): Ikonopisanie v Rossii do vtoroi poloviny XVII veka; Freski paperti Blagoveshchenskogo sobora v Moskve; Vliianie inostrannykh khudozhnikov na russkoe iskusstvo vo vtoroi polovine XVII veka; Zhivopisets Vasilii Poznanskii, ego proizvedeniia i ucheniki; Russkii zhanr XVII veka," 5-98.

19. *ZR,* 1906, No. 11-12, 149.

20. B. Dikovskii, "Neskol'ko slov ob severnykh tserkovnykh postroikakh shatrovogo perioda," *ZR,* 1907, No. 6, 59-62.

21. E. O., "Pomorskie rukopisi, ikh miniatiury i ornamentatsiia," *ZR,* 1907, No. 10, 19-23.

22. V. Rozanov, "Aleksandr Andreevich Ivanov," *ZR,* 1906, No. 11-12, 3-6.

23. *ZR,* 1907, No. 7-8-9.

24. A. Benua, "Sobranie M. I. Miatlevoi v S.-Peterburge," *ZR,* 1906, No. 11-12, 35-41.

25. A. I. Uspensky, "Starinnaia mebel gr. A. V. Olsufieva," *ZR,* 1907, No. 3, 29-33.

26. *ZR,* 1907, No. 11-12, 35-6.

27. K. A. Siunnerberg, review of S. Makovskii's *Stranitsy khudozhestvennoi, kritiki, ZR,* 1906, No. 6, 105.

28. *ZR,* 1906, No. 6, 78-80.

29. *ZR,* 1906, No. 2, 95-6.

30. *ZR,* 1906, No. 4, 76-9.

31. S. Makovskii, "Pamiatnik M. I. Glinke," *ZR,* 1906, No. 4, 92-4.

32. *ZR,* 1906, No. 3, 129. Rostislavov later wrote a book entitled *Kuindzhi* (St. Petersburg, 1914).

33. *ZR,* 1906, No. 5, 56-9.

34. On Čiurlionis, see Mark Etkind, *Mir, kak bol'shaia simfoniia* (Leningrad, 1970).

35. *ZR,* 1907, No. 6, 31-40.

36. *ZR,* 1907, No. 6, 32.

37. *ZR,* 1906, No. 2, 80-88.

38. Ibid., 80.

39. Ibid., 82.

40. Ibid., 85.

41. Ibid., 87.

42. Ibid.

43. See Alexandre Benois, *The Russian School of Painting,* translated by Avrahm Yarmolinsky (New York, 1916), 199.

44. Shervashidze was a painter and theatrical designer. He studied at the Moscow School of Painting, Sculpture, and Architecture, and from 1893 until 1906 under Jullien and Corman in Paris. After 1907 he designed sets for the Marinsky, Aleksandrinsky, and Starinny Theaters in Petersburg.

45. *ZR,* 1906, No. 6, 65.

46. Ibid., 68.

47. Ibid., 72.

48. D. V. Filosofov, "Misticheskii anarkhizm: dekadenstvo, obshchestvennost' i misticheskii anarkhizm," *ZR,* 1906, No. 10, 58-65.

49. Ibid., 60.

50. See Alexandre Benois, *Reminiscences of the Russian Ballet,* translated by Mary Britneva (London, 1941), 186.

51. *ZR,* 1906, No. 10, 66-72. For two contradictory descriptions of Voloshin, see Ivan Bunin, *Vospominaniia* (Paris, 1950), 186-7, and Marina Tsvetaeva, "Zhivoe i o zhivom (Voloshin)" in her *Proza* (Letchworth, 1969), 9-76.

52. Ibid., 72.

53. A. Rostislavov, "Individualizm Rerikha," *ZR*, 1907, No. 4, 8-10.

54. G. Tasteven, "Nitsshe i sovremennyi krizis (filosofskii etiud)," *ZR*, 1907, No. 7-8-9, 110-5.

55. Ibid., 110.

56. Ibid., 115.

57. *ZR*, 1907, No. 11-12, 75-84.

58. Ibid., 84.

59. *ZR*, 1907, No. 11-12, 37-46.

60. This approach had apparently been borrowed from *The Yellow Book*. See Katherine Lyon Mix, *Study in Yellow: The Yellow Book and its Contributors* (Lawrence, Kansas, 1960), 73.

61. A. Belyi, "9 pesen Gete N. Metnera," *ZR*, 1906, No. 4, 105-7.

62. *ZR*, 1906, No. 1, 98-103.

63. Ibid., 103.

64. Ibid., 101.

65. Ibid., 103.

66. Ibid., 101.

67. *ZR*, 1906, No. 2, 136-7.

68. An examination of the foreign contacts of, and contributions to *Vesy* is given in some detail in Georgette Donchin, *The Influence of French Symbolism on Russian Poetry* (The Hague, 1958), 49-66.

69. Il'ia Erenburg, *Liudi, gody, zhizn'* (Moscow, 1961), 168-9.

70. M. Voloshin, quoted in Ibid., 171.

71. *ZR*, 1906, No. 6, unpaged endpiece.

72. *ZR*, 1907, No. 2, 38-48; No. 3, 41-53.

73. *ZR*, 1907, No. 4, 60.

74. *ZR*, 1906, No. 7-8-9, 121-8; No. 10, 39-46.

75. *ZR*, 1907, No. 4, 32-45.

76. *ZR*, 1906, No. 11-12, 59-67.

77. *ZR*, 1906, No. 6, 43-52.

78. V. Rozanov, "Egipet," *ZR*, 1906, No. 5, 51-5.

79. A. Belyi, "Pis'mo iz Miunkhena," *ZR*, 1906, No. 11-12, 115-8.

80. "Mirovaia ekteniia," *ZR*, 1906, No. 3, 72-83.

81. "Venets lavrovy," *ZR*, 1906, No. 5, 43-50.

82. "Henrik Ibsen," *ZR*, 1906, No. 6, 73-5.

83. "Ob Uailde," *ZR*, 1906, No. 2, 91-4.

84. "Posleslovie k kommentariiu 'Legendy o velikom inkvizitore,'" *ZR*, 1906, No. 11-12, 97-101.

85. "Poeziia Ia. P. Polonskogo," *ZR*, 1906, No. 11-12, 102-6.

86. *Aleksandr Blok i Andrei Belyi. Perepiska* (Moscow, 1940), 166.

87. *ZR*, 1906, No. 11-12, 88-96.

88. "Karl V—dialog o realizme v iskusstve," *ZR*, 1906, No. 4, 61-7.

89. "Odna iz russkikh poetiko-filosofskikh kontseptsii," *ZR*, 1906, No. 7-8-9, 146-50.

90. "Iz starykh pisem," *ZR*, 1907, No. 2, 49-59.

91. Konst. Erberg, "Bezvlastie" *ZR*, 1907, No. 4, 46-63.

92. *ZR*, 1906, No. 4, 68-73; No. 5, 64-72.

93. *ZR*, 1907, No. 5, 47-55.

94. *ZR*, 1906, No. 11-12, 107-14.

95. *ZR*, 1907, No. 2, 60-4.

96. Sergei Krechetov, review of *Novye zvuki* by A. Raisky, and *K svetu i svobode* by Z. N.

Obolenskaia, *ZR,* 1906, No. 4, 110.

97. A. Belyi, review of P. V. Znamenskii, *Pravoslavie i sovremennaia zhizn',* ZR, 1906, No. 6, 101.

98. "Saadi," review of P. V. Arseniev, *Saltykov-Shchedrin, ZR,* 1906, No. 11-12, 155.

99. "Sigurd," review of eighth and ninth *Znanie* sborniki, *ZR,* 1906, No. 4, 112.

100. *ZR,* 1906, No. 4, 112. Dymov wrote a number of imitatively symbolist melodramas, and also worked on the magazine *Teatr i Iskusstvo* (St. Petersburg, 1901-16), where he was described as being "too much of an artist for editorial work." See A. R. Kugel, *List'ia s dereva—vospominaniia* (Leningrad, 1926), 34 ff.

101. For a description of this entire affair, see Maslenikov, *Frenzied,* 110 ff., or in more detail, Vladislav Khodasevich, "Konets Renaty," in his *Nekropol* (Brussels, 1940), 5-99.

102. For more on Chukovsky during this period, see Jeffrey Brooks, "The Young Kornei Chukovsky (1905-1914): A Liberal Critic in Search of Cultural Unity," *Russian Review* (January 1974), volume 33, No. 1, 50-62.

103. Letter to E. K. Medtner, quoted in A. N. Scriabin, *Pis'ma* (Moscow, 1965), 407.

104. *ZR,* 1906, No. 2, 136-7.

105. S. S. Prokofiev, *S. S. Prokofiev: Materialy, dokumenty, vospominaniia* (Moscow, 1961), 138.

106. *ZR,* 1906, No. 6, 84.

107. Konstantin Stanislavsky has left an interesting portrait of Sats' method of working on the music for Hamsun's play; see his *Moia zhizn' v iskusstve* (Moscow, 1962), 376.

108. S., "Moskovskaia muzykal'naia zhizn' " *ZR,* 1906, No. 10, 109.

109. I. A. S., "Satana v muzyke," *ZR,* 1907, No. 1, 65-7. For more on this, see Chapter 4.

110. I. A. S., "O vzaimootnoshenii muzyki i teksta v opere," *ZR,* 1907, No. 1, 71-3; "Ob opernykh nedorazumeniiakh voobshche," *ZR,* 1906, No. 2, 70-4.

111. Aleksandr Struve, "Muzykal'nye pis'ma (Moskva)," *ZR,* 1906, No. 3, 117.

112. Mizgir, "Musorgsky," *ZR,* 1906, No. 3, 84.

113. *ZR,* 1907, No. 1, 93.

114. *ZR,* 1906, No. 11-12, 125.

115. *ZR,* 1907, No. 6, 54-7.

116. Volfing, "Otgoloski iubileia Shumanna," *ZR,* 1906, No. 11-12, 126-7.

117. Koreshchenko, *ZR,* 1906, No. 2, 65.

118. Volfing, "Sixtus Beckmesser Redivivus," *ZR,* 1907, No. 2, 66.

119. Ibid., 69.

120. Ibid.

121. V. K., "Maks Reger," *ZR,* 1906, No. 2, 97-101.

122. V. K., "Muzykal'naia khronika Peterburga," *ZR,* 1906, No. 5, 66.

123. Andrei Belyi, *Mezhdu dvukh revoliutsii* (Moscow, 1934), 343.

124. Volfing, "Cagliostro v muzyke ('Etude' o 'novoi' muzyke)," *ZR,* 1907, No. 4, 67.

125. Ibid., 67.

126. Ibid., 68.

127. Volfing, "Modernizm v muzyke" *ZR,* 1907, No. 3, 68.

128. Ibid., 69.

129. *ZR,* 1907, No. 7-8-9, 116-21; No. 10, 58-65.

130. Ibid., 1907, No. 10, 62.

NOTES TO CHAPTER IV

1. *ZR,* 1907, No. 4, 74.

2. *ZR,* 1907, No. 6, 68.

3. *ZR*, 1907, No. 5, 63-74.
4. On this, see L. K. Erman, *Intelligentsiia v pervoi russkoi revoliutsii* (Moscow, 1966).
5. A. Blok, "O realistakh," *ZR*, 1907, No. 5, 63-4.
6. Ibid., 65.
7. Ibid., 67.
8. Ibid., 72.
9. See Chapter 3.
10. *Vesy*, 1907, No. 8, 78-9.
11. *ZR*, 1907, No. 7-8-9, 160.
12. For a discussion of this review, see Chapter 3.
13. *ZR*, 1906, No. 3, 131-2.
14. Ibid., 131.
15. Ibid.
16. Ibid., 132.
17. *Vesy*, 1906, No. 5, 87-9.
18. Ibid., 87.
19. Ibid., 88.
20. Ibid., 89.
21. *ZR*, 1906, No. 5, 80.
22. Ibid.
23. "Voprosy," *Vesy*, 1906, No. 6, 73-6.
24. Ibid., 73.
25. Ibid., 75.
26. Ibid., 76.
27. Pentaur, "*Zolotoe Runo*. 1907 No. 1 i 2," *Vesy*, 1907, No. 3, 74-6.
28. Ibid., 75-6.
29. Ibid., 76.
30. Ibid., 76-80.
31. Ibid., 76.
32. *ZR*, 1907, No. 4, 79-80.
33. Ibid., 1907, No. 4, 80.
34. Ibid.
35. Ibid.
36. *Vesy*, 1907, No. 6, 75-6.
37. Ibid., 76.
38. Andrei Belyi, *Vospominaniia o Bloke* (Moscow-Berlin, 1922-23), 498-9.
39. This is discussed in some detail with regard to Blok in V. N. Orlov, "Istoriia odnoi druzhby-vrazhdy," in *Aleksandr Blok i Andrei Belyi: Perepiska* (Moscow, 1940), xxvii ff.
40. Andrei Belyi, *Mezhdu dvukh revoliutsii* (Moscow, 1934), 245.
41. Ibid.
42. Ibid., 246.
43. Belyi continually resented his necessary dependence on the rich Maecenases and attacked the art patrons (Riabushinsky among them) in his "Khudozhniki oskorbiteliam" in *Vesy*, 1907, No. 1, 53-6.
44. Orlov, "Istoriia."
45. Belyi, *Mehzdu*, 247.
46. *ZR*, 1907, No. 10, 58-60.
47. 1907, No. 60, 66.
48. Belyi, *Vospominaniia*, 498-9.
49. Oleg Maslenikov, *The Frenzied Poets* (Berkeley and Los Angeles, 1952), quoting

Literaturnoe nasledstvo, volume 27-8 (Moscow, 1937), 384-5, 406.

50. Belyi, *Vospominaniia,* 506-7.

51. Maslenikov, *Frenzied,* 109.

52. *ZR,* 1907, No. 7-8-9, 160.

53. *Chas,* No. 24 (11 September 1907).

54. See Andreev's letter to Gorky, quoted in James B. Woodward, *Leonid Andreev: A Study* (Oxford, 1969), 117.

55. Blok letter to V. Ivanov, 5 September 1907, quoted in E. L. Belkind, "Blok i Viacheslav Ivanov," in *Blokovskii sbornik* (Tartu, 1971), volume 2, 373.

56. See Georgii Chulkov, *Gody stranstvii* (Moscow, 1930), 184.

57. Ibid., 396.

58. Uncertain date, quoted in G. G. Shmakov, "Blok i Kuzmin," *Blokovskii sbornik* (Tartu, 1971), volume 2, 360.

59. "Ot redaktsii," *ZR,* 1907, No. 7-8-9, 160.

60. *Vesy,* 1908, No. 2, 116.

61. "Ot redaktsii," *ZR,* 1907, No. 6, 68.

62. John Malmsted considers this the most likely reason; letter to the author, 8-24-76.

63. The announcement was made in *ZR,* 1907, No. 10, 86.

64. F. D. Reeve, *Aleksandr Blok* (New York, 1962), 220-1.

NOTES TO CHAPTER V

1. Mirsky has remarked that all Blok's articles should be called "lyrical essays." See D. S. Mirsky, "O proze Aleksandra Bloka," in A. A. Blok, *Sobranie sochinenii,* vol. 8 (Leningrad, 1936), ix ff.

2. *ZR,* 1906, No. 11-12, 107-14.

3. A. A. Blok, "Bezvremene," *ZR,* 1906, No. 11-12, 107.

4. Ibid., 107.

5. A. A. Blok, "O lirike," *ZR,* 1907, No. 6, 41-53.

6. Ibid., 41.

7. Ibid., 42.

8. Ibid., 43.

9. Ibid., 42-3.

10. Ibid., 47.

11. *ZR,* 1907, No. 7-8-9, 122-31.

12. Ibid., 128.

13. Ibid., 125

14. *ZR,* 1908, No. 3-4, 78-86; 1908, No. 5, 51-9.

15. *ZR,* 1907, No. 11-12, 91-8.

16. A. A. Blok, *Pis'ma k rodnym* (Moscow-Leningrad, 1927), volume 1, 182 (27 November 1907).

17. A. A. Blok, "Literaturnye itogi 1907 g.," *ZR,* 1907, No. 11-12, 92.

18. Ibid., 97.

19. George Putnam, "Aleksandr Blok and the Russian Intelligentsia," *Slavic and East European Journal,* Spring 1965, volume 9, No. 1, 33-4.

20. *ZR,* 1908, No. 2, 55-9.

21. Ibid., 57.

22. Ibid.

23. Ibid.

24. Ibid.

25. Ibid.

26. Ibid.

27. Ibid.

28. Ibid., 58. Blok's Nietzschean terminology was reflective of his interests at the time; he was especially taken with the Apollonian-Dionysian contrasts of *The Birth of Tragedy*, which he read in 1906, and upon which he planned to base a play, "Dionis Gipoboreiskii."

29. "Pis'mo o poezii," *ZR*, 1908, No. 7-8-9, 94-9; 1908, No. 10, 46-51.

30. "Solntse nad Rossiei," *ZR*, 1908, No. 7-8-9, 113-4.

31. "Rossiia i intelligentsiia," *ZR*, 1909, No. 1, 78-85. For a lengthier examination of this theme, see Putnam, "Aleksandr Blok."

32. *ZR*, 1907, No. 2, 60-4.

33. Blok letter to Belyi, 3 January 1907, in *Aleksandr Blok i Andrei Belyi: Perepiska* (Moscow, 1940), 167.

34. *ZR*, 1907, No. 5, 64.

35. See Blok's very appreciative article on Tolstoy in this regard, "Solntse nad Rossiei."

36. Blok, *Pis'ma k rodnym*, 27 November 1907, 182.

37. On this sense of apocalypticism, see Samual D. Cioran, *The Apocalyptic Symbolism of Andrei Belyi* (The Hague, 1973).

38. *ZR*, 1908, No. 11-12, 62-9.

39. A. A. Blok, *Zapisnye knizhki* (Leningrad, 1930), 29 October 1908, 92-3.

40. *ZR*, 1909, No. 1, 78-85.

41. Ibid., 84.

42. Blok, *Pis'ma k rodnym*, 14 December 1908, 240.

43. G. Chulkov, "Litsom k litsu," *ZR*, 1909, No. 1, 105-7.

44. D. S. Merezhkovskii, "Narod i intelligentsiia," *Rech'*, 16 November 1908.

45. For more on *Vekhi*, see Putnam, "Aleksandr Blok"; Nicolas Zernov, *The Russian Religious Renaissance of the Twentieth Century* (New York, 1963), 111-30; and Leonard Schapiro, "The *Vekhi* Group and the Mystique of Revolution," *The Slavonic and East European Review*, XXXIV, No. 82 (December 1955), 56-76.

46. M. A. Beketova, *Aleksandr Blok: Biograficheskii ocherk* (Petersburg, 1922), 118.

47. Mochulskii, *Blok*, 247-8.

48. For more on Blok's trip to Italy, see Lucy E. Vogel, *Aleksandr Blok: The Journey to Italy* (Ithaca, 1973).

49. V. A. Desnitskii, "Blok, kak literaturnyi kritik," in Blok, *Sobranie sochinenii*, vol. 10 (Leningrad, 1935), 5-6.

50. *Perepiska*, 220.

51. The speech, "O sovremennom sostoianii russkogo simvolizma," later appeared as an article in *Apollon*, 1910, No. 8, 21-30.

52. Blok published three collections of prose articles in 1918 and 1919, many of which were reworkings of his *Zolotoe Runo* articles in light of the 1917 revolutions: *Rossiia i intelligentsiia* (Moscow, 1918); *Katilina* (Petersburg, 1918); *Rossiia i intelligentsiia* (1907-1918), second edition (Petersburg, 1919).

NOTES TO CHAPTER VI

1. See James West, *Russian Symbolism* (London, 1970).

2. "Vesnoiu na severe," *ZR*, 1906, No. 11-12, 48-9; "Zhatva," *ZR*, 1907, No. 7-8-9, 67.

3. Including *Voprosy Zhizni* and *Novyi Put'*; see Georgii Chulkov, *Gody stranstvii* (Moscow, 1930), 66 ff.

4. Ibid., 87.

5. *Fakely*, vol. 1 (Petersburg, 1906).

6. Georgii Chulkov, "O misticheskom anarkhizme," *Voprosy Zhizni*, 1906, No. 7, 199-204.

7. Viacheslav Ivanov, "Krizis individualizma," *Voprosy Zhizni*, 1905, No. 7, No. 9.

8. See Georgii Chulkov, "Ob utverzhdenii lichnosti," *Fakely*, vol. 2 (Petersburg, 1907).

9. Andrei Belyi, "Georgii Chulkov 'O misticheskom anarkhizme,'" *ZR*, 1906, No. 7-8-9, 174-5.

10. Dmitrii Filosofov, "Misticheskii anarkhizm: Dekadenstvo, obshchestvennost', i misticheskii anarkhizm," *ZR*, 1906, No. 10, 58-65.

11. Ibid., 59.

12. Ibid., 65.

13. Chulkov, *Gody*, 183.

14. See, for example, A. Toporkov's "O novom realizme (Boris Zaitsev)," *ZR*, 1907, No. 10, 46-9.

15. Georgii Chulkov, "Pokryvalo Izidy," *ZR*, 1908, No. 5, 72.

16. Ibid. Similar ideas were expressed in the same writer's "Liliia i roza," *ZR*, 1908, No. 6, 51-4.

17. See "Predchuvstvie i predvestie," *ZR*, 1906, No. 4, 68-73, No. 6, 53-63; "Ty esi," *ZR*, 1907, No. 7-8-9, 100-2; "Dve stikhii v sovremennom simvolizme," *ZR*, 1908, No. 3-4, 86-94; "Drevnii uzhas—po povodu kartiny L. Baksta 'Terror Antiquus' (publichnaia lektsiia)," *ZR*, 1909, No. 4, 51-65; "O russkoi idee," *ZR*, 1909, No. 1, 85-93. West has characterized Ivanov's theories of "realistic symbolism" as being "not...a systematically expressed esthetic, but...scattered literary-critical writings and isolated essays on philosophical and theoretical questions, produced very often in a spirit of polemic or of self-defense." *Russian Symbolism*, 107.

18. For a detailed examination of Ivanov's theories, see West, *Russian Symbolism*.

19. V. Briusov, "Vekhi IV: Fakely," *Vesy*, 1906, No. 5, 56.

20. Ibid., 284.

21. V. Briusov, "Vekhi V. Misticheskie anarkhisty," *Vesy*, 1906, No. 8, 43-7

22. "Detskaia svistulka," *Vesy*, 1907, No. 8, 54-8; "Shtempelevannaia kalosha," *Vesy*, 1907, No. 5, 59-62; "O propovednikakh, epikureitsakh, misticheskikh anarkhistakh i t. p.," *ZR*, 1907, No. 1, 61-4; "Volnootpushchenniki," *Vesy*, 1908, No. 2, 69-72; "O pianstve slovesnom," *Arabeski* (Moscow, 1911), 358-61.

23. See Belyi's "Khudozhniki oskorbiteliam," *Vesy*, 1907, No. 1, 53-6.

24. "Detskaia svistulka," 55.

25. Ibid., 58.

26. A. Belyi, review of *Tsvetnik or*, *Vesy*, 1907, No. 6, 67.

27. Ibid., 70.

28. Chulkov even appeared in Belyi's novel *Serebriannyi golub* of 1909 as Semen Chukholka, a confused proponent of mystical anarchism.

29. A. Belyi, "Aleksandr Blok. Liricheskie dramy," *Vesy*, 1908, No. 5, 66.

30. On this period in Blok's life, see, for example, his *Zapisnye knizhki* (Leningrad, 1932).

31. *ZR*, 1907, No. 2, 76.

32. *Obrazovanie*, 1908, No. 8, 67; quoted in Pavel Gromov, *Geroi i vremia* (Leningrad, 1961), 479.

33. Chulkov, *Gody*, 375-6; dated Shakhmatovo, 17 August 1907.

34. See Chapter 5.

35. E. Semenov, "Le mysticisme anarchique," *Le Mercure de France*, No. 242 (16 July 1907), 361-4.

36. Chulkov, *Gody*, 393.

37. *ZR*, 1907, No. 7-8-9, 102.

38. "Delo domashnee," *Tovarishch*, 23 September 1907.

39. Chulkov, *Gody*, 184.

40. *ZR*, 1908, No. 1; 61-4.

41. Ibid., 61.

42. For more on Gorodetsky (from a contemporary Soviet point of view), see S. M. Mashinskii, "Sergei Gorodetskii," in Sergei Gorodetskii, *Stikhotvoreniia i poemy* (Leningrad, 1974), 5-52.

43. Serzh Geliotropov, "Razsuzhdenie o starosti, kriticheskikh priemakh i tak voobshche," *ZR*, 1908, No. 3-4, 125-7.

44. S. Gorodetskii, "Glukhoe vremia," *ZR*, 1908, No. 6, 69-70; "Amin," *ZR*, 1908, No. 7, 105-7.

45. *ZR*, 1909, No. 1, 93-101.

46. Ibid., 94.

47. S. Gorodetskii, "Blizhaishaia zadacha russkoi literatury," *ZR*, 1909, No. 4, 66-81.

48. See Chulkov, *Gody*, 183.

49. Empirik, "O 'chistom simvolizme,' teurgizme i nigilizme," *ZR*, No. 5, 77-8.

50. Empirik, "Sfinks bez zagadki," *ZR*, 1908, No. 11-12, 85-6.

51. Ibid., 86. The article was written in response to V. Bykov (Briusov), "Iz zhurnalov," *Vesy*, 1908, No. 10, 103-5.

52. G. T., "Po zvezdam (po povodu sbornika statei Viach. Ivanova)," *ZR*, 1909, No. 6, 74-6.

53. Ibid., 76.

54. Genrikh Tasteven, "Vozrozhdenie stilia (po povodu sbornika rasskazov Georgiia Chulkova)," *ZR*, 1909, No. 11-12, 87-9; in the same issue, the untitled review of a recent collection of Chulkov's stories, 102-3.

55. G. T., "Religiozno-filosofskie tendentsii 'Anatemy,'" *ZR*, 1909, No. 7-8-9, 142.

56. See Chulkov, *Gody*, 74.

57. See, for example, Belyi, *Arabeski*, 488-9.

58. Georgii Chulkov, "Iskhod," *ZR*, 1908, No. 7-8-9, 99-105. Gorodetsky's books *Iar* and *Perun* (both 1907) expressed his interests in old Slavonic mythology and the lives of simple people. Chulkov wrote of *Iar* later: "Mythology and folklore were not a subject of study for Gorodetsky; they were for him a subject of recollections." *Gody*, 166.

NOTES TO CHAPTER VII

1. *ZR*, 1906, No. 7-8-9, 121-8;, No. 10, 39-46.

2. Andrei Belyi, *Nachalo veka* (Moscow, 1933), 375.

3. E.g., see L. K. Erman, *Intelligentsiia v pervoi russkoi revoliutsii* (Moscow, 1966), 132.

4. *ZR*, 1906, No. 5, ii.

5. *ZR*, 1906, No. 10, i.

6. For an interesting discussion of this story, see Renate Schilk Bialy, "Devices for the Incongruous: A Study of A. M. Remizov's Prose," Ph. D. dissertation, UCLA, 1974, 52-61.

7. *ZR*, 1907, No. 1, 74.

8. On the "Devil" theme in Russian symbolist literature, see for example, A. E. Redko, *Literaturno-khudozhestvennye iskaniia v kontse XIX-nachala XX veka* (Leningrad, 1924), and among others, Olga Matich, *Paradox in the Religious Poetry of Zinaida Hippius* (Munich, 1972), especially pp. 92-9.

9. S. Makovskii, "Golubaia roza," *ZR*, 1907, No. 5, 25-8.

10. Ibid., 25.

11. Ibid., 26.

12. Ibid., 27.

13. A. Rostislavov, "Vystavochnoe tvorchestvo," *ZR*, 1907, No. 1, 76-7. Diaghilev's and Benois' *Mir Iskusstva* exhibitions had fulfilled Rostislavov's conditions, of course, but they were still notable exceptions. On the Union, see Vladimir Lapshin, *Soiuz russkikh khudozhnikov* (Leningrad, 1974).

14. Unpublished memoirs of Anatolii Arapov, quoted in John E. Bowlt, "Nikolai Riabushinsky: Playboy of the Eastern World," *Apollo* (December 1973), 491.

15. *ZR*, 1907, No. 4, 81.

16. N. Tarovatyi, "Na vystavke 'Mir Iskusstva,'" *ZR*, 1906, No. 3, 124.

17. For a detailed description of these works, see John E. Bowlt, "The 'Blue Rose' Movement and Russian Symbolist Painting," Ph. D. dissertation, University of St. Andrews, 1972.

18. Sergei Shcherbatov, *Khudozhnik v ushedshei Rossii* (New York, 1955), 40.

19. S. Glagol, "Golubaia roza," *Moskovskii Ezhednevnik*, No. 14 (7 April 1907), quoted in John E. Bowlt, "Russian Symbolism and the 'Blue Rose' Movement," *Slavonic and East European Review* (April 1937), 180.

20. I. Grabar, "Golubaia roza," *Vesy*, 1907, No. 5, 94-5.

21. Ibid., 96.

22. S. Makovskii, *Siluety russkikh khudozhnikov* (Prague, 1922), 133.

23. Valentin Serov, *Perepiska* (Leningrad-Moscow, 1937), 374.

24. Ibid., 374-5.

25. Camilla Gray feels Mercereau helped Riabushinsky with this, but there seems little justification for such a conclusion. Larionov's role in organizing the exhibition should also be mentioned here: Waldemar George says that Larionov "organized" the exhibition "with Riabushinsky's help" in his *Larionov* (Paris, 1966) and is supported in his view by Tamara Talbot Rice (*A Concise History of Russian Art*, New York, 1963) and François Daulte (introduction to the catalog of the Larionov exhibition, Musée Toulouse-Lautrec, Albi, June-September 1973). For Larionov to have held such a position of authority within the exhibition committee seems unlikely, although he did play an increasingly important role in the later *Zolotoe Runo* exhibitions. George's facts on this early period are questionable in any case, since he also says that Larionov was the creator of the *Golubaia roza* group, which is absolutely untrue.

26. For a list of works in the Morozov-Shchukin collections, see: Sergei Makovskii, "Frantsuzskie khudozhniki iz sobraniia I. A. Morozova," *Apollon*, 1912, No. 3-4, 5-16; Iakov Tugendkhol'd, "Frantsuzskoe sobranie S. I. Shchukina," *Apollon*, 1914, No. 1-2, 5-46.

27. Michael Ginsburg, "Art Collectors of Old Russia: The Morozovs and the Shchukins," *Apollo*, December 1973, 474.

28. Ibid., 482.

29. *ZR*, 1908, No. 6, 78. "French: Bonnard, Van Dongen, Van Gogh, Rouault, Valloton, Vuillard; Russians: Kuznetsov, Larionov, V. Milioti, Sarian, Riabushinsky, Utkin, etc." For a list of the works appearing in all three *Zolotoe Runo* exhibitions, see Valentine Marcadé, *Le Renouveau de l'art pictural russe 1863-1914* (Lausanne, 1971), 288-96.

30. *ZR*, 1908, No. 7-8-9.

31. For more on these articles, see Chapter 8.

32. (?) Matov, "Salon Zolotogo Runa," *Russkii Artist*, 27 April 1908, No. 14, quoted in Bowlt, "The 'Blue Rose' Movement and Russian Symbolist Painting," 282.

33. *ZR*, 1908, No. 10.

34. Igor Grabar, "Salon Zolotogo Runa," *Vesy*, 1908, No. 6, 91-4.

35. *ZR*, 1908, No. 7-8-9, 121.

36. Ibid.
37. Ibid.
38. Ibid., 122.
39. Ibid., 123.
40. Ibid.
41. *ZR*, 1908, No. 7-8-9, 124.
42. S. Iu., *ZR*, 1909, No. 2-3, 112-3.
43. M. L., *ZR*, 1909, No. 2-3, 113-4.
44. Introduction to the catalog of the "Salon Zolotoe Runo" (Moscow, 1909), quoted in Bowlt, "The 'Blue Rose' Movement and Russian Symbolist Painting," 308.
45. Empirik, "Neskol'ko slov o vystavke Zolotogo Runa," *ZR*, 1909, No. 2-3, i-iii.
46. Ibid., i.
47. Ibid., iii.
48. A list of paintings sold from the exhibition was given in *ZR*, 1909, No. 2-3, 116.
49. Gray, *Experiment*, 88.
50. An interesting book on Falk has appeared in East Germany: Dmitrii Sarabjanow, *Robert Falk* (Dresden, 1974).
51. *ZR*, 1909, No. 1, No. 2-3.
52. This final exhibition ran from 27 December 1909 to 31 January 1910.
53. Martiros Sarian, *Iz moei zhizni* (Moscow, 1970), 115-24.
54. A. Toporkov, "O tvorcheskom i sozertsatel'nom estetizme (po povodu vystavki Zolotoe Runa)," *ZR*, 1909, No. 11-12, 69-74.
55. Ibid., 74.
56. On this, see Bowlt, "The 'Blue Rose' Movement and Russian Symbolist Painting," 318.
57. Vladimir Markov, *Russian Futurism* (Berkeley and Los Angeles, 1968), 35.
58. Robert Goldwater, in his *Primitivism in Modern Painting* (New York, 1938), has noted that the first book on children's art was published in Italy in 1887 and translated into German in 1906. At the same time, there was a sudden growth in interest in the art of the child in England and Germany, "the direct result of an expansion of the educational system toward the inclusion of the poorer classes, and the consequent changes in curriculum." (187) In Russia, of course, the interest was considerably more theoretical, rather than being based on such social developments.
59. "Ob azbuke v kartinakh Aleksandra Benua," *ZR*, 1906, No. 3, 134.
60. "Dvazhdy dva—piat' (o rebenke i o genii)," *ZR*, 1907, No. 10, 43-5.
61. "Otkroveniia detskikh igr," *ZR*, 1907, No. 10, 68-75.
62. N. N., "Peterburgskaia khronika," *ZR*, 1908, No. 7-8-9, 119.
63. On this, see Bialy, "Remizov."
64. Jacob Bronowski, *The Ascent of Man* (Boston, 1973), Chapter 13, "The Long Childhood," *passim*.

NOTES TO CHAPTER VIII

1. On the foreign interests of other Russian modernist periodicals, see Georgette Donchin, *The Influence of French Symbolism on Russian Poetry* (The Hague, 1958), Chapter 2.
2. *ZR*, 1908, No. 6, 21-50.
3. E. Zagorskii, "Prometei molodoi Polshii," *ZR*, 1908, No. 10, 54-59.
4. "Tirtei," *ZR*, 1907, No. 2, 31-37; "Stezeiu Kaina," *ZR*, 1907, No. 11-12, 50-57.
5. "K etike pola," *ZR*, 1907, No. 11-12, 63-67.

6. "Den' sudnyi," *ZR*, 1909, Nos. 1-12.

7. See Irena Szwede, "The Works of Stanislaw Przybyszewskj and Their Reception in Russia at the Beginning of the XX Century," Ph.D. dissertation, Stanford University, 1970.

8. See Czeslaw Milosz, *The History of Polish Literature* (New York, 1969), 332. In his "K etike pola," 63, Przybyszewski wrote: " 'In the beginning there was sex. There is nothing besides it and everything is in it alone.' I wrote these words 17 years ago in my first book and they are still just as true today."

9. See, for example, Przybyszewski's manifesto for his Krakow journal *Zycie (Life)*, "Confietor" (1 January 1899); translated in Milosz, *History*, 330.

10. *ZR*, 1908, No. 10, 62-65.

11. "Ob Uailde," *ZR*, 1906, No. 2, 91-94.

12. *ZR*, 1908, No. 5, 66-72.

13. "Tvochestvo i mysl' (po povodu knigi A. Bergsona *Tvorcheskaia evoliutsiia*)," *ZR*, 1909, No. 5, 52-62.

14. "Novye tendentsii frantsuzskoi zhivopisi" (translated by Tasteven), *ZR*, 1908, Nos. 7-8-9, I-IV; No. 10, I-IV; No. 11-12, i-viii.

15. "Ustremleniia novoi frantsuzskoi zhivopisi," *ZR*, 1908, No. 7-8-9, v-xiii.

16. "Impressionizm i novye iskaniia (zametka)," *ZR*, 1908, No. 7-8-9, xvii-ix.

17. See *ZR*, 1909, No. 1: illustrations (5-14); "Pol Gogen," i-ii; "Otryvki iz *Noa-Noa*," ii-vii (continued 1909, No. 6, 68-71); *Noa-Noa* had been republished in France in 1908, and the *Zolotoe Runo* publishing house hoped to issue a complete Russian translation of the book.

18. "Pol Gogen, kak skulptor," *ZR*, 1909, No.7-8-9, 132-35; No. 10, 47-52.

19. "Iz perepiski Van Goga (pis'ma k bratu Teodoru)," *ZR*, 1908, No. 7-8-9, xiii-xvi; "Pis'ma Van Goga—pis'ma k E. Bernard," *ZR*, 1909, No. 2, 80-86. The translation was made from a German edition.

20. *ZR*, 1909, No. 5, 63-69; No. 6, 64-68. This article was the basis for Denis' well-known book *Théories: Du Symbolisme et de Gauguin vers un nouvel ordre classique* (Paris, 1957), 98-108.

21. Maurice Denis, *Journal, tome II* (1905-1920) (Paris, 1957), 98-108.

22. Gauguin, quoted in Charles Gauss, *The Aesthetic Theories of French Artists* (Baltimore, 1966), 54.

23. Denis warned artists to return to the essential elements of art, to rid art of its anecdotal, documentary character and make it a reflection of the important truths of the universe. His definition of a painting as being "essentially a flat surface covered with colors assembled in a certain order" can be seen as a fundamental tenet of modern abstractionist art. For Denis, art was to translate nature into "iconic" language, art was to be the subjective deformation of nature (see his *Théories*). Yet he called the Pont Aven school (of which he was the principal theorist) one of "Néo-traditionnisme" that was leading to classicism. These ideas found some expression as well elsewhere in *Zolotoe Runo*: Evgenii Anichkov's "Poslednie pobegi russkoi poezii" (*ZR*, 1908, No. 2, 45-55; No. 3-4, 103-12) described decadence's transformation into classicism, and while the editors printed a disclaimer saying that they disagreed with Anichkov's article "in its evaluation of the role and significance of 'classical decadence'" (*ZR*, 1908, No. 3-4, 103), G.T. (undoubtedly Tasteven) repeated Anichkov's interpretation of decadence transforming itself into a new classicism in his "Po zvezdam" (*ZR*, 1909, No. 6, 76). As with so many issues, it appears *Zolotoe Runo* had not quite made up its mind about what its position on this one should be.

24. Andrei Belyi, *Mezhdu dvukh revoliutsii* (Moscow, 1934), 222.

25. John Russell, *The World of Matisse* (New York, 1969), 96.

26. Alfred Barr, Jr., *Matisse: His Art and His Public* (New York, 1966), 106.

27. Alexandre Mercereau, "Anri Matiss i sovremennaia zhivopis'," *ZR*, 1909, No. 6, I-III.

28. "Zametki khudozhnika," *ZR*, 1909, No. 6, iii-x; the article had originally appeared in the *Grande revue*, 25 December 1908.

29. This is Barr's translation of the original French text; *Matisse*, 122.

30. Ibid., 123.

31. Volfing, "Vagnerofskie festshpili 1907 g. v Miunkhene (zametki nevagnerista)," *ZR*, 1907, No. 7-8-9, 103-9; No. 10, 50-57; 1908, No. 1, 65-70; No. 2, 59-62; No. 3-4, 112-17.

32. "Modernizm v muzyke," *ZR*, 1908, No. 5, 60-65.

33. "Estrada," *ZR*, 1908, No. 11-12, 77-79.

34. "Po povodu osennego salona," *ZR*, 1908, No. 10, 69-73.

35. *ZR*, 1909, No. 2-3, 119-20.

36. G.T., "Persidskaia zhivopis'," *ZR*, 1908, No. 3-4, 38abc.

37. Aleksandr Uspenskii, "Rezba po kosti," *ZR*, 1908, No. 11-12, 23-28.

38. "P'ianost' solntsa," *ZR*, 1908, No. 3-4, 69-77; "S Balearskikh beregov—putevaia pautina," 1908, No. 7-8-9, 86-93.

39. "Siena," *ZR*, 1908, No. 3-4, 67-69; "Fezole," 1908, No. 7-8-9, 83-85.

40. "Kukol'noe tsarstvo," *ZR*, 1908, No. 6, 69-74.

41. V. M-i, "O Pavle Kuznetsove (Neskol'ko slov)," *ZR*, 1908, No. 6, 3-4.

42. A. Rostislavov, "Lanseray," *ZR*, 1908, No. 11-12, 9-10.

43. N. Vrangel', "Nikolai Alekseevich Lomtev (1818-1858)," *ZR*, 1909, No. 10, ix.

44. P. Muratov, "Staroe i molodoe na poslednikh vystavkakh," *ZR*, 1908, No. 1, 88.

45. A. Rostislavov, "Khudozhniki v teatre," *ZR*, 1909, No. 7-8-9, I-VII.

46. Anastasia Chebotarevskaia, "Aisedora Dunkan v prozreniiakh Fridrikha Nitsshe," *ZR*, 1909, No. 4, 81-83.

47. B. Diks, "Na rasputi—neskol'ko slov o sovremennom teatre," *ZR*, 1908, No. 2, 62-64. V. Meierkhol'd, "Iz pisem o teatre," *ZR*, 1908, No. 7-8-9, 108-10. N. N. Evreinov, "Teoriia monodramy," *ZR*, 1909, No. 4, 87.

48. S. A., "Muzyka," *ZR*, 1909, No. 4, 90.

49. N. Zhiliaev, "Ob opere voobshche (po povodu postanovki 'Zolotogo petushka')," *ZR*, 1909, No. 10, 63. See also his "N. A. Rimskii-Korsakov," *ZR*, 1908, No. 7-8-9, 114-16.

NOTES TO CHAPTER IX

1. Mark Etkind, *Aleksandr N. Benua* (Moscow-Leningrad, 1965), 80.

2. Graf Aleksis Zhasminov (V. Burenin), "Moia sobstvennaia duma," *Novoe Vremia*, 23 February 1907, quoted in N. Ashukin, *Valerii Briusov* (Moscow, 1929), 217-18.

3. Belyi has acidly described the situation from his own point of view; see his *Mezhdu dvukh revoliutsii* (Moscow, 1934), 246.

4. See P. A. Berlin, *Russkaia burzhuaziia v staroe i novoe vremia* (Moscow, 1922), 292 ff.

5. See A. A. Sidorov, *Russkaia grafika nachala XX veka* (Moscow, 1969), 155.

6. *ZR*, 1908, No. 7-8-9, 126.

7. *ZR*, 1906, No. 11-12, 161.

8. Ibid.

9. See *ZR*, 1908, No. 10, 75; the issue seized was 1908, No. 7-8-9.

10. *ZR*, 1908, No. 2, 135; No. 7-8-9, 126.

11. See "Moskva i Peterburg," *Rech'*, 22 October 1909.

12. See Sergei Makovskii, *Na parnasse serebriannogo veka* (Munich, 1962).

13. Georgette Donchin, *The Influence of French Symbolism on Russian Poetry* (The Hague, 1958), 71.

14. Redaktsiia, "Vstuplenie," *Apollon*, 1909, No. 1, 4.

15. "Ot redaktsii," *Apollon,* 1910, No. 4, 52.

16. "Vstuplenie," 4.

17. Denis Mickiewicz, "*Apollo* and Modernist Poetics," *Russian Literature Triquarterly,* No. 1 (1971), 229.

18. Empirik, "O Peterburgskom 'Apollonizme' (pis'mo iz Peterburga)," *ZR,* 1909, No. 7-8-9, 136.

19. Ibid., 137.

20. *Apollon,* 1909, No. 1, 5-11.

21. Empirik, "O Peterburgskom," 137.

22. Ibid.

23. Ibid., 138.

24. V. Milioti, "Zabytye zavety," *ZR,* 1909, No. 4, iii-vi.

25. S. G., "Po povodu 'Khudozhestvennyh pisem' G-na A. Benua," *ZR,* 1909, No. 11-12, 90-93.

26. S. Gorodetskii, "Formotvorchestvo," *ZR,* 1909, No. 10, 52-58.

27. "Khronika," *ZR,* 1909, No. 10, 67.

28. "Pechalnyi iubilei," *ZR,* 1909, No. 4, 93-94. The occasion was Briusov's lecture asserting that Gogol was not a realist. *Zolotoe Runo* defended him from the attacks of the utilitarians.

29. *ZR,* 1908, No. 10, 75.

30. A. L., "Gazetnye kritiki v roli politsii nravov," *ZR,* 1909, No. 11-12, 97-98.

31. See the letter from Komissarzhevskaia to *Zolotoe Runo: ZR,* 1908, No. 10, 76.

32. *ZR,* 1909, No. 11-12, 84-85.

33. G. Chulkov, "Moskva i demon," *ZR,* 1909, No. 6, 71-74.

34. Ibid., 72.

35. Ibid., 74.

36. *ZR,* 1909, No. 7-8-9, 97.

37. Letter to the editors from Valery Briusov, *Vesy,* 1909, No. 2, 89.

38. On Briusov's decision and his changing position, see Martin Rice, *Valery Briusov and the Rise of Russian Symbolism* (Ann Arbor, 1975), 90ff.

39. *ZR,* 1909, No. 6, 79.

40. *Vesy,* 1909, No. 12, 189-90.

41. Georgii Chulkov, "Vesy," *Apollon,* 1910, No. 7, 19-20.

42. S. Gorodetskii, "Stado palachai," *ZR,* 1909, No. 12, 85.

43. "Ot redaktsii," *ZR,* 1909, No. 11-12, 105.

44. The following portraits were commissioned by, and appeared in, *Zolotoe Runo:* 1906, No. 1, "Konstantin Balmont" by Valentin Serov; No. 2, "Konstantin Somov" by Lev Bakst; No. 7-8-9, "Valery Briusov" by Mikhail Vrubel; 1907 No. 1, "Andrei Belyi by Lev Bakst; No. 3, "Viacheslav Ivanov" by Konstantin Somov; No. 4, "Nikolai Roerich" by Alexander Golovin; No. 7-8-9, "Alexei Remizov" by Boris Kustodiev; No. 11-12, "Fedor Sologub," by Boris Kustodiev, "Konstantin Balmont" by a unidentified artist; 1908, No. 1, "Alexander Blok" by Konstantin Somov; No. 6, "Pavel Kuznetsov" self-portrait (this portrait was most likely not commissioned by *Zolotoe Runo*); No. 10, "Vsevolod Meyerhold (as Pierrot)" by Nikolai Ulianov; No. 11-12, "Evgeny Lanseray" by Konstantin Somov; 1909, No. 1, "Boris Zaitsev" by Nikolai Ulianov; No. 7-8-9, "Leonid Andreev" by Valentin Serov; No. 11-12, "Mikhail Vrubel" by Valentin Serov. In addition, "Mikhail Kuzmin" by Konstantin Somov was commissioned by the magazine, but had not appeared by the time of *Zolotoe Runo's* discontinuation, and was eventually published in *Apollon.*

45. "Ot redaktsii," *ZR,* 1909, No. 11-12, 105-6.

46. Ibid., 106.

47. Ibid.

48. Ibid.

49. Ibid., 107.

50. It should be noted here that *Vesy* received a much larger treatment in *Apollon* than did *Zolotoe Runo*. In addition to the Chulkov article already mentioned, Kuzmin wrote on *Vesy*'s "artistic prose" (1909, No. 9, 35-41), Gumilev on poetry in *Vesy* (1910, No. 9, 42-44), and N. Vrangel on art in *Vesy* (1910, No. 9, 17-18).

51. A. Rostislavov, "Zolotoe Runo," *Apollon*, 1910, No. 9, 43.

NOTES TO CHAPTER X

1. N. Bachtin, quoted in Lionel Kochan, *Russia in Revolution* (London, 1966), 147.

2. Il'ia Erenburg, *Liudi, gody, zhizn'* (Moscow, 1966), 45-6.

3. Ibid., 46.

4. Briusov, quoted in Dimitrii Maksimov, *Poeziia Valeriia Briusova* (Leningrad, 1940), 200.

5. See Leonid Timofeev, *Aleksandr Blok* (Moscow, 1957), 66.

6. See Chapter 2.

7. See Chapter 2.

8. See Chapter 2.

9. *ZR*, 1907, No. 7-8-9, 110-5.

10. See Robert Goldwater, "Primitivism in Modern Art," in *World Cultures and Modern Art* (Munich, 1972), 241.

11. Eventually, of course, this primitivism would find its fullest expression in Igor Stravinsky, in particular his "Le Sacré du Printemps" of 1913.

12. See James West, *Russian Symbolism* (London, 1970), on these ideas of Ivanov's.

13. Albert Guérard wrote that anarchy rather than estheticism was most indicative of the years 1890-1914 in Europe as a whole; see his *Art for Art's Sake* (New York, 1936), 69.

14. Blok, quoted in Vladimir Orlov, *Aleksandr Blok* (Moscow, 1956), 108.

15. Aleksandr Blok, *Sobranie sochinenii*, volume 5 (Moscow-Leningrad, 1962), 206-7.

16. *ZR*, 1907, No. 4, 32-45.

17. P. Pertsov, *Literaturnye vospominaniia* (Moscow-Leningrad, 1933), 266.

18. Joan D. Grossman, *Edgar Allan Poe in Russia* (Würzburg, 1973), 168.

19. A not dissimilar development was taking place at much the same time in Vienna: see Carl Schorske, "Cultural Hothouse," *New York Review of Books*, volume 22, No. 20 (11 December 1975), 39-44.

20. Viacheslav Ivanov, "Zavety simvolizma," *Apollon*, 1910, No. 8, 5-20.

21. V. Briusov, "O 'rechi rabskoi.' V zashchitu poezii," *Apollon*, 1910, No. 9, 31-4.

22. See Martin P. Rice, *Valery Briusov and the Rise of Russian Symbolism* (Ann Arbor, 1975), 117.

23. Aleksandr Blok, "O nastoiashchem sostoianii russkogo simvolizma," *Apollon*, 1910, No. 8, 21-30.

24. Mikhail Kuzmin, "O prekrasnoi iasnosti," *Apollon*, 1910, No. 4, 5-10.

25. "Nasledie simvolizma i akmeizm," *Apollon*, 1913, No. 1, 42-5.

26. *Apollon*, 1913, No. 1, 48.

27. Linda Koreska-Hartmann, *Jugendstil—Stil der 'Jugend'* (Munich, 1969), 13.

28. Edward Lucie-Smith, *Symbolist Art* (New York, 1972), 55. See also Henderik Roelof Rookmaaker, *Synthetist Art Theories* (Amsterdam, 1959).

29. Borisov-Musatov, quoted in Alla Rusakova, *Borisov-Musatov* (Leningrad, 1974), 75.

30. Sergei Gorodetskii, "Vospominaniia o Bloke," *Pechat' i revoliutsiia*, 1922, No. 1, 84.

31. D. S. Mirsky, *Contemporary Russian Literature* (New York, 1926), 183.

32. See Wladyslawa Jaworska, "The Aesthetic of the Pont-Aven School," Chapter XII of her *Gauguin and the Pont-Aven School* (London, 1972).

33. Goldwater, "Primitivism," 241.

34. Virginia Woolf, quoted in Irving Howe, "The Idea of the Modern," in his *Literary Modernism* (New York, 1967), 15.

BIBLIOGRAPHY

I. Major literary works and artistic essays and articles appearing in *Zolotoe Runo;* authors listed in alphabetical order, their works listed chronologically; short book reviews, notices, and poems are not included; with the exception of articles, genres are identified.

A. M. "Astarta Vostoka i pozdneishie otrazheniia etogo kul'ta," 1906, No. 11-12, 127-8.

A. Sh. [Aleksandr Shervashidze]. "Vystavka Tarkhova," 1906, No. 6, 91-2.

Andreev, Leonid. "Eleazar," 1906, No. 11-12, 59-67 (story).

Anichkov, Evgenii. "Poslednie pobegi russkoi poezii," 1908, No. 2, 45-55; No. 3-4, 103-112.

Auslender, Sergei. "Koldun," 1906, No. 6, 41-2 (story).

_____ "Iz Peterburga," 1907, No. 7-8-9, 147-8 (letter); similar letters in 1907, No. 10, No. 11-12; 1908, No. 1, No. 2, No. 3-4; 1909, No. 1.

_____ "Mest Dzhirolamo Markeze," 1907, No. 10, 38-42 (novella).

_____ "Kukol'noe tsarstvo," 1908, No. 6, 70-4.

_____ "Kupidonova poviazka," 1908, No. 7-8-9, 72-8 (story).

Bachinskii, A. "O sbornike 'Svobodnaia sovest' ', " 1906, No. 1, 145-8 (review).

_____ "Fichte 'Naznachenie cheloveka,' " 1906, No. 2, 131-3 (review).

Bal'mont, Konstantin. "Ozherel'e," 1906, No. 1, 38-41; No. 2, 40-2; No. 4, 37-9; No. 5, 23-5; No. 6, 23-5 (poems).

_____ "Dva slova ob Amerike," 1906, No. 1, 72-6 (letter).

_____ "Chelovecheskaia povest' Kvichei-Maiev," 1906, No. 1, 78-89; No. 2, 45-57.

_____ "Ob Uailde," 1906, No. 2, 91-4.

_____ "Fleity iz chelovecheskikh kostei," 1906, No. 6, 43-52.

_____ "Solovei Budimirovich," 1906, No. 10, 28-30 (poem).

_____ "Rdianye zvezdy," 1907, No. 7-8-9, 91-9.

_____ "Khorovod vremen," 1907, No. 11-12, 37-49 (poems).

_____ "Chuvstvo rasy v tvorchestve," 1907, No. 11-12, 58-9.

_____ "Nashe literaturnoe segodnia," 1907, No. 11-12, 60-2.

_____ "Tvardovskii. Taina vechnoi iunosti," 1908, No. 1, 54-60.

_____ "Belyi lebed'," 1908, No. 3-4, 39-43 (poem).

_____ "P'ianost' solntsa," 1908, No. 3-4, 69-77.

_____ "Lirika pola. Mysli i oshchushcheniia," 1908, No. 5, 38-43; 1909, No. 1, 67-77.

_____ "S Balearskikh beregov," 1908, No. 7-8-9, 86-93.

_____ "Vasen'ka," 1908, No. 11-12, 42-5 (story).

_____ "Sibilla," 1909, No. 10, 28-31.

Belyi, Andrei [Boris Bugaev]. "Goremyki," 1906, No. 1, 49-52 (poems).

_____ "Past' nochi (otryvok mysterii)," 1906, No. 1, 62-71.

_____ "O 'Sbornik statei po filosofii estestvoznaniia,'" 1906, No. 1, 150-3 (review).

_____ "Dostoevskii," 1906, No. 2, 89-90.

———— "A. L.Volynskii 'Dostoevskii,'" 1906, No. 2, 127-30 (review).

———— "Kaleka," 1906, No. 3, 43-5 (poems).

———— "Rozovye girliandy," 1906, No. 3, 63-6.

———— "Mirovaia ekteniia," 1906, No. 3, 72-83.

———— "Venets lavrovy," 1906, No. 5, 43-50.

———— "Genrik Ibsen," 1906, No. 6, 73-5.

———— "Kust'," 1906, No. 7-8-9, 129-35 (story).

———— "Printsip formy v estetike," 1906, No. 10, 88-96.

———— "Pis'mo iz Miunkhena," 1906, No. 10, 115-17.

———— "O propovednikakh, gastronomakh, misticheskikh anarkhistakh i t.d.," 1907, No. 1, 61-4.

———— "Epitafiia," 1907, No. 3, 37-40 (poems).

———— "Melankholiia," 1908, No. 3-4, 44-7 (poems).

Benois, Aleksandr. "Khudozhestvennye eresi," 1906, No. 2, 80-8.

———— Pervaia vystavka internatsional'nogo obshchestva akvarelistov v Parizhe," 1906, No. 3, 94-6.

———— "Sobranie M. I. Miatlevoi v S-Peterburge," 1906, No. 11-12, 35-41.

———— "Khudozhestvennoe znachenie Venetsianova," 1907, No. 7-8-9, 29-32.

———— "Otvet Filosofovu," 1908, No. 3-4, 99-103.

Blok, Aleksandr. "Kraski i slova," 1906, No. 1, 98-103.

———— "O knige Valeriia Briusova 'Stefanos,'" 1906, No. 1, 136-40 (review).

———— "Bezvremen'e," 1906, No. 11-12, 107-14.

———— "Devushka rozovoi kalitki i murav'inyi tsar," 1907, No. 2, 60-4.

———— "Korol' na ploshchadi," 1907, No. 4, 32-45 (play).

———— "O realistakh," 1907, No. 5, 63-74.

———— "O lirike," 1907, No. 6, 41-53.

———— "O drame," 1907, No. 7-8-9, 122-33.

———— "Literaturnye itogi 1907 g.," 1907, No. 11-12, 91-100.

———— "Za gran'iu proshlykh let," 1908, No. 1, 31-40 (poems).

———— "Tri voprosa," 1908, No. 2, 55-9.

———— "O teatre," 1908, No. 3-4, 78-86; No. 5, 51-9.

———— "Solntse nad Rossiei," 1908, No. 7-8-9, 113-4.

———— "Pis'mo o poezii," 1908, No. 7-8-9, 94-8.

———— "Voprosy, voprosy, voprosy," 1908, No. 11-12, 62-9.

———— "Rossiia i intelligentsiia," 1909, No. 1, 78-84.

Briusov, Valerii. "Nadpisi k kartinam," 1906, No. 3, 39-41 (poems).

———— "Karl V," 1906, No. 4, 61-7.

———— "Otzvuki antichnogo," 1906, No. 10, 25-7 (poems).

———— "Sestry," 1906, No. 10, 47-53 (story).

Chebotarevskaia, Anastasiia. "Tvorimoe tvorchestvo," 1908, No. 11-12, 56-61.

———— "Aisedora Dunkan v prozreniakh Fridrikha Nitsshe," 1909, No. 4, 81-2.

Chereda, Iurii. "Sinee," 1906, No. 5, 37-42 (story).

Chukovskii, Kornei. "Peterburgskie teatry," 1907, No. 2, 75-6; No. 3, 75-6.

Chulkov, Georgii [see also Boris Kremnev]. "Razoblachennaia magiia," 1908, No. 1, 61-4.

———— "Semena buri," 1908, No. 2, 25-38 (play).

———— "Sestra," 1908, No. 3-4, 51-5 (story).

———— "Pokryvalo Izidy," 1908, No. 5, 66-72.

———— "Liliia i roza," 1908, No. 6, 51-4.

———— "Iskhod," 1908, No. 7-8-9, 99-105.

———— "Litsom k litsu," 1909, No. 1, 105-7.

_____ "Moskva i demon," 1909, No. 6, 71-3.

_____ "O liricheskom tragedii," 1909, No. 11-12, 51-4.

Denis, Maurice. "Ot Gogena i Van-Goga k klassitsizmu," 1909, No. 5, 63-8; No. 6, 64-7.

Dikovskii, B. "Neskol'ko slov o 'Balaganchike' A. Bloka," 1907, No. 7-8-9, 141-2.

_____ "Na rasputi (Neskol'ko slov o sovremennom teatre)," 1908, No. 2, 63-4.

Dymov, Osip. "Peterburgskie teatry," 1906, No. 2, 104-7.

_____ "Vesennee bezumnie," 1906, No. 3, 53-9 (story).

_____ "Peterburgskie teatry," 1906, No. 3, 103-7.

_____ "Konstantin Somov," 1906, No. 7-8-9, 151-3.

_____ "Peterburgskie teatry," 1906, No. 10, 79-80; No. 11-12, 137-8.

E. I. K. "Iz muzykal'noi zhizni Moskvy," 1907, No. 4, 77-8.

E. O. "Pomorskie rukopisi, ikh miniatiury i ornamentatsiia," 1907, No. 10, 19-23.

Eiges, K(onstantin?). "Muzyka i estetika," 1906, No. 5, 60-3.

_____ "Osnovnaia antinomiia muzykal'noi estetiki," 1906, No. 11-12, 122-5.

_____ "Muzyka, kak odno iz vysshikh misticheskikh perezhivanii," 1907, No. 7, 54-7.

_____ "Krasota v iskusstve," 1909, No. 11-12, 61-8.

Empirik [Genrikh Tasteven]. "Prichiny odnoi literaturnoi metamorfozy," 1907, No. 4, 79-80.

_____ "O kul'turnoi kritike," 1907, No. 5, 75.

_____ "O chistom simvolizme, teurgizme i nigilizme," 1908 No. 5, 77-9.

_____ "Sfinks bez zagadki," 1908, No. 11-12, 85-6.

_____ "Neskol'ko slov o vystavke Zolotogo Runa," 1909, No. 2-3, i-iii.

_____ "Pis'mo iz Peterburga," 1909, No. 7-8-9, 136-40.

Erberg, Konstantin [Konstantin Siunnerberg]. "Bezvlastie," 1907, No. 4, 46-63.

_____ "Dvazhdy dva piat'," 1907, No. 10, 43-5.

_____ "Otchetnaia vystavka v Akademii khudozhestv," 1907, No. 11-12, 104-5.

_____ "Pis'ma o tvorchestve," 1908, No. 11-12, 79-81.

Esmer-Valdor, N. [Alexandre Mercereau]. "Khudozestvennyi poselok vo Frantsii," 1907, No. 10, 81-2.

_____ "Salon d'Automne (pis'mo iz Parizha)," 1907, No. 11-12, 116.

_____ "Po povodu osennego Salona," 1908, No. 10, 69-72.

Filosofov, Dmitrii. "Khudozhestvennaia zhizn' Peterburga," 1906, No. 1, 106-11.

_____ "Misticheskii anarkhizm," 1906, No. 10, 58-65.

_____ "Iskusstvo i gosudarstvo," 1907 No. 6, 31-40.

_____ "Kniaz' A.I. Urusov," 1907, No. 10, 66-70.

_____ "Tozhe tendentsiia," 1908, No. 1, 71-6.

G.T. [Genrikh Tasteven]. "Po zvezdam," 1909, No. 6, 74-6.

_____ "Anatema Leonida Andreeva," 1909, No. 7-8-9, 141-2.

Geliotropov, Serzh [Sergei Gorodetskii]. "Razsuzhdenie o starosti, kriticheskikh priemakh i tak voobshche," 1908, No. 3-4, 125-7.

Gertsyg, E. "Besoiskatel'stvo v tikhom omute," 1909, No. 2-3, 95-9.

Gauguin, Paul. "Otryvki iz Noa-Noa," 1909, No. 1, I-VII; No. 6, 68-70.

Gorodetskii, Sergei [see also Serzh Geliotropov]. "Stikhi o Sviatoi Liubvi," 1907, No. 5, 32-7 (poems).

_____ "Ogon' za reshetkoi," 1908, No. 3-4, 95-8.

_____ "Prostaia skazka," 1908, No. 5, 27-30 (poems).

_____ "Glukhoe vremia," 1908, No. 6, 69-70.

_____ "Amin'," 1908, No. 7-8-9, 105-7.

_____ "Shuba," 1909, No. 1, 56-62 (story).

_____ "Idolotvorchestvo," 1909, No. 1, 93-100.

_____ "Blizhaishaia zadacha russkoi literatury," 1909, No. 4, 66-80.

—— "Formotvorchestvo," 1909, No. 10, 52-8.

—— "Stado palachei (pamiati Vrubelia)," 1909, No. 11-12, 86.

—— "Po povodu khudozhestvennykh pisem Aleksandra Benua," 1909, No. 11-12, 90-2.

Hippius, Zinaida [Z. Gippius]. "Ivan Ivanovich i chert," 1906, No. 2, 58-75 (story).

—— "Net i da," 1906, No. 7-8-9, 142-5 (play).

Iartsev, P. "Moskovskie teatry," 1907, No. 7-8-9, 149-51.

—— "Teatral'noe iskusstvo i stsenicheskoe tvorchestvo," 1907, No. 10, 78-80.

Imgardt, D. "Zhivopis' i revoliutsiia," 1906, No. 5, 56-9.

Ivanov, Viacheslav. "Predchuvstviia i predvestiia," 1906, No. 4, 68-73; No. 6, 53-63.

—— "O veselom remesle i umnom veselii," 1907, No. 5, 47-55.

—— "Ty esi," 1907, No. 7-8-9, 100-2.

—— "Son Melampa," 1907, No. 10, 31-5 (poem).

—— "Dve stikhii v sovremennom simvolizme," 1908, No. 3-4-5, 86-94.

—— "Sporady," 1908, No. 11-12, 70-3.

—— "O russkoi idee," 1909, No. 1, 85-92; No. 2-3, 87-94.

—— "Iz tsikla 'Pristrastiia'," 1909, No. 2-3, 77-9 (poems).

—— "Antichnyi uzhas (po povodu kartiny L. Baksta)," 1909, No. 4, 51-65.

K.R. "O I. Gofmane i fortepiannoi igre," 1907, No. 1, 68-70.

Karatygin, Viacheslav [see also V.K.]. "Muzykal'naia zhizn' Peterburga," 1906, No. 11-12, 139-42.

—— "Maskarad," 1907, No. 7-8-9, 116-21; No. 10, 58-65.

Kirienko-Voloshin, M. [Maksimilian Voloshin]. "Individualizm v iskusstve," 1906, No. 10, 66-73.

Kondrat'ev, Aleksandr. "Orfei," 1906, No. 3, 60-2 (story).

—— "Satiressa," 1906, No. 4, 45-53 (story).

—— "Afrodita zastupnitsa," 1906, No. 7-8-9, 120ab (story).

—— "Famirid," 1908, No. 1, 44-53; No. 2, 39-44.

Kozhevnikov, Petr. "Khvala devushke," 1908, No. 3-4, 63-6 (story).

Krechetov, Sergei [Sergei Sokolov]. "Apologety kul'tury," 1906, No. 3, 131-3.

Kremnev, Boris [Georgii Chulkov]. "Snezhnaia deva," 1908, No. 10, 51-4.

Krinitskii, Mark. "Slepets," 1906, No. 5, 31-6 (story).

Kursinskii, A. [see also A. Kur-skii]. "L. Andreev, tt. II i III, Rasskazy," 1906, No. 5, 84-6.

Kur-skii, A. [A. Kursinskii]. "Moskovskie dramaticheskie teatry," 1906, No. 10, 82-3; No. 11-12, 144; 1907, No. 1, 77; No. 2, 85.

Kuzmin, Mikhail. "Povest' ob Elevsippe," 1906, No. 11-12, 68-79 (story).

—— "Iz pisem devitsy Klary Val'mon k Rosalii Tiutelmaier," 1907, No. 1, 37-8 (story).

—— "Ten' Fillidy," 1907, No. 7-8-9, 83-7 (story).

—— "Venok vesen," 1908, No. 7-8-9, 67-71 (poems).

—— "Dvoinoi napersnik," 1908, No. 10, 27-37 (story).

—— "Nezhnyi Iosif," 1909, No. 1, 49-55; No. 2-3, 58-76; No. 4, 15-36; No. 5, 35-43; No. 6, 42-56; No. 7-8-9, 104-25; 10, 19-27 (novella).

Maestro [Vasilii Rozanov]. "To zhe, no drugimi slovami," 1907, No. 1, 56-60.

Makovskii, Sergei. "Pamiatnik M. I. Glinke," 1906, No. 4, 92-3.

—— "N. Rerikh," 1907, No. 4, 3-7.

—— "Golubaia roza," 1907, No. 5, 25-8.

Malakhieva-Mirovich, V. "Dva lika," 1908, No. 7-8-9, 111-2.

—— "O Meterlinke," 1908, No. 10, 62-5.

Matisse, Henri. "Zametki khudozhnika," 1909, No. 6, iii-x.

Medtner, N. "Romans na slova Andreia Belogo," 1908, No. 1, 70abcd.

Meierkhol'd, Vsevolod. "Pis'ma o teatre," 1908, No. 7-8-9, 108-10.

Mercereau, Alexandre [see also Esmer-Valdor]. "Henri Matisse i sovremennaia zhivopis'," 1909, No. 6, i-iii.
_____ "Monticelli," 1909, No. 11-12, i-vii.
Merezhkovskii, Dmitrii. "Starinnye oktavy," 1906, No. 1, 31-7; No. 2, 31-9; No. 3, 31-8; No. 4, 25-32 (poems).
_____ "Vse protiv vsekh," 1906, No. 1, 90-7.
Milioti, Vasilii [see also V. M-i and V. M-ti]. "Dve vystavki," 1907, No. 4, 78.
_____ "Zabytye zavety," 1909, No. 4, iii-vi.
_____ "Risunki Vrubelia," 1909, No. 5, i-ii.
Milioti, Vasilii and Likiardopulo, M. "Moskovskie vystavki," 1906, No. 11-12, 143-4.
Minskii, N. "Idea Solomei," 1908, No. 6, 55-8.
Mire [Aleksandr Moiseev]. "Pavliny," 1906, No. 6, 31-3 (story).
_____ "Propovednik smerti," 1907, No. 5, 45-6 (story).
Mizgir [Boris Popov]. "Mozart," 1906, No. 1, 126-8.
_____ "Musorgskii," 1906, No. 3, 84-7.
Morice, Charles. "Novye tendentsii frantsuzskogo iskusstva," 1908, No. 7-8-9, i-iv; No. 10, i-iv; No. 11-12, i-viii.
_____ "Gogen, kak skul'ptor," 1909, No. 7-8-9, 132-5; No. 10, 47-51.
Muratov, Pavel. "O vysokom khudozhestve," 1907, No. 11-12, 75-90.
_____ "Staroe i molodoe na poslednikh vystavkakh," 1908, No. 1, 87-90.
_____ "Novye priobreteniia Tretiakovskoi gallerei," 1908, No. 1, 72-4.
_____ "Solnechnye chasy," 1908, No. 10, 60-2.
_____ "Onore Dome," 1908, No. 11-12, 73-6.
N. G. "Neskol'ko slov o Ge," 1909, No. 4, i-iii.
N. Zh. [Nikolai Zhiliaev]. "Eduard Grig," 1907, No. 7-8-9, 134-8.
_____ "Rimskii-Korsakov," 1908, No. 7-8-9, 114-6.
Novikov, Ivan. "V slobode," 1906, No. 7-8-9, 136-41 (story).
_____ "Pchely prichastnitsy," 1908, No. 10, 38-45.
Petrovskaia, Nina. "Moskovskie teatry," 1906, No. 1, 117-22.
_____ "Moskovskaia teatral'naia zhizn'," 1906, No. 2, 111-4; No. 3, 119-22.
Potemkin, P. "Ee venki (liricheskaia poema)," 1909, No. 5, 15-18 (poem).
Przybyszewski, Stanislaw. "Tirtei," 1907, No. 2, 31-7 (poem in prose).
_____ "Stezeiu Kaina," 1907, No. 11-12, 50-7 (poem).
_____ "K etike pola," 1907, No. 11-12, 63-7.
_____ Den'sudnyi, 1909, No. 1, 19-48; No. 2-3, 31-57; No. 4, 15-36; No. 5, 21-34; No. 6, 15-41; No. 7-8-9, 37-103 (novel).
Remizov, Aleksei. "Pozhar," 1906, No. 4, 54-60 (story).
_____ "Posolon'," 1906, No. 7-8-9, 121-7; No. 10, 39-46 (stories).
_____ "Chertik," 1907, No. 1, 39-52 (story).
_____ "Zanofa," 1907 No. 5, 41-4 (story).
_____ "Belun," "Nezhit," "Khovala," 1907, No. 7-8-9, 73-5 (stories).
_____ "Maka," 1907, No. 7-8-9, 76-82 (story).
_____ "Krov'," "Zadushnitsy," "Vedogon," 1908, No. 1, 41-3 (stories).
_____ "Pod krovom nochi. Sny," 1908, No. 5, 31-7 (story).
_____ "Kak Kot Kotofeich otpustil nas k Moriu-Okeanu," 1908, No. 11-12, 46-9 (story).
_____ "Tragediia ob Iude, printse Iskaiotskom," and "Prilozhenie—Skazanie o Iude predatele," 1909, No. 11-12, 15-50 (play and story).
Roerich, Nikolai. "Zapisnye listki," 1906, No. 2, 95-6; No. 4, 76-9; No. 6, 78-81; No. 7-8-9, 156-9; 1907, No. 6, 58-63.

Roerich, Nikolai, and Makovskii, Sergei, and Golubev, V. "Na Iaponskoi vystavke," 1906, No. 1, 111-7.
Rostislavov, Aleksandr. "Deiatel'nost' Akademii," 1906, No. 6, 88-90.
_____ "V muzee Aleksandra III," 1906, No. 11-12, 118-21.
_____ "Nabroski o khudozhestvennykh delakh," 1906, No. 11-12, 136-7; 1907, No. 3, 73-4; No. 4, 79; No. 10, 72; No. 11-12, 106.
_____ "O khudozhestvennom obrazovanii," 1907, No. 2, 78-9.
_____ "Individualizm Rerikha," 1907, No. 4, 8-10.
_____ "Vystavochnye absiurdy," 1907, No. 10, 71-2.
_____ "Deshevoe khudozhestvo," 1907, No. 11-12, 105.
_____ "Lansere," 1908, No. 11-12, 9-10.
_____ "Ne v konia korm," 1908, 11-12, 84-5.
_____ "Ob uchenicheskoi vystavke v akademii," 1908, No. 11-12, 87-8.
_____ "Khudozhniki v teatre," 1909, No. 7-8-9, i-viii.
Rozanov, Vasilii [see also Maestro]. "Egipet," 1906, No. 6, 51-5.
_____ "Odna iz russkikh poetiko-filosofskikh kontseptsii," 1906, No. 7-8-9, 146-50.
_____ "A. A. Ivanov," 1906, No. 11-12, 3-6.
_____ "Posleslovie k kommentariiu Legendy o velikom inkvizitore F. Dostoevskogo," 1906, No. 11-12, 97-101.
_____ "M. V. Nesterov," 1907, No. 2, 3-7.
_____ "Iz starykh pisem," 1907, No. 2, 49-59; No. 3, 54-62.
Sadovskoi, Boris. "Leshii," 1906, No. 7-8-9, 119-20 (story).
_____ "Poeziia A. P. Polonskogo," 1906, No. 11-12, 102-6.
_____ "Lamia," 1907, No. 5, 38-40 (story).
Sats, Il'ia. "Muzykal'nye zametki," 1906, No. 3, 114-6; No. 4, 87-9.
_____ "Moskovskaia muzykal'naia zhizn'," 1906, No. 10, 80-1; No. 11-12, 145-6.
_____ "Satana v muzyke," 1907, No. 1, 65-7.
_____ "O vzaimootnoshenii muzyki i teksta v opere," 1907, No. 1, 71-3; No. 2, 70-4.
_____ "Moskovskaia muzykal'naia khronika," 1907, No. 2, 81-4; No. 3, 78-80.
Shervashidze, Aleksandr [see also A. Sh.]. "Individualizm i traditsiia," 1906, No. 6, 64-72.
_____ "Aleksandr Benua," 1906, No. 10, 3-6.
_____ "Vystavka russkogo khudozhestva v Parizhe," 1906, No. 11-12, 130-2.
Shinskii, N. [Nikolai Riabushinskii]. "Iskusstvo, ego druzia i vragi," 1908, No. 7-8-9, 120-1.
_____ "V rode skazki," 1909, No. 10, 32-6 (story).
Siunnerberg, Konstantin [see also Erberg]. "Sukhie list'ia," 1906, No. 1, 124-6.
_____ "Khudozhestvennaia zhizn' Peterburga," 1906, No. 3, 98-102; No. 4, 80-2; No. 5, 64; No. 6, 82-3; No. 10, 75; No. 11-12, 134-5; 1907, No. 1, 76; No. 2, 76-7; No. 3, 72.
_____ "Parizhskie gazety o russkoi vystavke," 1906, No. 11-12, 133-4.
_____ "Simvolicheskii teatr," 1907, No. 1, 78-9.
Skif [Sergei Sokolov]. "Vystavka Moskovskogo tovarishchestva khudozhnikov," 1906, No. 2, 117-9.
Sologub, Fedor [Fedor Teternikov]. "Prizyvaiushchii zveria," 1906, No. 1, 53-6 (story).
_____ " 'Ia,' kniga sovershennogo samoutverzhdeniia," 1906, No. 2, 76-9 (story).
_____ "Tela i dusha," 1906, No. 6, 34-40 (story).
_____ "Chelovek cheloveku—d'iavol," 1907, No. 1, 53-5.
_____ "Dar mudrykh pchel," 1907, No. 2, 38-48; No. 3, 41-53 (play).
_____ "Smert' po ob'iavleniiu," 1907, No. 6, 26-30 (story).
_____ "Mechta Don-Kikhota," 1908, No. 1, 79-80.
_____ "Bagrianyi pir zari," 1908, No. 2, 21-3 (poems).
_____ " 'Kremnev' (povest' v stikhakh)," 1908, No. 11-12, 32-41 (poem).

Solov'ev, Sergei. "Vesniani," 1906, No. 10, 54-7 (story).

Sredin, Aleksandr. "O Borisove-Musatove," 1906, No. 3, 67-71.

_____ "Starinnye vyshivki," 1906, No. 3, 88-93.

_____ "M. V. Nesterov. Biograficheskii ocherk," 1907, No. 1, 7-8.

Stolitsa, Liubov'. "Raduga," 1907, No. 7-8-9, 88-90.

Struve, Aleksandr. "Muzykal'nye pis'ma," 1906, No. 2, 114-7; No. 3, 117-8.

Suslov, N. "Religiia i gotika," 1906, No. 7-8-9, 154-5.

Svetlov, Valerian. "Peterburgskii balet," 1907, No. 10, 77-8.

Tarovatyi, Nikolai. "Na akvarel'noi vystavke v Moskve," 1906, No. 1, 123-4.

_____. "Na vystavke 'Mir Iskusstva,' " 1906, No. 3, 123-4; No. 5, 72-3.

Tasteven, Genrikh [see also G. T. and Empirik]. "Eduard Gartman," 1906, No. 6, 76-7.

_____ "Nitsshe i sovremennyi krizis," 1907, No. 7-8-9, 110-5.

_____ "Persidskaia zhivopis'," 1908, No. 3-4, 38abc.

_____ "Impressionizm i novye iskaniia," 1908, No. 7-8-9, xvii-xix.

_____ "Vozrozhdenie stilia," 1909, No. 11-12, 87-9.

Toporkov, A. "Grani," 1906, No. 11-12, 80-7 (story).

_____ "O novom realizme i o B. Zaitseve," 1907, No. 10, 46-9.

_____ "Noch'iu," 1908, No. 3-4, 56-62 (story).

_____ "Tvorchestvo i mysl'," 1909, No. 5, 52-62.

_____ "O tvorcheskom i sozertsatel'nom estetizme," 1909, No. 11-12, 69-74.

Troitskii, V. "Emalevye izdeliia v Rossii," 1909, No. 10, i-viii.

Uspenskii, Aleksandr. "Drevne-russkaia zhivopis' (XV-XVIII vv.)," 1906, No. 7-8-9, 5-98.

_____ "Bes," 1907, No. 1, 21-7.

_____ "Starinnaia mebel' gr. A. V. Olsuf'eva," 1907, No. 3, 29-33.

_____ "A. G. Venetsianov," 1907, No. 7-8-9, 33-40.

_____ "Rez'ba po kosti," 1908, No. 11-12, 23-8.

V.K. [Viacheslav Karatygin]. "M. Reger," 1906, No. 2, 97-101.

_____ "Muzykal'naia khronika Peterburga," 1906, No. 3, 108-13; No. 4, 83-6; No. 5, 65-8; No. 6, 84-7; No. 7-8-9, 160-3; No. 10, 76-8; 1907, No. 1, 81-3; No. 2, 79-80; No. 3, 76-7; No. 4, 74-6; No. 5, 75; No. 7-8-9, 139-40; No. 11-12, 101-3.

_____ "O Gogole," 1909, No. 2-3, 108-11.

V. M-i [Vasilii Milioti]. "O priemakh khudozhestvennoi kritiki," 1907, No. 5, 76-7.

_____ "Pol'skaia starina v Rumiantsevskom muzee," 1907, No. 11-12, 35-6.

V. M-ti [Vasilii Milioti]. "O 'Soiuze,' " 1908, No. 1, 94-6.

_____ "O Pavle Kuznetsove," 1908, No. 6, 3-4.

Van Gogh, Vincent. "Iz perepiski s druziami," 1908, No. 7-8-9, XIII-XVI; 1909, No. 2-3, 80-6.

Volfing [Emilii Medtner]. " 'Skupoi rytsar' i 'Francheska da Rimini,' " 1906, No. 1, 122-3.

_____ "Muzykal'naia vesna," 1906, No. 5, 69-71.

_____ "Otgoloski iubileia Shumana," 1906, No. 11-12, 126-7.

_____ "Sixtus Beckmesser redivivus," 1907, No. 2, 65-9.

_____ "Modernizm i muzyka," 1907, No. 3, 63-71.

_____ "Kaliostro v muzyke," 1907, No. 4, 64-73.

_____ "Vagnerofskie 'festshpili' 1907 g. v Miunkhene," 1907, No. 7-8-9, 103-9; No. 10, 50-7; 1908, No. 1, 65-70; No. 2-3-4, 59-62.

_____ "Rakhmaninov, kak ispolnitel'," 1908, No. 2, 75-6.

_____ "Modernizm v muzyke," 1908, No. 5, 60-5.

_____ "Estrada," 1908, No. 11-12, 77-9; 1909, No. 2-3, 100-8; No. 5, 44-51.

_____ "O muzykal'noi kritike," 1909, No. 6, 57-63; No. 7-8-9, 126-31; No. 10, 37-46.

_____ "Dom pesni," 1909, No. 11-12, 75-83.

Voloshin, Maksimilian [see also M. Kirienko-Voloshin]. "Pervaia vystavka internatsional'nogo obshchestva akvarelistov v Parizhe," 1906, No. 3, 96-7.

———— "Karrier," 1906, No. 4, 74-5.

———— "Terre antique," 1907, No. 4, 27-9 (poems).

———— "K. F. Bogaevskii," 1907, No. 10, 24-30.

———— "Otkrovenie detskikh igr," 1907, No. 11-12, 68-74.

———— "Demony razrusheniia i zla," 1908, No. 6, 59-69.

———— "Novye ustremleniia frantsuzskoi zhivopisi," 1908, No. 7-8-9, v-xii.

———— "Horomedan," 1909, No. 11-12, 55-60.

Vorotnikov, A. P. "Tvoreniia Vrubelia v Kirillovskom khrame," 1906, No. 4, 90-1.

———— "Teatr Komissarzhevskoi v Moskve," 1907, No. 7-8-9, 153-4.

Vrangel', N. N. "Venetsianov i ego shkola," 1907, No. 7-8-9, 61-4.

———— "Miniatiury imperatorskogo Ermitazha," 1908, No. 2, 15-20.

———— "Iakov Fedorovich Kapkov," 1908, No. 5, 3-4.

———— "Nikolai Alekseevich Lomtev," 1909, No. 10, ix-x.

Wyspianski, Stanislaw. "Sud'i," 1908, No. 6, 21-50 (play).

Zagorskii, E. "Prometei molodoi Pol'shi," 1908, No. 10, 54-9.

Zaitsev, Boris. "Mif," 1906, No. 3, 47-52 (story).

———— "Sienna," 1908, No. 3-4, 67-9.

———— "Italiia. Fiezole," 1908, No. 7-8-9, 83-5.

Zhiliaev, N. [see also N. Zh.]. "Ob opere voobshche (po povodu postanovki 'Zolotogo petushka')," 1909, No. 10, 59-64.

II. Other Works

Aleksandr Blok i Andrei Belyi: Perepiska. Moscow, 1940.

Alpatov, Mikhail. The Russian Impact on Art. Translated by Ivy Litvinov. New York, 1950.

Anderson, Troels. Moderne russisk kunst 1910-1930. Copenhagen (?), 1967.

Andreev, Leonid. Pis'ma. Leningrad, 1924.

Annenkov, Iurii. Dnevnik moikh vstrech. New York, 1966. 2 volumes.

Ashukin, N. Valerii Briusov. Moscow, 1929.

Asmus, V. "Filosofiia i estetika russkogo simvolizma." Literaturnoe nasledstvo. Volume 27-28. Moscow, 1937.

Bakst, Lev. Serov i ia v Gretsii. Berlin, 1923.

Barr, Alfred H., Jr. Matisse: His Art and His Public. New York, 1936.

Beaumont, Cyril W. Serge Diaghilev. London, 1933.

Bedford, C. Harold. "D. S. Merezhkovsky: The Forgotten Poet." The Slavonic and East European Review, XXXVI, No. 86 (1957), 159-80.

———— "Dmitrii Merezhkovsky, the Intelligentsia and the Revolution of 1905." Canadian Slavonic Papers, III (1958), 27-42.

———— The Seeker: D. S. Merezhkovsky. Lawrence (Kansas), 1975.

Beketova, M. A. Aleksandr Blok: Biograficheskii ocherk. Petersburg, 1922.

———— Aleksandr Blok i ego mat'. Leningrad-Moscow, 1925.

Belikov, Pavel, and Kniazeva, Valentina. Rerikh. Moscow, 1972.

Bel'kind, E. L. "Blok i Viacheslav Ivanov." Blokovskii sbornik. Volume 2. Tartu, 1971. 364-84.

Belousov, Ivan. Literaturnaia sreda: Vospominaniia 1880-1928. Moscow, 1928.

———— Ushedshaia Moskva. Moscow, 1927.

Belyi, Andrei [Boris Bugaev]. Arabeski. Moscow, 1911.

———— "Detskaia svistulka." Vesy, 1907, No. 8, 54-8.

———— "Khudozhniki oskorbiteliam." Vesy, 1907, No. 1, 53-6.

———— Mezhdu dvukh revoliutsii. Moscow, 1934.

———— Nachalo veka. Moscow, 1933.

———— "Shtempelevannaia kalosha." Vesy, 1907, No. 5, 59-62.

_____ "Volnootpushchenniki." *Vesy*, 1908, No. 2, 69-72.

_____ "Vospominaniia ob Aleksandre Aleksandroviche Bloke." *Zapiski mechtatelei*, No. 6 (Petersburg, 1922), 7-122.

_____ *Vospominaniia o Bloke*. Moscow-Berlin, 1922-23.

Benois, Alexandre. *Memoirs*. Translated by Moura Budberg. London, 1964. 2 volumes.

_____ *Reminiscences of the Russian Ballet*. Translated by Mary Britnieva. London, 1941.

_____ *The Russian School of Painting*. Translated by Avrahm Yarmolinsky. New York, 1916.

_____ *Vozniknovenie "Mir Iskusstva."* Leningrad, 1928.

_____ *Zhizn' khudozhnika; vospominaniia*. New York, 1955. 2 volumes.

Berberova, Nina. *Alexandre Blok et son temps*. Paris, 1947.

Berdyaev, Nicolas. *Dream and Reality: An Essay in Autobiography*. New York, 1951.

Berlin, P. A. *Russkaia burzhuaziia v staroe i novoe vremia*. Moscow, 1922.

Bezzubov, V. I. "Aleksandr Blok i Leonid Andreev." *Blokovskii sbornik*. Volume I. Tartu, 1964. 226-320.

Bialik, B. A. et al, editors. *Russkaia literatura kontsa XIX-nachala XX veka: devianostye gody*. Moscow, 1968.

_____ *Russkaia literatura kontsa XIX-nachala XX veka: 1901-1907*. Moscow, 1971.

_____ *Russkaia literatura kontsa XIX-nachala XX veka: 1908-1917*. Moscow, 1972.

Bialik, B. A., editor. *Literaturno-esteticheskie kontseptsii v Rossii kontsa XIX-nachala XX v*. Moscow, 1975.

Bialy, Renate Schilk. "Devices for the Incongruous: A Study of A. M. Remizov's Prose." Ph.D. dissertation. UCLA, 1974.

Bill, Valentine. "The Morozovs." *Russian Review*, XIX, No. 2 (April, 1955), 109-16.

_____ *The Forgotten Class*. New York, 1959.

Billington, James. *The Icon and the Axe*. New York, 1967.

Blok, Aleksandr. "O sovremennom sostoianii russkogo simvolizma." *Apollon*, 1910, No. 8, 21-30.

_____ *Pis'ma Aleksandra Bloka*. Leningrad, 1925.

_____ *Pis'ma Aleksandra Bloka k E. P. Ivanovu*. Moscow, 1936.

_____ *Pis'ma Aleksandra Bloka k rodnym*. Leningrad, 1927. 2 volumes.

_____ *Zapisnye knizhki*. Leningrad, 1930.

Bonneau, S. *L'universe poétique d'Alexandre Blok*. Paris, 1946.

Botkina, Aleksandra. *Pavel Mikhailovich Tretiakov v zhizni i iskusstve*. Moscow, 1960.

Bowers, Faubion. *Scriabin*. Tokyo, 1969. 2 volumes.

Bowlt, John E. "The 'Blue Rose' Movement and Russian Symbolist Painting." Ph.D. dissertation, University of St. Andrews, 1972.

_____ "The World of Art." *Russian Literature Triquarterly*, 1972, No. 4, 183-218.

_____ "Neo-primitivism and Russian Painting." *The Burlington Magazine*, v. 116, No. 853 (March 1974), 133-40.

_____ "Nikolai Ryabushinsky: Playboy of the Eastern World." *Apollo*, XCVIII, No. 142 (December 1973), 486-93.

_____ "Russian Symbolism and the 'Blue Rose' Movement." *The Slavonic and East European Review*, LI, No. 123 (April 1973), 161-81.

_____ "Synthecism and Symbolism: The Russian *World of Art* Movement." *Forum for Modern Language Studies* (St. Andrews, Scotland), IX, No. 1 (January 1973), 35-48.

_____ "Two Russian Maecenases: Savva Morozov and Princess Tenisheva." *Apollo*, XCVIII, No. 142 (December 1973), 444-53.

Bowra, Cecil M. *The Heritage of Symbolism*. London, 1959.

Bristol, Evelyn. "The Lyric Poetry of Fedor Sologub." Ph.D. dissertation, UC Berkeley, 1959.

Briusov, Valerii. *Dnevniki 1891-1910.* Moscow, 1927.
———. "Kliuchi Tain." *Vesy,* 1906, No. 1, 3-21.
———. "O 'rechi rabskoi.' V zashchitu poezii." *Apollon,* 1910, No. 9, 31-4.
———. "Posledniaia rabota Vrubelia." Vrubel', Mikhail. *Perepiska. Vospominaniia o khudozhnike.* Leningrad, 1963. 263-9.
———. "Vekhi IV: Fakely." *Vesy,* 1906, No. 5, 54-8.
———. "Vekhi V. Misticheskie anarkhisty." *Vesy,* 1906, No. 8, 43-7.
———. *Za moim oknom.* Moscow, 1913.
Brodskii, N. L., editor. *Literaturnye manifesty ot simvolizma k oktiabriu.* Moscow, 1929.
Bronowski, Jacob. *The Ascent of Man.* Boston, 1973.
Brooks, Jeffrey. "The Young Kornei Chukovsky, 1905-1914: A Liberal Critic in Search of Cultural Unity." *Russian Review.* v. 33, No. 1 (January 1974), 50-62.
Buckle, Richard. *In Search of Diaghilev.* London, 1955.
Bunin. Ivan. *Vospominaniia.* Paris, 1950.
Buryshkin, Pavel. *Moskva kupecheskaia.* New York, 1954.
Bushmin, A. S. et al, editors. *Istoriia russkoi literatury.* v. 10. Moscow-Leningrad, 1954.
V. Bykov [Valerii Briusov]. "Iz zhurnalov." *Vesy,* 1908, No. 10, 103-5.
Carter, A. E. *The Idea of Decadence in French Literature 1830-1900.* Toronto, 1958.
Cassou, Jean. "The Climate of Thought." Jean Cassou, Emil Langui, Nicolaus Pevsner. *Gateway to the Twentieth Century.* New York, 1962. 5-115.
Chekhov, Anton. *Letters of Anton Chekhov.* Translated by Michael Henry Heim in collaboration with Simon Karlinsky. New York, 1973.
Cherepakhov, Matvei and E. M. Fingerit. *Russkaia periodicheskaia pechat' (1895-oktiabr' 1917).* Moscow, 1957.
Chernyshevskii, Nikolai. *Esteticheskie otnosheniia iskusstva k deistvitel'nosti.* Moscow, 1948.
Chukovskii, Kornei. *Ot Chekhova do nashikh dnei.* Petersburg, 1909.
Chulkov, Georgii. *Gody stranstvii.* Moscow, 1930.
———. *Nashi sputniki.* Moscow, 1922.
———. *O misticheskom anarkhizme.* Petersburg, 1906.
———. "Ob utverzhdenii lichnosti." *Fakely.* v. 2. Petersburg, 1907, 1-26.
———. "Vesy." *Apollon,* 1910, No. 7, 15-20.
Cioran, Samuel. *The Apocalyptic Symbolism of Andrej Belyj.* The Hague, 1973.
Curtiss, John S. *Church and State in Russia; The Last Years of the Empire 1900-17.* New York, 1940.
Davies, Ivor. "Primitivism in the First Wave of the Twentieth-Century Avant Garde in Russia." *Studio International.* v. 186, No. 958 (September 1973), 80-4.
Denis, Maurice. *Journal. Tome II (1905-1920).* Paris, 1957.
Deschartes, O. [Olga Shor]. "Viacheslav Ivanov." *Oxford Slavonic Papers.* Volume 5 (1954), 41-58.
Desnitskii, V. A. "A. Blok, kak literaturnyi kritik." Aleksandr Blok. *Sobranie sochinenii.* v. 10. Leningrad, 1935. 5-15.
Desnitskii, V. A. and Muratova, K. D., editors. *Revoliutsiia 1905 goda i russkaia literatura.* Moscow-Leningrad, 1956.
Diaghilev, Sergei. "Slozhnye voprosy." *Mir Iskusstva,* 1899, No. 1, 1-11.
———. "V chas itogov." *Vesy,* 1905, No. 4, 45-6.
Diakonitsyn, L. F. *Ideinye protivorechiia v estetike russkoi zhivopisi kontsa 19-nachala 20 v.* Perm, 1966.
Dikman, M. I. "Blok—kritik." *Istoriia russkoi kritiki.* B. P. Gorodetskii et al, editors. Moscow-Leningrad, 1958. 2 volumes. Volume 2, 646-64.

Donchin, Georgette. *The Influence of French Symbolism on Russian Poetry.* The Hague, 1958.

Efros, Abram. *Profili.* Moscow, 1930.

Erenburg, Il'ia. *Liudi, gody, zhizn'.* Moscow, 1966.

Erlich, Victor. *The Double Image: Concepts of the Poet in Slavic Literatures.* Baltimore, 1964.

_____ "Russian Symbolism and Polish Neo-Romanticism: Notes on Comparative Nomenclature of Slavic Modernism." Victor Terras, editor. *American Contributions to the Seventh International Congress of Slavists.* Volume 2: Literature and Folklore. The Hague, 1973. 181-97.

Erman, L. K. *Intelligentsiia v pervoi russkoi revoliutsii.* Moscow, 1966.

Etkind, Mark. *Aleksandr N. Benua.* Moscow-Leningrad, 1965.

_____ *Mir kak bol'shaia simfoniia.* Leningrad, 1970.

Fedorov, Andrei. *Teatr A. Bloka i dramaturgiia ego vremeni.* Leningrad, 1972.

Filosofov, Dmitrii. *Slova i zhizn'.* Petersburg, 1909.

Flam, Jack D., editor. *Matisse on Art.* London, 1973.

Gauss, Charles Edward. *The Aesthetic Theories of French Artists.* Baltimore, 1966.

Geib, Katharina. *Aleksej Mikhajlovič Remizov—Stilstudien.* Munich, 1970.

George, Waldemar. *Larionov.* Paris, 1966.

Ginsburg, Michael. "Art Collectors of Old Russia: The Morozovs and the Shchukins." *Apollo,* XCVIII, No. 142 (December 1973), 470-85.

Gippius, Zinaida. See Hippius.

Gofman, Modest, editor. *Kniga o russkikh poetakh poslednogo desiatiletiia.* Petersburg-Moscow, 1908.

Goldwater, Robert. "Primitivism in Modern Art." *World Cultures and Modern Art: Exhibition on the Occasion of the XXth Olympiad.* Siegfried Wichmann, director. Munich, 1972. 240-4.

_____ *Primitivism in Modern Painting.* New York, 1938.

Gol'tsev, Viktor. "Aleksandr Blok kak literaturnyi kritik." *Novyi mir,* 1931, No. 1-3, 163-73.

Gomberg-Verzhbinskaia, E. P. *Russkoe iskusstvo i revoliutsiia 1905 g.* Leningrad, 1960.

Gorbachev, G. E. *Kapitalizm i russkaia literatura.* Leningrad, 1925.

Gornitskaia, N. S. "Briusov-kritik." *Istoriia russkoi kritiki.* B. P. Gorodetskii et al, editors. Leningrad, 1958. 2 volumes. Volume 2, 629-45.

Gorodetskii, B. P., main editor. *Istoriia russkoi poezii.* Volume 2: "Russkaia poeziia vtoroi poloviny XIX veka." Leningrad, 1969.

Gorodetskii, Sergei. "Nekotorye techeniia v sovremennoi russkoi literature." *Apollon,* 1913, No. 1, 46-50.

_____ "Vospominaniia o Bloke." *Pechat' i revoliutsiia.* 1922, No. 1, 75-87.

Grabar, Igor'. "Golubaia roza." *Vesy,* 1907, No. 5, 93-6.

_____ *Moia zhizn'. Avtomonografiia.* Moscow-Leningrad, 1937.

_____ *Pis'ma 1891-1917.* Moscow, 1974.

_____ "Salon Zolotogo Runa." *Vesy,* 1908, No. 6, 91-4.

Gray, Camilla. *The Russian Experiment in Art 1863-1922.* New York, 1970.

Gromov, Pavel. *A. Blok: Ego predshestvenniki i sovremenniki.* Leningrad, 1966.

_____ *Geroi i vremia.* Leningrad, 1961.

Grossman, Joan Delaney. *Edgar Allan Poe in Russia: A Study in Legend and Literary Influence.* Würzburg, 1973.

Grover, Stuart R. "The World of Art Movement in Russia." *Russian Review,* v. 32, No. 1 January 1973), 28-42.

Guenther, Johannes von. *Ein Leben in Ostwind.* Munich, 1969.

Guérard, Albert L. *Art for Art's Sake.* New York, 1936.

Gumilev, Nikolai. "Nasledie simvolizma i akmeizm." *Apollon,* 1913, No. 1, 42-5.
───── "Poeziia v 'Vesakh.' " *Apollon,* 1910, No. 9, 42-4.
Gurian, Waldemar. "The Memoirs of Bely." *Russian Review,* v. III (1943), 95-103.
Gusarova, Alla. *Mir Iskusstva.* Leningrad, 1972.
Harcave, Sidney. *The Russian Revolution of 1905.* New York, 1964.
Haskell, Arnold L. (with Walter Nuvel). *Diaghileff, His Artistic and Private Life.* New York, 1935.
Hilton, Allison. "Matisse in Moscow." *Art Journal,* XXIX, No. 2 (Winter 1969-70), 166-73.
Hippius [Gippius], Zinaida. *Dmitrii Merezhkovskii.* Paris, 1951.
───── *Literaturnyi dnevnik 1899-1907.* Petersburg, 1908.
───── *Zhivye litsa.* Prague, 1925.
Hoover, Marjorie L. *Meyerhold: The Art of Conscious Theater.* Amherst (Mass.), 1974.
Howe, Irving. "The Idea of the Modern." In his *Literary Modernism.* New York, 1967.
Iaremich, S. P. *Mikhail Aleksandrovich Vrubel': zhizn' i tvorchestvo.* Moscow, 1911.
Isakov, S. *1905 god v satire i karikature.* Leningrad, 1928.
Istoriia Moskvy. Volume 5: "Period imperializma i burzhuazno-demokraticheskikh revoliutsii." Edited by A. M. Pankratova. Moscow, 1955.
Istoriia russkogo iskusstva. Volume 10: 1 and 2. Edited by N. P. Lapshina and G. G. Pospelov. Moscow, 1969.
Ivanov, Razumnik V. *Aleksandr Blok. Andrei Belyi.* Petersburg, 1919.
Ivanov, Viacheslav and Gershenzon, M. *Perepiska iz dvukh uglov.* Petersburg, 1921.
───── *Po zvezdam.* Petersburg, 1909.
───── "Zavety simvolizma." *Apollon,* 1910, No. 8, 5-20.
Ivoilov, Vladimir. *Aleksandr Aleksandrovich Blok.* Petersburg, 1922.
Jackson, Holbrook. *The Eighteen Nineties.* New York, 1927.
Jaworska, Wladyslawa. *Gauguin and the Pont-Aven School.* London, 1972.
Jullian, Philippe. *Dreamers of Decadence: Symbolist Painters of the 1890's.* Translated by Robert Baldick. New York, 1971.
───── *The Symbolists.* Translated by Mary Anne Stevens. London, 1973.
Karlinsky, Simon. "The Dostoevsky of Russian Poetry." *Nation,* 21 August 1972, 117-9.
───── "Introduction: The Gentle Subversive." *Letters of Anton Chekhov.* Translated by Michael Heim in collaboration with Simon Karlinsky. New York, 1973.
───── *Marina Cvetaeva: Her Life and Art.* Berkeley, 1966.
Kaun, Alexander. *Leonid Andreev: A Critical Study.* New York, 1924.
Khodasevich, Vladislav. *Nekropol'.* Brussels, 1939.
Kisch, Cecil. *Alexander Blok, Prophet of Revolution.* London, 1960.
Klimoff, Eugene. "Alexandre Benois and His Role in Russian Art."*Apollo,* XVIII, No. 142 (December 1973), 460-9.
───── "Russian Architecture: 1880-1910."*Apollo,* XVIII No. 142 (December 1973), 436-43.
Kluge, Rolf-Dieter. *Westeuropa und Russland im Weltbild Aleksandr Bloks.* Slavistische Beiträge, v. 27. Munich, 1967.
Kochan, Lionel. *Russia in Revolution: 1890-1918.* London, 1966.
Kodrianskaia, Natal'ia. *Aleksei Remizov.* Paris, 1957.
Kogan, Dora. *Mamontovskii kruzhok.* Moscow, 1970.
───── "Novye techeniia v zhivopisi 1907-1917." *Istoriia russkogo iskusstva.* Volume 10-2. Edited by N. P. Lapshina and G. G. Pospelov. Moscow, 1969.
Kogan, P. *Ocherki po istorii noveishei russkoi literatury.* Volume 3; Moscow, 1911. Volume 4; Moscow-Leningrad, 1929.
Kopshitser, Mark. *Valentin Serov.* Moscow, 1967.
Koreska-Hartmann, Linda. *Jugendstil—Stil der 'Jugend.'* Munich, 1969.

Kramer, Hilton. " 'The World of Art' in Exile." *New York Times* (3 May 1970), 23.

Kranikhfel'd, Vladimir. "Zolotoe Runo." *Mir Bozhii*, 1906, No. 4, 57-62.

Kugel', A. R. *List'ia s dereva—Vospominaniia.* Leningrad, 1926.

Kuzmin, Mikhail. "Khudozestvennaia proza 'Vesov.' " *Apollon*, 1910, No. 9, 35-41.

—— "O prekrasnoi iasnosti." *Apollon*, 1910, No. 4, 5-10.

—— "Vospominaniia o N. N. Sapunove." *N. Sapunov. Vospominaniia. Kharakteristiki.* Moscow, 1916, 43-53.

Lapshin, Vladimir. *Soiuz russkikh khudozhnikov.* Leningrad, 1974.

Lapshina, N. P. "Mir Iskusstva." *Russkaia khudozhestvennaia kul'tura kontsa XIX-nachala XX veka.* A. D. Alekseev et al, editors. Moscow, 1969. 2 volumes. Volume 2, 129-62.

Lehmann, A. G. *The Symbolist Aesthetic in France 1885-1895.* Oxford, 1968.

Lelevich, G. *V. Ia. Bruisov.* Moscow-Leningrad, 1926.

Levinson, André. *Bakst: The Story of the Artist's Life.* London, 1923.

Lidin, Vladimir. *Pisateli: Avtobiografii i portrety sovremennykh russkikh prozaikov.* Moscow, 1928.

Lifar, Sergei. *Diagilev i s Diagilevom.* Paris, 1928.

—— *Stradnye gody.* Paris, 1935.

Lobanov, Viktor. *Kanuny.* Moscow, 1968.

—— *Khudozhestvennye gruppirovki za poslednie 25 let.* Moscow, 1930.

—— *Knizhnaia grafika E. E. Lansere.* Moscow, 1948.

—— *1905 god i zhivopisi.* Moscow, 1922.

Loguine, Tatiana. *Gontcharova et Larionov.* Paris, 1971.

Lucie-Smith, Edward. *Symbolist Art.* New York, 1972.

Maguire, Robert A. "Macrocosm or Microcosm? The Symbolists on Russia." Charles A. Moser, editor. *Russia: The Spirit of Nationalism (Review of National Literatures).* Volume 3, No. 1 (Spring 1972). New York, 125-52.

Makovskii, Sergei. "Frantsuzskie khudozhniki iz sobraniia I. A. Morozova."*Apollon*, 1912, No. 3-4, 5-16.

—— *Na parnasse "Serebrianogo veka."* Munich, 1962.

—— *Portrety sovremennikov.* New York, 1955.

—— *Siluety russkikh khudozhnikov.* New York, 1955.

—— *Stranitsy khudozhestvennoi kritiki.* Petersburg, 1909.

Maksimov, Dmitrii. *Briusov: Poeziia i pozitsiia.* Leningrad, 1969.

—— "Kriticheskaia proza Bloka." *Blokovskii sbornik.* Volume I. Tartu, 1964. 28-97.

—— *Poeziia Valeriia Briusova.* Leningrad, 1940.

—— *Revoliutsiia 1905 goda i russkaia literatura.* Moscow-Leningrad, 1950.

Maksimov, V. E. *Ocherk istorii noveishei russkoi literatury.* Moscow-Leningrad, 1925.

—— *Iz proshlogo russkoi zhurnalistiki.* Leningrad, 1930.

Mamontov, Vsevolod. *Vospominaniia o russkikh khudozhnikakh.* Moscow, 1950.

Marcadé, Valentine. *Le Renouveau de l'art pictural russe 1863-1914.* Lausanne, 1971.

Markov, Vladimir. "Balmont: A Reappraisal."*Slavic Review.* v. 28, No. 2 (June 1969), 221-64.

—— *Russian Futurism: A History.* Berkeley and Los Angeles, 1968.

Martin, Elizabeth Puckett. "The Symbolist Criticism of Painting: France, 1880-1895." Ph. D. dissertation. Bryn Mawr, 1948.

Mashbits-Verov, Iosif. *Russkii simvolizm i put' Aleksandra Bloka.* Kuibyshev, 1969.

Mashinskii, S. "Put' poeta." Sergei Gorodetskii. *Stikhotvoreniia i poemy.* Moscow, 1960. 3-32.

—— "Sergei Gorodetskii." Sergei Gorodetskii. *Stikhotvoreniia i poemy.* Leningrad, 1974. 5-52.

Maslenikov, Oleg. *The Frenzied Poets—Andrei Bely and the Russian Symbolists.* Berkeley and Los Angeles, 1952.
_____ "Ruskin, Bely, and the Solovyovs." *Slavonic and East European Review,* XXXV, No. 84 (1956), 15-23.
_____ "The Young Andrei Bely and the Symbolist Movement in Russia (1901-1909)." Ph.D. dissertation, UC Berkeley, 1942.
Matich, Olga. *Paradox in the Religious Poetry of Zinaida Hippius.* Munich, 1972.
Meierkhol'd, Vsevolod. *Stat'i, pis'ma, rechi, besedy.* Moscow, 1968. 2 volumes.
Merezhkovskii, Dmitrii. "O prichinakh upadka i o novykh techeniiakh sovremennoi russkoi literatury." *Polnoe sobranie sochinenii.* Volume XVIII. Moscow, 1914, 175-276.
Michel Larionov et son temps. Catalogue of the Musée Toulouse-Lautrec (Albi) exhibition, June-September, 1973.
Mickiewicz, Denis. "*Apollo* and Modernist Poetics." *Russian Literature Triquarterly,* 1971, No. 1, 226-61.
Miele, Franco. *L'Avanguardia Tradita: Arte Russa dal XIX al XX secolo.* Rome, 1973.
Mihajlov, Mihajlo. "Russian Modernism." *Russian Themes.* Translated by Marija Mihajlov. New York, 1968. 264-87.
Mikhailovskii, Boris. *Izbrannye stat'i o literature i iskusstve.* Moscow, 1968.
_____ *Russkaia literatura XX veka.* Moscow, 1939.
Miliukov, Paul. *Outlines of Russian Culture.* Translated by Valentine Ughet and Eleanor Davis. New York, 1942. 3 volumes.
Miller, Margaret. *The Economic Development of Russia 1905-1914.* London, 1926.
Milner, John. *Symbolists and Decadents.* London, 1971.
Milosz, Czeslaw. *The History of Polish Literature.* New York, 1969.
Mirskii, Dmitrii. *Contemporary Russian Literature 1881-1925.* New York, 1926.
_____ "O proze Aleksandra Bloka." Aleksandr Blok. *Sobranie sochinenii.* Volume 8. Leningrad, 1936. ix-xxvi.
Mix, Katherine Lyon. *A Study in Yellow: The Yellow Book and Its Contributors.* Lawrence (Kansas), 1960.
Mochul'skii, Konstantin. *Aleksandr Blok.* Paris, 1948.
_____ *Andrei Belyi.* Paris, 1955.
_____ *Valerii Briusov.* Paris, 1962.
Nedoshvin, G. A. et al. "Vvedenie." *Istoriia russkogo iskusstva.* Edited by N. P. Lapshina and G. G. Pospelov. Volume 10:1. Moscow, 1969. 7-42.
Nemirovich-Danchenko, Vladimir. *Iz proshlogo.* Moscow, 1936.
Nestyev, Israel. *Prokofiev.* Translated by Florence Jonas. Stanford, 1960.
Newcombe, Josephine. *Leonid Andreev.* New York, 1973.
Nordau, Max. *Entartung.* Berlin, 1892-93. 2 volumes.
Oberländer, Erwin, editor. *Russia Enters the Twentieth Century: 1894-1917.* New York, 1971.
Orlov, Vladimir. "Aleksandr Blok i Andrei Belyi v 1907 g." *Literaturnoe nasledstvo.* Volume 27-28. Moscow, 1937. 371-408.
_____ *Aleksandr Blok: Ocherk tvorchestva.* Moscow, 1956.
_____ "Istoriia odnoi druzhby-vrazhdy." *Aleksandr Blok i Andrei Belyi: Perepiska.* Moscow, 1940, v-lxiv.
1940. v-lxiv.
_____ *Put'i i sud'by.* Moscow, 1963.
Ostroumova-Lebedeva, A. P. *Avtobiograficheskie zapiski 1900-16.* 3 volumes. Moscow, 1935-51.
Pachmuss, Temira. *Zinaida Hippius: An Intellectual Profile.* Carbondale (Illinois), 1971.

_____, ed. *Selected Works of Zinaida Hippius*. Carbondale (Illinois), 1972.

Pakhomov, N. P. *Abramtsevo*. Moscow, 1969.

Patterson, Rodney Lee. "The Early Poetry of Konstantin Dmitrievič Balmont." Ph.D. dissertation. UCLA. 1969.

Pentaur [Valerii Briusov]. "Zolotoe Runo. 1907 Nos. 1 i 2." *Vesy,* 1907, No. 3, 74-6.

Pertsov, Petr. *Literaturnye vospominaniia 1890-1902*. Moscow-Leningrad, 1933.

Petrov, V. N. "Mir Iskusstva." *Istoriia russkogo iskusstva*. Volume 10:1. Edited by N. P. Lapshina and G. G. Pospelov. 341-485.

Piast, V. [Vladimir Pestovskii]. *Vstrechi*. Moscow, 1929.

Podobedova, Ol'ga. *Igor' Emmanuilovich Grabar*. Moscow, n.d.

Poggioli, Renato. *The Phoenix and the Spider*. Cambridge (Mass.), 1957.

_____ *Poets of Russia*. Cambridge, 1960.

_____ *The Theory of the Avant-Garde*. Translated by Gerald Fitzgerald. Cambridge, 1968.

Pogorelova, B. " 'Skorpion' i 'Vesy.' " *Novyi zhurnal*. Volume 40 (1955), 168-73.

Pruzhan, Irina. *Konstantin Somov*. Moscow, 1972.

_____ *Lev Samoilovich Bakst*. Leningrad, 1975.

Putnam, George. "Aleksandr Blok and the Russian Intelligentsia." *Slavic and East European Journal*. Volume 9, No. 1 (Spring 1965), 29-46.

Red'ko, A. E. *Literaturno-khudozhestvennye iskaniia v kontse XIX-nachala XX v.* Leningrad, 1924.

Reeve, F. D. *Aleksandr Blok: Between Image and Idea*. New York, 1962.

Riabushinskii, Vladimir. "Kupechestvo moskovskoe." *Den' russkogo rebenka*. San Francisco, 1951. 168-89.

Rice, Martin P. *Valery Briusov and the Rise of Russian Symbolism*. Ann Arbor, 1975.

Rice, Tamara Talbot. *A Concise History of Russian Art*. New York, 1963.

Roberts, Spencer E., editor. *Essays in Russian Literature: The Conservative View: Leontiev, Rozanov, Shestov*. Athens (Ohio), 1968.

Rodina, Tat'iana. *Aleksandr Blok i russkii teatr nachala XX veka*. Moscow, 1972.

Rookmaaker, Henderik. *Synthetist Art Theories*. Amsterdam, 1959.

Rosenthal, Bernice G. "The Artist as Prophet and Revolutionary: Dmitrii Sergeevich Merezhkovsky and the 'Silver Age'." Ph. D. dissertation, UC Berkeley, 1970.

_____ *Dmitrii Sergeevich Merezhkovsky and the Silver Age: The Development of a Revolutionary Mentality*. The Hague, 1975.

Rostislavov, Aleksandr. "Zolotoe Runo." *Apollon,* 1910, No. 9, 42-4.

Rozanov, Vasilii. *Sredi khudozhnikov*. Petersburg, 1914.

Rusakova, Alla. *Borisov-Musatov*. Moscow, 1975.

Russell, John. *The World of Matisse 1869-1954*. New York, 1969.

Russkaia khudozhestvennaia kul'tura kontsa XIX-nachala XX veka (1895-1907). A. D. Alekseev et al, editors. 2 volumes. Moscow, 1968-69.

Sabaneev, Leonid. *Modern Russian Composers*. Translated by Judah A. Joffe. New York, 1927.

Sarab'ianov, Dmitrii. *Russian Painters of the Early Twentieth Century (New Trends)*. Leningrad, 1973.

_____ *Russkaia zhivopis' kontsa 1900-kh-nachala 1910-kh godov*. Moscow, 1971.

Sarabjanow, Dmitrii [Dmitrii Sarab'ianov]. *Robert Falk*. Dresden, 1974.

Sar'ian, Martiros. *Iz moei zhizni*. Moscow, 1970.

Schapiro, Leonard. "The *Vekhi* Group and the Mystique of Revolution." *Slavonic and East European Review,* XXXIV, No. 82 (December 1955), 56-76.

Schmidt, Alexander. *Valerij Brjusovs Beitrag zur Literatur-theorie*. Munich, 1963.

Schorske, Carl E. "Cultural Hothouse." *The New York Review of Books.* Volume 22, No. 20 (11 December 1975), 39-44.
Semenov, E. "Le mysticisme anarchique." *Le Mercure de France,* No. 242 (16 July 1907), 361-4.
Serov, Valentin. *Perepiska 1884-1911.* Leningrad-Moscow, 1937.
Shcherbatov, Sergei. *Khudozhnik v ushedshei Rossii.* New York, 1955.
Shlifstein, S. I., editor. *S. S. Prokof'ev: materialy, dokumenty, vospominaniia.* Moscow, 1961.
Shmakov, G. G. "Blok i Kuzmin." *Blokovskii sbornik.* Volume 2. Tartu, 1971. 341-64.
Sidorov, Aleksei. *Russkaia grafika nachala XX veka.* Moscow, 1969.
Siunnerberg, Konstantin. *Tsel' tvorchestva.* Moscow, 1913.
Skriabin, Aleksandr. *Pis'ma.* Moscow, 1965.
Slonim, Marc. *From Chekhov to the Revolution: Russian Literature 1900-1917.* New York, 1962.
―――― *Russian Theater: From the Empire to the Soviets.* New York, 1961.
Sokolova, N. I., editor. *Puti razvitiia russkogo iskusstva kontsa XIX-nachala XX veka.* Moscow, 1972.
Solov'ev, Boris. *Poet i ego podvig: Tvorcheskii put' Aleksandra Bloka.* Moscow, 1968.
Solzhenitsyn, Alexander. *The Gulag Archipelago: I-II.* Translated by Thomas P. Whitney. New York, 1974.
Spencer, Charles. *Leon Bakst.* London, 1973.
―――― (with Philip Dyer and Martin Battersby). *The World of Serge Diaghilev.* Chicago, 1974.
Stacy, R. H. *Russian Literary Criticism: A Short History.* Syracuse, 1974.
Stanislavskii, Konstantin. *Moia zhizn' v iskusstve.* Moscow, 1962.
Stepun, Fedor. *Vergangenes und Unvergängliches.* Munich, 1948.
Sternin, Grigorii. *Khudozhestvennaia zhizn' Rossii na rubezhe XIX-XX v.* Moscow, 1970.
―――― *Ocherki russkoi satiricheskoi grafiki.* Moscow, 1964.
Strakhovsky, Leonid I. *Craftsmen of the Word: Three Poets of Modern Russia (Gumilev, Akhmatova, Mandelstam).* Westport (Conn.), 1949.
Szwede, Irena. "The Works of Stanislaw Przybyszewski and Their Reception in Russia at the Beginning of the XX Century." Ph.D. dissertation, Stanford University, 1970.
Tenisheva, Mar'ia. *Vpechatleniia moei zhizni.* Paris, 1933.
Timofeev, Leonid. *Aleksandr Blok.* Moscow, 1957.
Tovarishch German [Zinaida Gippius]. "Zolotoe Runo." *Vesy,* 1906, No. 2, 81-3.
―――― "Zolotomu runu." *Vesy,* 1906, No. 5, 87-9.
Treadgold, Donald W. *The West in Russia and China.* Volume 1: Russia, 1472-1917. Cambridge (Mass.), 1973.
Trotskii, Lev. *1905.* Translated by Anya Bostock. New York, 1971.
Tschöpl, Carin. *Vjačeslav Ivanov: Dichtung und Dichtungs-theorie.* Munich, 1968.
Tsvetaeva, Marina. *Proza.* Letchworth (UK), 1969.
Tuchman, Barbara. *The Proud Tower.* New York, 1967.
Tugendkhol'd, Iakov. "Frantsuzskoe sobranie S. I. Shchukina." *Apollon,* 1914, No. 1-2, 5-46.
Valentinov, N. [Nikolai Volskii]. *Dva goda s simvolistami.* Stanford, 1969.
Vengerov, S. A., editor. *Russkaia literatura XX v. 1890-1910.* Moscow, 1914-16.
Vogel, Lucy E. *Aleksandr Blok: The Journey to Italy.* Ithaca, 1973.
Volkov, Anatolii. *Russkaia literatura XX veka: Dooktiabrskii period.* Moscow, 1966.
Vrangel', N. "Iskusstvo v 'Vesakh.' " *Apollon,* 1910, No. 10, 17-18.
Vrubel', Mikhail. *Perepiska. Vospominaniia o khudozhnike.* Leningrad, 1963.

Wallis, Mieczyslaw. *Secesja.* Warsaw, 1974.

Weidlé, Wladimir. *Russia: Absent and Present.* Translated by A. Gordon Smith. London, 1952.

West, James. "Neo-Romanticism in the Russian Symbolist Esthetic." *Slavonic and East European Review.* July, 1973. 413-27.

_____ *Russian Symbolism: A Study of Viacheslav Ivanov and the Russian Symbolist Aesthetic.* London, 1970.

Woloschin, Margarita. *Die Grüne Shlange.* Stuttgart, 1954.

Woodward, James B. *Leonid Andreev: A Study.* Oxford, 1969.

Zaitsev, Boris. *Dalekoe.* Washington, D.C., 1965.

Zernov, Nicolas. *The Russian Religious Renaissance of the Twentieth Century.* London, 1963.

_____ *Three Russian Prophets: Khomiakov, Dostoevsky, Soloviev.* London, 1944.

Zhuravleva, A. "Mir Iskusstva." *Istoriia russkogo iskusstva.* N. G. Mashkovtsev et al., editors. 2 volumes. Moscow, 1960. Volume 2, 381-401.

Zlobin, Vladimir. *Tiazhelaia dusha.* Washington, D.C., 1970.

Zorgenfrei, V. A. "Aleksandr Aleksandrovich Blok." *Zapiski mechtatelei.* No. 6 (Petersburg, 1922), 123-54.